GOD IS IN THE KITCHEN
What's He Cooking Up for Me?

Ginger Estavillo Umali

WestBow Press
A DIVISION OF THOMAS NELSON
& ZONDERVAN

Copyright © 2015 Ginger Estavillo Umali.

Cover image by Ginger Estavillo Umali

All rights reserved. No part of this book may be used or reproduced by any means, graphic, electronic, or mechanical, including photocopying, recording, taping or by any information storage retrieval system without the written permission of the author except in the case of brief quotations embodied in critical articles and reviews.

This book is a work of non-fiction. Unless otherwise noted, the author and the publisher make no explicit guarantees as to the accuracy of the information contained in this book and in some cases, names of people and places have been altered to protect their privacy.

Scripture taken from the Holy Bible, NEW INTERNATIONAL VERSION®. Copyright © 1973, 1978, 1984, 2011 by Biblica, Inc. All rights reserved worldwide. Used by permission. NEW INTERNATIONAL VERSION® and NIV® are registered trademarks of Biblica, Inc. Use of either trademark for the offering of goods or services requires the prior written consent of Biblica US, Inc.

Scripture taken from *The Message*. Copyright © 1993, 1994, 1995, 1996, 2000, 2001, 2002. Used by permission of NavPress Publishing Group.

WestBow Press books may be ordered through booksellers or by contacting:

WestBow Press
A Division of Thomas Nelson & Zondervan
1663 Liberty Drive
Bloomington, IN 47403
www.westbowpress.com
1 (866) 928-1240

Because of the dynamic nature of the Internet, any web addresses or links contained in this book may have changed since publication and may no longer be valid. The views expressed in this work are solely those of the author and do not necessarily reflect the views of the publisher, and the publisher hereby disclaims any responsibility for them.

Any people depicted in stock imagery provided by Thinkstock are models, and such images are being used for illustrative purposes only. Certain stock imagery © Thinkstock.

ISBN: 978-1-5127-1143-1 (sc)
ISBN: 978-1-5127-1144-8 (hc)
ISBN: 978-1-5127-1142-4 (e)

Library of Congress Control Number: 2015914571

Print information available on the last page.

WestBow Press rev. date: 10/05/2015

To my mom, Carol,
who loved and believed
in a Nobody like me.

To my husband, Alvin
who handpicked this Nobody
and called her beautiful.

To my children,
Colleen, Pajo, and Chiara
who transformed this Nobody
into a Somebody.

Contents

MENU 1: Mercy and Grace

1. Beyond Smears and Flaws … {1}
2. Roaches in the Ark … {7}
3. His Face … {17}
4. Against the Tide … {23}
5. Nanoo! Nanoo! … {33}
6. Treasures from Out of the Blue … {39}

MENU 2: Faith

7. The Long Trip Home … {47}
8. Declaration of Dependence … {59}
9. Unshaken Faith … {67}
10. Big God in a Candy Wrap … {73}
11. The Armor of God … {81}
12. Snapshots of Eternity … {91}
13. Soar Like an Eagle … {103}

MENU 3: Holiness in Relationships

14. Of Burps, ABC's, & Ladybug Eyelashes … {113}
15. Who Wins? … {121}

16. Tongue under Lockdown　　{ 127 }
17. Salute to Mothers　　{ 133 }

MENU 4: Christian Living

18. Choices　　{ 141 }
19. Where Beauty Lies　　{ 151 }
20. Our Father Who Art in Heaven　　{ 159 }
21. Lead Us Not into Temptation　　{ 167 }
22. If I Could Change Things　　{ 173 }
23. The Lord Is My Shepherd　　{ 179 }
24. Through Heaven's Gates　　{ 187 }

MENU 5: Love

25. Loved Beyond Boundaries　　{ 197 }
26. When a Bandage Is Not Enough　　{ 211 }
27. Love in Broken Cups　　{ 219 }
28. Beyond Rhyme or Reason　　{ 225 }
29. The Power of "Small"　　{ 233 }

MENU 6: Strength in Suffering

30. Shortcuts　　{ 239 }
31. Even Death Cannot Part　　{ 245 }
32. When God Says "No"　　{ 253 }
33. Of Boats and Bridges　　{ 261 }
34. He Knows Your Heart　　{ 269 }
35. Crucified　　{ 277 }
36. In the Quietness of the Night　　{ 287 }
37. Running on Empty　　{ 293 }
38. Are We There Yet?　　{ 299 }

MENU 7: Godly Character

39. The Litterbug, the Onlooker, & a Dose of Integrity   { 307 }
40. Just Pull the Plug   { 313 }
41. On My Own Hiking Shoes   { 321 }
42. Earthen Wares   { 325 }
43. Judging by the Looks ... and the Tooth   { 343 }
44. Dunk   { 353 }
45. Of Pixels, Quilts, & Homecoming Misconceptions   { 357 }

Introduction

Click ... Click ... Click

"Why do you keep cutting my nails but you don't cut yours, Mama?" my ten-year old son asked randomly, right in the middle of our nail-clipping time.

"I do tidy up my nails. See? I just trimmed it yesterday." I stretched my arms before me and splayed my fingers for his inspection.

"But your nails are still long," Pajo eyed my fingers with a mixture of curiosity and mild protest. "You don't trim it down to the skin, just like mine. You cut mine too short. I don't even have nails left to scratch or pick my nose!"

Amused and distracted by the urgency of his need, I groped for a reasonable reply. "Ladies are allowed to grow their nails longer."

"Why?"

"So that we'll look beautiful."

"Why do you need to look beautiful?" Short answers never satisfy this boy.

I almost impulsively said, "So that we can attract men!" But this little Mr. Witty might pounce on me with a rebuff, "What business do you have attracting men when you are already married."

I rummaged in my brain but smart wordplays eluded me, so I settled on the quickest alternative. Why do people need to look beautiful? "So that we can be loved."

It was a wimpy answer, and I only realized it the same second the words rolled out of my tongue. Too late! I couldn't do a U-turn and sing a different tune.

"But Mama ..." Pajo breathed out with eyes rolling. "I already love you! So go ahead and cut your nails!"

This story started out as a thigh-slapping rib tickler. But long after the humour grew stale, Pajo's one-liner still chimed in my head—"I already love you!"

Immediately, it was no longer my son's voice but God's voice that resonated like the staccato on a drum. "Come as you are. Even without the pretense, I already love you."

God is constantly inviting us to come to Him—whether we have flashy nail art or snipped nails with grungy engine grease underneath. The invitation stands. Come despite your sinfulness and neurotic thoughts. Come even with your encumbering baggage and conflicted hearts. Come with your crosses, traumas, and thorns. You can never be phony before God because there is no camouflage you can hide behind that He can't see through. There is no dark bunker you can retreat into where the brilliance of His floodlight can't invade. There is no false front He can't penetrate, no mystery He can't unshroud, and no mask He can't peel. From whichever oblique angle He inspects, you are beautiful.

Broken,
Warped,
Imperfect,
And beautiful.

As you read through the pages of this book, I invite you to come as you are, reach deep into the void in your soul, and unload everything to a God who calls you 'beloved'. May the true stories in this book prompt you to also be honest about your own pains, and believe that it is impossible, even for the worst vagabond, to stray far from His compass. Be confident. There is a soft spot in God's big heart reserved only for you.

As I was drafting the manuscript of *God is in the Kitchen*, there were many occasions when my mind went blank, and all creativity flew out the window. There was no allegory to demystify or ink to splatter on paper. I couldn't even draw a speech bubble on a comic I lazily doodled. The first-person narration became a no-person narration because the writer rocketed off into oblivion. During the thick of my writer's block, anyone who approached me with a penny-for-your-thoughts bargain lost in a cockamamie game. Since my brain had no thoughts, I could as well be unconscious.

After a few minutes of staring at an empty notepad, I let out a sigh—or should I say, I heaved a very, very deep sigh. I must have exhaled so noisily for I shattered the silence and broke my husband's concentration.

"What's the matter?" Alvin rarely unglues his eyes from the computer screen when he's busy working. But that night, he spun around with a probing look.

"I don't know what I'm doing." As I massaged my temple, I foolishly hoped that my gift of gab, which was sucked into a black hole, could travel faster than the speed of light and sink back into my brain.

"You're lucky," he said. "At least you're forgiven."

"What do you mean?" Now it was my turn to look at him curiously.

"Remember what Jesus said when he was hanging on the cross at Calvary? 'Forgive them Father for they do not know what they're doing.' Well then. You're forgiven!"

As I replayed this light-hearted evening with my husband, I marvelled at how quickly spiritual truth pops out of mundane activities. Of course, Alvin wasn't preaching a sermon when he spontaneously whipped the gag line. He was just goofing around. Still, I thought to myself, there are times when schedules are predictable. Nothing is out of the ordinary, yet God can handpick those dull moments to teach a priceless lesson or speak an uplifting word.

Now that's what this book is about. *God Is In The Kitchen: What's He Cooking Up For Me?* is a devotional memoir that seeks to put into form the wealth of insights sprinkled by God in the strangest places, under the most mediocre circumstances. God doesn't idly loiter around the outer fringes of our lives then jump back into the center of the ring only when a miracle needs to happen.

God is in the everyday.

His warehouses of miracles empty out to vulnerable hearts that care to see them through the lens of faith. Even as you cook meals, wash dishes, and wipe down gooey yogurt from a toddler's sticky face, God talks. His Spirit can move and unsteel you right smack in the middle of a vegetable-slicing, grease-scrubbing, baby-tantrum-stopping moment.

Sometimes intense and thought-provoking, at other times comical, these inspirational stories mirror the hand of God in daily life. It is my prayer that you will retreat from this book refreshed from tip to toe—with your heart ablaze and thumping madly for love of sweet Jesus. May the Holy Spirit ignite each word in this book to the point where you will also be conscious of His glory and timely intrusion into your otherwise predictable, ho-hum days.

Remember, you are the reason God is smitten.

Yes, you!

The beloved ... and the forgiven!

Chapter 1

Beyond Smears and Flaws

We used to live in a cramped apartment where every single nook and cranny served a purpose. Much of the flurry of activity happened in the kitchen, and the six-seat dining table was the most important piece of furniture we learned to use in unconventional ways. It served as Colleen's study desk and the babies' diaper changing table. Other times, it was a game table for many family Scattergories and Scrabble nights. With all the flyers and local publications strewn over the top, you could say it was a magazine rack as well. Since we frequently rested Chiara's carrier on it, the dining table doubled up as the baby's bed.

And, oh, I forgot. We served our meals there too—that is, if we were lucky to find a few functional square inches.

One evening, Colleen sat on one side of the dining table, shoulders hunched over her homework. She spread out a sheet of long, bright white paper on which she gingerly sketched with felt pens and crayons. With detailed finishing touches, my little student

MENU 1: MERCY AND GRACE

dolled up a superb work of art any mother would be proud to flaunt in a frame.

As this was happening, my husband, Alvin, entered the dining room and positioned Pajo on the change pad beside Colleen. Right in the middle of a diaper change, seconds before the baby was completely wrapped, my boy tinkled. Up blasted pee like a rocket on a mission to Mars.

With perfect trajectory, the leak landed unexpectedly on Colleen's elaborate drawing. Like deadly lava, it swallowed everything in its path. Before long, Colleen's art, reduced to one chaotic splash of color, was no longer the Rembrandtesque showcase I thought it was.

As could be expected, Colleen kicked up a storm. The clock was ticking, and she didn't look forward to pulling an all-nighter.

I handed Colleen another sheet from the computer armoire and encouraged her to draw a simpler version. Problem was, our paper was a tad shorter and a shade darker. My fussy daughter was afraid her teacher would nitpick and question her about it.

"Just be honest and tell her what happened," I said. "I bet she'll understand."

Colleen managed to finish her project while muttering under her breath, "Pajo, you silly goose!"

The finished product wasn't as meticulously crafted as the original, but she decided that it would do.

In school, Colleen jumped at the first opportunity to explain. "I'm so sorry, Mrs. Lucas. But my brother peed on my homework."

"I've heard many different excuses from students during my entire career," she said with an amused curl on her lips. "But that sure is one excuse I've never heard before."

The incident became a classic joke among the school staff. Whenever Colleen bumped into teachers along the hallway, they would laugh, give her a knowing wink, or say things like "I heard what happened to your homework" or "I gotta meet that brother of yours."

Despite the substandard project Colleen turned in, Mrs. Lucas was gracious enough to give her an A. It was a decent reward not only for the homework she submitted or the earlier sketch Pajo redecorated, but it was also a suitable encouragement for Colleen, who embraced honesty as gospel truth.

The following school year, my then grade-six daughter had another assignment. By this time, Pajo had already learned bladder control. As an adventurous toddler who wanted to explore his tiny world, he found thrill in mimicking everything his big sister did.

Whenever Colleen squeaked in delight, he too shrieked like a fingernail-scratched chalkboard. Whenever big sister wrote, Pajo also squiggled on his own paper. When his sister showed some rhythmic moves, he also bobbed his head and bounced his shoulders in a way that would shame the best hip-hopper in *So You Think You Can Dance*.

One evening, Colleen left her finished artwork on top of the dining table. In her absence, Pajo's curious fingers crawled from its hiding place like a hairy tarantula and snatched the unsuspecting victim from its cradle.

With a green felt marker, he scrawled on the back of the paper like he was in a rapture. Pajo wreaked havoc in lesser time than it took to say "shazam!" All Colleen could do was scratch her head and wail, "Oh no, not again you silly goose!"

This time, Colleen didn't bother to redo her work; at least, the damage was done on the backside. She decided to submit her work as it was—lock, stock, and barrel—with no apologies for the mess Pajo created.

A couple of days later, Mr. Kirk, her grade-six teacher, who also heard about the legendary "pee" fiasco, held the homework up to Colleen's face.

MENU 1: MERCY AND GRACE

"See this, Colleen?" the teacher said with a broad grin. "I gave you an A!"

Then he turned the paper over and showed off the flipside with all its messy hieroglyphs. With an even wider grin, he announced, "And I gave your brother a B-minus!"

As I look back at the magnanimous response of both teachers, I'm reminded of the way God handles our own failures.

You see, our lives are also disfigured by splashes of error. Doodles of sin and imperfection spoil our work. Even when we put our best effort, our ungodly urges still prevail against us.

We can't get over the hump of our mistakes and live joyfully again because we swim in a pool of guilt.

However, regardless of the weak spots in our character, God gives us an A. Yes, despite the foibles, God gives his children a second chance—even a third or a hundredth!

God isn't infuriated and bent out of shape when we backslide. He looks past our mistakes because mercy is His name.

In the first epistle to Timothy, the apostle Paul writes,

> Here is a trustworthy saying that deserves full acceptance: Christ Jesus came into the world to save sinners—of whom I am the worst. But for that very reason I was shown mercy so that in me, the worst of sinners, Christ Jesus might display his immense patience as an example for those who would believe in him and receive eternal life. (1 Timothy 1:15–16 New International Version)

You may think like Paul and consider yourself the worst of sinners. Looking at the person sitting next to you, you judge that he can't possibly be messed up as badly as you are.

Friend, your neighbour isn't the yardstick by which you measure how far you've fallen from grace. God's holiness alone is the litmus test that determines the acidity and foulness in you.

Since we are called to be perfect as our heavenly Father is perfect, it might seem then that all of us will fall short. All of us will lose face, bummed in the pit of humiliation. We'll all be damned for judgment, deserving of His justice.

That's all true!

There's no denying it.

However, as Paul also said, Jesus came to save a stiff-necked people. It is precisely because we are corrupted that mercy tracked us down.

Though it is within God's power and advantage to smite us for our guile, He did the unthinkable and showed compassion instead—because mercy can't be mercy unless it is given to the wicked.

Mercy can't be redeeming unless it pays off our debts.

Mercy can't pump new life unless it chips the smut off our calcified hearts.

Mercy can't bail us out of trouble unless we are first in trouble.

Mercy can't bring hope unless it erases the black soot off our darkened future.

Yes, mercy isn't mercy unless it is given to the shamefully rotten, undeserving person.

Therefore, dear sister, get a clean sheet of paper and redraw your life with new, crisp colours. Your bighearted, broad-minded God is asking you to start afresh.

You may have hidden from sight because of guilt. But by God's mercy, get back into the game now!

Brother, reconcile with God and then jump-start your engines again. Don't give up because of a past misstep. Overcome

MENU 1: MERCY AND GRACE

the fear of rejection and hurdle the self-condemnation. Bring your best foot forward and begin the march on the double.

Tomorrow is looking better than today.

Because mercy is already there.

And He will do whatever it takes to see us rise from our brokenness—even when it means looking beyond smears and flaws.

```
            Jesus said,
"It is not the healthy who need a doctor,
            but the sick.
   But go and learn what this means:
     'I desire mercy, not sacrifice.'
  For I have not come to call the righteous,
           but sinners."
            Matthew 9:12-13
```

CHAPTER 2

Roaches in the Ark

I don't know from which bug cockroaches evolved. I don't really care which creepy crawly, bird, amoeba, or fish ancestor they call grandpa. I just want to understand why Noah bothered to bring them in the ark.

For me, these pests have no other function in life than to be just that—pests! I won't mind if roaches drown in the flood. I won't object if they become part of every predator's food chain. For me, the faster cockroaches slam into extinction, the better.

But believe it or not, one day these roaches served a higher purpose. As repulsive as these critters are, they taught me a lesson I couldn't learn any other way.

Many years ago, before our family migrated to Canada, we frequently visited an uptown mall in the heart of a bustling business district. Adjacent to the multi-level shopping center was a parkade with exit pay booths manned by uniformed attendants.

One afternoon, after a few hours of window-shopping, I walked back to the parking building to drive home. The rush-hour

MENU 1: MERCY AND GRACE

traffic outside the complex caused a slow build up of vehicles at the parking pay station. Cars that tried to weave out of the lot couldn't inch through the exits since the highway was clogged.

As I was about to engineer the car out of my slot, a man in a silver sedan screeched to a halt in front of me from out of nowhere. He whizzed by so unexpectedly that he would have smashed my fenders if I didn't pound on the brakes. Either the driver didn't see me pushing forward because he was in a hurry to get around the highway gridlocks, or he was just rude and wanted to get ahead of the pay booth queue.

On impulse, I honked the horn in fair warning. I wanted to let the man know that if he wasn't careful, he could have caused trouble. However, that single beep pushed his buttons the wrong way. He flew into a rage. If looks could melt, I'd be a pool of fatty cholesterol by now.

To even the score, the man revved and stopped his car less than a foot away from my front bumper. He purposely did so in order to trap me on the spot. He completely blocked my path, jammed the exit, and caused a bottleneck of cars behind him. By then, I was about to hit the roof too. His actions were barbaric and totally unwarranted.

After a three-minute deadlock, I hooted again—longer this time. All the vehicles at the pay booth had already been processed. The way was clear in front of him, and by not cruising forward, he was holding hostage a dozen other drivers behind him. I wanted so badly to go home already, but the wicked driver didn't budge. He was obviously trying to pick a fight.

On the verge of losing my cool, I rolled down my windows and asked, "What's the problem?"

To my utter disbelief, his passenger stepped out of the car and pointed an accusing finger to my face. The broad-shouldered woman in her mid-thirties was foaming at the mouth as she jumped into a shameless, jaw-dropping tirade.

"What's YOUR problem?!" she shouted back. Without taking a second to swallow, she fired profanities in rapid succession like a trigger-happy, machine-gun-toting madman.

I felt the warm rush of blood to my cheeks as I finally lost my temper. I tell you, her vulgar diatribe made me manic enough to chew nails and spit rivets. Nobody had ever cursed me in my entire life, and this choleric stranger had no license to lash her unruly tongue the way she did.

That very instant, I saw her as one big, foul-mouthed cockroach I wanted so much to whack. My anger made me think of uncouth people as grubby vermin that didn't deserve to live. Again, I asked Noah, "Why didn't you squash the roaches with your heel when you had the chance?"

Noah didn't give me an answer.

But God did.

He stated the obvious—we're not in paradise.

We have to live with both the pleasant and the unpleasant. We need to love abrasive and obnoxious people. Yes, we have to accept cockroaches as an ordained part of creation and love them for who they are. God meant them to ride the ark too—because hateful critters bring out the worst in us. In the process, they magnify our areas of growth and the virtues we lack.

In this case, I needed to develop patience and tolerance. It was not a Christian thing for me to pay back a punch with a slap. Even though I didn't physically harm my offenders, I attacked them in the ambit of my mind.

Honestly, I really wanted to slice the woman's tongue and bite the man's nose. I was tempted to give in to any criminal instincts that lay dormant inside my body. It was madness, I know! But thank

MENU 1: MERCY AND GRACE

God for these cockroaches in wheels, I saw clearly the areas of my character that needed a revamp.

A year later, my cockroaches made a grand re-entry. And how quickly they reproduced!

As my family and I were getting ready for permanent relocation, we dispatched most of our furniture and personal effects to an international freight forwarder. However, we still had a few boxes left which we scheduled to bring to the company for air transport.

Alvin and I, together with a couple of friends, loaded the cargo on a pick-up truck before we proceeded to the airport. We took a short cut and passed through gated communities, as we normally did when we wanted to avoid traffic in the highway.

We were nearly at the exit when two armed, uniformed men flagged us down. In broad daylight, they stepped in front of our convoy and signalled for us to pull over. Thinking that they were police officers, we moved to the shoulder and waited for further instructions.

Upon their approach, my friend asked, "What's the matter, sir? What did we do wrong?"

"I'm sorry, but you cannot drive through," one man replied. "This is a private road, and you need a sticker to pass."

A closer look at his uniform indicated that he wasn't affiliated with the police force. He was an employee of the neighbourhood council, tasked to patrol the gates.

"But we're from this neighbourhood," my friend reasoned.

A legal agreement existed between neighbouring communities that we could move across boundaries without the identifying stickers on the windshield. We crossed these same roads countless times before without any hold-ups or interrogation.

If we were already allowed to set foot inside the complex through the other barricaded entrance, did it make sense that we couldn't go out? Somehow, their logic was shifty.

"What do you have in the back?" Just one look at the other man's sinister smirk and we knew he eyed our cargo with evil intent. "The boxes are marked 'Canada'. Are you going to Canada?"

"Sir, we're just delivering these to the airport." My friend tried to be as polite as possible. He didn't want to delay our trip by provoking the caretakers.

The men circled the pick-up truck then lingered at the back where they inspected the boxes and talked in hushed tones. One of them mumbled something in his two-way radio. Within minutes, five more uniformed men arrived.

Time was ticking, and these people were detaining us for no apparent reason. If we didn't move ahead, we would be late for our appointment.

"Can we go now?" my husband asked.

"No!" the newcomer said a little too tigerishly. "We can't release you until you pay five hundred."

"What!" Alvin and I almost said in chorus. "What for?" Five hundred was an awfully big amount you wouldn't want to spend shopping, let alone throw away on shady deals.

"That's the rule here. If you want to pass through, you have to pay us the fee. Otherwise, you'll have to leave your goods behind."

What in the world?! What kind of baloney regulation was that? Something smelled fishy, and the dubious personalities in front of us began to shrink into the cockroaches I so reviled.

Corruption in the country has burgeoned so far and wide; you could stare at it even at the grassroots level. Plainly, these men were trying to use our shipment as bait to extort money.

MENU 1: MERCY AND GRACE

Alvin and I would never succumb to threats. With heated words, we debated our way out of the scam they set up.

The bullies used flare-ups, outbursts, and many forms of intimidation to badger us into paying. A couple of the men fingered their holsters as if to remind us they were armed and ready. More uniformed guards crawled out of their dark holes. Believing they had strength in numbers, many became doubly arrogant.

There's only so much belligerence even the most mild-mannered person could take. Push the wrong buttons further, even a worm will turn.

By then, my whole body was trembling in mixed fear and anger. I stormed out of the car, a notepad and pen in tow. I approached my enemies one by one and started jotting down the names stitched on their uniforms.

Every single molecule in my body was so incensed. I wanted to press charges against these sociopathic busybodies. If that didn't work, I intended to cut these men down to size by sending an editorial to any widely-circulated newspaper.

Pumped for battle, I was ready to pull out all the stops to prick their conscience and bring an end to this outrageous villainy!

When two guards took notice, they instinctively concealed their nameplates. Soon, everyone whacked their breasts like they were making a pledge of allegiance or something. They looked really funny that way.

"What are you doing?" the guy's voice was shaky. He dodged me even as he spoke.

I didn't say a word. I was livid beyond description.

One man provoked me and said, "Go ahead. Write down our names. Let's see who cares. Who do you think you're trying to scare here?"

The men's war of words chewed more hours than we anticipated. By then, we were awfully late, yet the confrontation was nowhere close to a settlement.

Since I was the only lady among a deluge of a dozen or more bullet-loaded cockroaches, my friend feared for my safety.

"Ginger, go back inside the car, please," he pleaded. "Go in, and tell Alvin to drive ahead. We'll take care of this."

I looked apprehensively at my dear brother. "What are you going to do?" I whispered.

"I'll handle it. Just go."

Alvin started the ignition and slowly steered the car away from the curb. To my surprise, none of the patrols blocked us. After a couple of minutes, the truck also pulled out and tailed us straight to the airport.

Apparently threatened, my friend finally caved in and paid the price for our road access and protection. The bullies had a grand slam, but it was a shallow one obtained under duress.

This was a harrowing experience that made me glad our family was all packed and ready to fly. I wanted to leave everything behind, cockroaches and all.

But then again, the Lord reminded me. Pain and suffering are significant parts of man's growth. I can flee to the farthest corners of Never Never Land, but there's no escaping their clutches.

Let's lay it on the line. Life is a cycle of peaks and valleys.

It is a social mixture of bullies and saints.

A dance between good and evil.

A harvest of wheat and weeds.

If we choose only butterflies and cute ladybugs and decide to swat all the despicable roaches in our lives, where would our balance be? How do we learn our lessons if our lives are a steady mountaintop encounter? How else can we witness the Lord's victory over pain if there is no pain to bear?

MENU 1: Mercy and Grace

The Lord teaches us in the gospels,

> Love your enemies, do good to those who hate you, bless those who curse you, pray for those who mistreat you. If someone slaps you on one cheek, turn to them the other also. If someone takes your coat, do not withhold your shirt from them. Give to everyone who asks you, and if anyone takes what belongs to you, do not demand it back. Do to others as you would have them do to you. (Luke 6:27–31)

Sounds so counter-intuitive, doesn't it? Does it make sense to love the person who wronged you? Can you look with kindness at someone who damaged your property, cheated you out of wealth, took advantage of your weaknesses, maligned your good name, humiliated you in public, or worse, killed your family?

We are not instinctively wired to extinguish our hatred. Anger is the first gut reaction that surfaces when an unwanted person tramples upon our rights.

It's almost like a Pavlovian response for us to take an eye for an eye without thinking of consequences. Human as we are, we also gravitate towards the pain and replay the events in our minds as if such dominating thoughts provide gratification.

The wound decays.

The irritation festers.

It sparks us to throw counterblows on our assailants, to give them a taste of their own bitter pill.

Hate, however, frustrates our growth. It eats us up and destroys our physical equilibrium, sometimes causing depression and all sorts of heartaches. Spiritually, anger gnaws at our souls too and sabotages the good that resides within.

God knows this only too well. This is why He urgently implores us to love the unlovable. God wants us to crack down on our grudges.

"Get even" is not a proverb.

It is a signpost that points to a bigger calamity.

Friend, don't give yourself a death sentence. Waiting for that payback time is a wasteful way to live. Revenge isn't the answer. There is nothing sweet in it that will permanently console.

God bids you, instead, to love the antagonists in your life. As an apt response, you need to at least try even if your feelings rebel against it. Even little attempts create huge ripples.

How do you love, you ask?

The first step in loving your enemies is to stop calling them cockroaches!

I use this term in its broadest figurative sense to cover all sorts of foulness creative people coin. Some call their enemies rascals or lunatics. Others cuss with many bleep-worthy swear words which primetime TV broadcasters censor.

Whatever it is, drop the filth.

Because, truth to tell, God loves all His children even if they are obnoxious enough to be called vermin.

Do you remember that pain-in-the-neck neighbour or the shrewd colleague who offended you? They are diamonds in the rough. They are all saints in the making. They just don't know it yet.

What else can you do?

Pray!

Pray for your attackers. It may be difficult to "bless those who curse you" as prescribed in verse twenty-eight. It may be a tall order to turn the other cheek when the first slap still stings like crazy. But you can pray.

Yes, this much, you can do.

If you used to debate with your enemies until you bled, pray now until you heal.

MENU 1: MERCY AND GRACE

However, pray the right way. Don't pray that a gaping sinkhole suddenly yawns and eats your enemy alive. Don't wish that the bully's nose gets flattened by a steamroller, nor should you pray for a meteorite to descend upon your foe and singe her hair to a peppercorn curl.

Don't ambush your sworn enemy with ill wishes and use God as an accomplice. You're exacting retribution simply by praying bad luck to rain on all the black sheep in your life.

Instead, pray for a renewal of his mind. Ask for a change of heart, that this man will elevate his life from mediocrity to virtue and become a living saint.

Nail this message down, my friend. Prayer not only delivers mercy upon your enemies but melts your heart as well. Soon enough, you'll be mellowed to the point of extending charity and warmth upon them.

You will no longer look at the tyrant as one who inflicted wounds, but as a victim who, likewise, suffered hurt and thus acted out of his own brokenness.

With fresh perspective, you'll see him as a damaged vessel in need of healing grace.

>   If your enemy is hungry, give him food to eat;
>   if he is thirsty, give him water to drink.
>   In doing this,
>   you will heap burning coals on his head,
>   and the Lord will reward you.
>   Proverbs 25:21-22

Chapter 3

His Face

It was a dark, cold night with the shimmer of the moon dimmed by the thickness of the clouds. I stood in front of our apartment building, dragging a heavy bag of junk from my kitchen.

The solitary lamp post in the front driveway barely lit the huge metal waste bin. While I was a few paces away from the dumpster, a series of thumping and thrashing sounds echoed from within the bin.

A dark shadow popped its toque-covered head from atop the pile of garbage. A dingy man in threadbare clothes jumped out with scraps of mouldy, putrid food. He looked at the morsels with ravenous eyes, obviously his first meal for the day. Before I could breathe a word, he ran off towards the next garbage bin down the block.

This was my first encounter with a homeless person in an urbanized street, in a country that boasted of economic wealth. The touching image of an abandoned survivor seemed misplaced. It was a dark blot on a first-rate landscape.

MENU 1: MERCY AND GRACE

Yet, the truth remained. There were drifting outcasts around me. And what a sacred moment it was to step inside their territory and learn from their disadvantage!

I immediately ran back into our apartment and threw open the kitchen cupboards. My daughter filled a bag with cans of cooked beans and tuna chunks, a box of Fruit Loops cereals, packets of easy-to-prepare oatmeal, and granola bars. She quickly scribbled a note and taped it on the bag.

"To the person looking for food in the garbage, these are for you."

The message was short but it was flooded with sympathy. The gesture was almost a heroic sacrifice. You see, we too were reeling from the blow of a personal recession. The provisions we surrendered were donations we ourselves received from the food bank. My daughter pleaded with me to share of her own want, unmindful of the empty dinner table we might have afterwards.

I left the grocery bag conspicuously at the base of the garbage container hoping that the same man would come again to reclaim it. Later, though, I was surprised that a different homeless fellow recovered the loot.

Yes, we were excited to have served another. But I wondered—how many more beggars are out there making banquets of worm-eaten apples and decayed, mildew-reeking bread?

I was so unsettled, and the feeling persisted to the very pit of my stomach.

Weeks passed, and we decided to move out of our rented apartment. I dragged loads of used cartons into the trunk of our car, ready to dispose of them at the dumpster. I decided that it was less strenuous for me to just bring the car up to the driveway than to heave the bulky boxes with my bare hands.

It was a chilly, shadowy night once again. The temperature was more freezing which was so uncharacteristic of spring. I parked the car on the curb, opened the trunk, and started to retrieve the cartons.

Suddenly, a six-foot man walked out of obscurity into my full view. His shoulder-length, ash-blonde hair was entangled in knots and must have never felt the slide of a fine-tooth comb. His clothes were ripped in many places, revealing muscles that were peppered with tattoos. His red eyes were as clouded as the lamps in medieval sepulchres; I wondered if he was sleep-deprived or if he had a sniff of illicit drugs.

As he slowly approached, I noticed that his face was severely banged up with purple, red, and blue bruises. Although fresh scabs formed on top of nasty cuts on his face and hands, one could still see tinges of blood oozing from them.

"Oh great!" I thought to myself. "What am I doing here with a bummer who obviously just had a fight?"

I shivered, partly from the cold wind, partly from fear. Alone with this stranger at nearly ten in the evening, I was more scared than a worm bait wiggling within a whisker of a trout's wide-open mouth. I didn't know if I was going to run back into the car and lock myself in or just calmly stand my ground and wait.

He stared at me, and all I could think of was "I'll be mugged! He's going to beat me up!"

He was like a cougar, ready to pounce on his motionless prey. At least that was what I predicted.

In a few seconds, the man found his voice. "Ma'm, would you like me to help you with those?" he asked.

I was taken aback by the politeness in his tone. He gave me a huge grin that revealed crooked yellow teeth under a neglected moustache.

I shot him back an uncertain smile and nodded my head. He reached for the cartons and with the swiftness of a gazelle, jumped

MENU 1: Mercy and Grace

over the five-foot metal bin. He collected his rancid food and completed the routine by throwing in my trash.

"Is there anything else I can help you with?" he asked.

"No," I managed to say feebly. "Thank you."

He walked away and retrieved a plastic bag of empty recyclable bottles and soda cans which, I deduced, he collected from many disposal sites. By estimation, he would be lucky to pocket a dollar of refund from the bottle depot—a precious amount he would probably scrimp for a meal.

Driven by remorse for my outrageous judgment of him, I called him back. "Excuse me sir. But would you like to have more bottles? I have two full bags in my apartment which I can give to you."

The homeless wanderer turned back, and the expression on his face was one that I could never forget. His eyes lit up with anticipation, like a child ready to tear open tinsel-wrapped presents on Christmas Eve. The sound of hope quickened his pulse like one who fortuitously stepped into a land of milk and honey.

Eyes bright with newborn expectation, he said, "Oh thank you very much!"

He stressed every word as if punctuating it would drive across his point more clearly.

I ran inside the building, stealing a glance at the man as I went through the foyer. This same person whom I prejudged to be an addicted thug ready to smash my face and blow my car to kingdom come, stood politely outside the entryway.

Even as I inadvertently granted him access by opening the door wide, he didn't ease himself in to take advantage of the heated coziness of the lobby. This same man whom I thought would use every dishonest trick in the book just to survive, stood patiently outside, braving near-zero temperatures with flimsy clothing. He briskly rubbed his hands together to warm himself. Cloudy mists spewed from his mouth at his every breath.

I came back shortly with two extra-large garbage bags of refundable bottles that could give him at least five dollars more. Then I handed him another bag of fresh food and a medium-sized container of warm mushroom soup.

I peered searchingly at his face, and he stared tenderly back. There were no more words exchanged, for his mouth quivered and tears started to roll, leaving streaks down his dirty cheeks.

Here was a man, pushed to the precipice of despair, renewed with hope because of a small bag of food. The same man I condemned to be a nuisance eager for a rough-and-tumble fight was bruised because he had to scrounge for his food with bare hands. His lacerations were, no doubt, knifed by the shards of glass and serrated tin cans in the dumps.

I had to fight back my own tears—mixed tears of shame at the evil thoughts that crossed my mind and tears of gladness.

Yes. Pure, unadulterated gladness.

For that night, I saw the gentle, loving face of Jesus. His head was crowned with unkempt and knotted hair. His eyes were red with exhaustion. And His features, battered by deprivation.

Yes, I saw Jesus' face.

And he smiled back at me.

Then the righteous will answer him,
"Lord, when did we see you hungry and feed you,
or thirsty and give you something to drink?
When did we see you a stranger and invite you in,

MENU 1: MERCY AND GRACE

>or needing clothes and clothe you?
>When did we see you sick
>or in prison and go to visit you?"
>The King will reply, "Truly I tell you,
>whatever you did for one of the least
>of these brothers and sisters of mine,
>you did for me."
>Matthew 25:37-40

CHAPTER 4

Against the Tide

Speaking from personal experience, Liesl once observed how awkward it was to uphold Christian principles in a secular organization where politics-thirsty workaholics swarm like hornets. I couldn't agree more.

It is almost an ambitious pursuit to be Christian in our hedonistic generation. It's like sneezing with your eyes open, or saying the letter M without your lips touching. It can't be done without looking awfully silly! Many of us are uncomfortable with speaking church language in the office. Inserting God in a conversation can get as clumsy as a butter-fingered waitress balancing a tray-load of plates.

Sometimes, it feels like you're a tug-o-war amateur, with brawny athletes of the winning team outnumbering your side of the rope. In this cutthroat match, we see two players: the followers of Christ versus the advocates of secularism.

One position campaigns for non-negotiable truth. They defend the gospel from cynics who ridicule its existence and seek

MENU 1: MERCY AND GRACE

its collapse. Though accused as intolerant, these people never water down biblical teaching to fit their skins. As people who sink their roots deeply into virtue, they don't bend over backwards and reshape principles to please those who disagree. Though given a bad press, nit-picked, or wrongfully judged, they stand their ground.

Authentic Christians.

They go by that name.

And for them, a diluted morality that switches with the seasons is a weak standard by which to live.

The other position pushes for variable standards. They are proponents of popular culture who get sucked in by strong undercurrents of relativism. Morality is debatable, and the crowd is free to swing its vote towards the party with the loudest voice.

On the pretext of freedom of choice, the individual decides what is right or wrong depending on what suits his life story. For such men, a little compromise doesn't hurt. It stands to reason that, for harmony's sake, a little bending of rules is good. What will it hurt to give or take a few principles to reach a mutual settlement between conflicting views?

And so, for this team, God's hard-and-fast commandments are not the touchstones on which decisions are based. Behaviour is dictated by social media, world view, peer pressure, political correctness, personal comfort, instant gratification, self-worship, pride, and a host of other warped philosophies.

I say this is a fierce tug-o-war ... one that Liesl encountered daily in her workplace. In that company, idle talk and sexually-tinted jokes were the trendy forms of entertainment. Pointless tittle-tattle punctuated every channel of communication. Slanderous humour received an attentive audience. Laughter added fuel to the fire and stirred up more risqué jokes.

No one dared to point out the impropriety of any conversation. To do so would be suicidal. Like a scarlet letter, the protester would carry a stigma. Wet blanket. Party pooper. Bore. Grinch. Those would be the kindest labels you'd hear.

Liesl knew only too well.

Because she was that one person who wore the scarlet letter.

The story started when Liesl decided to join the boys for coffee during one afternoon break. Typically, she kept her distance from them. That particular day, though, she worked through the lunch hour and her hunger already escalated to a migraine.

Liesl's colleagues were efficient workers, but it was on account of these men that the culture of vulgarity thrived in the office. And so it happened that during coffee break, one of the guys set the ball in motion. While chit-chat was tame at the onset, it wasn't clean for long.

Soon, one colleague enlightened the group on the sexual implications of different mannerisms. The open trade of ideas flipped from bearable to repulsive. The remarks left a tart taste in the mouth. As if these weren't enough, the men gyrated and twerked to add visual interest. Being the only lady in the group, Liesl felt awkward, to say the least. Though she wasn't the subject of the banter, she felt like every cell of her female anatomy was stripped for public study.

Any person could only be broadminded to a certain degree. Push one's latitudes for liberality a little further, and one's values would be put in jeopardy. Liesl was at that juncture.

She knew that she had to politely excuse herself or her thoughts would cave in to lust.

Apparently, her reaction made their blood boil. Never before had anyone openly showed distaste for their brand of entertainment by walking out. What Liesl did must have been a bold slap to their ego.

MENU 1: MERCY AND GRACE

After this incident, Liesl noticed a marked shift in the way her coworkers related with her. Their usual warmth was replaced with aloofness. All civility was wiped out. What remained was a stoical façade that brought across the message, "Go away! You don't belong here!"

From then on, life in the office became an emotionally tough season for Liesl. She approached them with a hearty "good morning" but was dodged with a blank stare. Whenever she broke the ice and struck a conversation, they turned their backs like she had a plague.

There was an isolated incident when halfway through a filthy joke, one colleague cynically interrupted, "Warning! Someone might walk out again!"

The intention wasn't really to halt the fun but to brashly insult the lone soldier who dared to put faith in action.

Liesl braved all levels of meanness towards which I counseled her to throw a snappy comeback. Instead of anger, I encouraged her to retaliate with forgiveness. If the bullies knew their purposeless intimidation had the efficacy to prick her nerves, then Liesl would have given them added ammunition.

Liesl didn't cave in to pressure. Still, with cold shoulders foreseeable in the agenda, the thought of walking through the door each morning weighed heavily on her shoulders. What modicum of inspiration she had was worn down pretty fast. She was a dead battery, and she literally jump-started herself to work everyday.

One Thursday afternoon, all the singles quietly organized a Friday night out at the hottest bar in the metro. Everyone was invited—except Liesl. While drumming on the computer, she overheard one associate say, "How about Liesl? Did anyone ask her?"

The voice was a decibel above a whisper but audible enough. That was their mistake! Realizing that the statement reached her ears with perfect clarity, they kept up appearances. Feigning kindness, they extended an invitation that was too weak; it might as well have snorted out of their noses.

Despite the begrudged offer, Liesl accepted. She was totally unmindful of the repercussions of her decision. Honestly, she acted on pride alone and didn't think too far ahead. However, as soon as she yielded to peer pressure, God tugged at her senses with a word of warning.

> You, dear children, are from God and have overcome them, because the one who is in you is greater than the one who is in the world. They are from the world and therefore speak from the viewpoint of the world, and the world listens to them. We are from God, and whoever knows God listens to us; but whoever is not from God does not listen to us. This is how we recognize the Spirit of truth and the spirit of falsehood. (1 John 4:4–6)

What precise timing! Despite the strong force of culture in the workplace, God expects His children to be stubborn in holiness. The Lord, who dwells in the hearts of His people, has greater influence than any worldly stronghold that pulls men to the throes of immorality.

It was this word of Scripture that revived Liesl from her temporary loss of sensibility. Never mind if she was criticized for being too Victorian in prudishness. Who would care if they called her Ms. Goody-Two-Shoes? It didn't matter if they flung mud and labeled her a bore, a bummer, or a puritan. God wanted Liesl to dismiss the insults and tap on to His grace of forbearance.

MENU 1: MERCY AND GRACE

Knowing that Liesl would make a monkey out of her faith if she joined the party, God seized matters into His own hands. That Thursday, her early afternoon muscle pains, runny nose, and chills deteriorated into a full-blown flu. Traveling home in the thick of a heavy downpour required extra effort. She could hardly budge an inch. The following day, her condition slid further downhill, and she had no choice but to call in sick.

The Friday night drinking spree went ahead as originally planned. But God singled Liesl out through illness to spare her from malicious talk or whatever rubbish He knew was waiting to happen with such wild company.

However, Liesl's inability to show up that night spurred further name-calling and gossip. It was their backhanded response to her cheekiness in accepting the dare.

"It's a good thing you didn't come. You gave us a chance to talk about you." The woman's barb was as razor-sharp as her glare.

Liesl tried her best to fend off the offensive blow with a laugh, but somehow, anger poisoned her mind. The disposition to love those with abrasive manners was dampened by an urge to get even. She wanted to pay back dirt with dirt. It took all the grace of heaven for Liesl to glue her tongue to her palate so it wouldn't lick the high-and-mighty look off that woman's face.

Liesl gave this girl her phoniest smile which, you bet, looked too wacky for words. How could it not look absurd? Have you ever seen someone smolder in the heart, foam at the mouth, and still smile like a fool? Liesl was the nuttiest fruitcake for doing exactly that!

Onwards from that day, Liesl was determined to take an indifferent stand. She urged herself to interact with them only as the job dictated. Otherwise, she stayed invisible. It was an escapist's temper, yes—a very comfortable deal which the Lord didn't applaud.

My friend, perhaps this day finds you in a similar pit. People around you sputter at your face, throw stones of judgment, and kick you while you're down. You feel listless, your spirit sucked dry. You drag your feet, ready to drop at the minutest pinch, because you're out of gas, crippled by the fight.

Sister, dry those tears. Brother, don't limp through your day. Take courage in the Lord's word. As it is written,

> Live such good lives among the pagans that, though they accuse you of doing wrong, they may see your good deeds and glorify God on the day he visits us.
> (1 Peter 2:12)

Ride through this persecution with your head looking up!

Truth is, you are surrounded by bruised people who carry on hostilities with their sin-impaired reasoning. You are right where God rooted you; there's no mistake about it. God planted you along the warpath, right in the middle of this contradiction, among mudslingers.

It's because the Lord is using you in His redeeming work—a peacemaker among wolves.

Work is in progress, so keep still.

Do not worry. Though you grunt and sweat, you'll never shed blood in this battle. God already sacrificed His Son to take your place in the bloodbath.

Remember, your enemies are not shooting you down, but Christ who lives in you. The disdain and condescension you think you suffer has fallen upon God's face. The apostle Paul wrote it in his epistle,

> For God did not call us to be impure, but to live a holy life. Therefore, anyone who rejects this instruction does not reject a human being but God,

MENU 1: MERCY AND GRACE

> the very God who gives you his Holy Spirit. (1 Thessalonians 4:7–8)

You wonder ... how do you make things right and regain your enemy's respect?

Maintain a gentle spirit in the face of opposition. By bearing peace in your heart, you will put your detractors to shame. The network of lies they weave will have no power against you because your humble tone will prove them wrong.

There is no easy way around this. For sure, it is no picnic. It is self-contradictory to stay positive when people treat you like slime, and yet, this is what God demands—

To create glory out of adversity,

Trade beauty for ashes,

Draw righteousness out of the fallen, and

Capture wisdom through life's crookedness.

Yes, it is possible to turn the gray days into life-giving blues, greens, and yellows. This is what God's redemptive work is all about. For your part, Paul encourages,

> Make it your ambition to lead a quiet life: You should mind your own business and work with your hands ... so that your daily life may win the respect of outsiders. (1 Thessalonians 4:11–12)

This is what God taught, and this is what Liesl learned to do.

The fruit?

The unholy mess in the office eventually cleared. God transfigured Liesl's mourning into joy, but not until she was frayed to near breaking point. He had Liesl pass through an agonizing test to see how much refinement her character could gain. Though she stubbornly bargained with God to lighten the yoke, He was solid in His purpose. Day in and out, she pleaded for the grace to ignore the scars and love the bullies.

Gradually, the ice thawed. The duplicity in interactions adjusted in a mind-blowing way. The tension that used to fill the air slowly lifted, replaced by laughter once more—the uncolored and wholesome kind this time!

Friends returned Liesl's smiles with equally guileless smiles. Attempts at conversation, no longer wasted, blossomed into seeds sown on fertile ground. For throughout this conflict, her colleagues' cocky disguises lifted to reveal Christ-hungry hearts ... hearts searching for answers.

God breathed life into their friendship. And though the transformation took months, it didn't matter.

God swapped Liesl's ashes of pain with a crown of beauty, His redemptive mission complete.

It was a hard-won victory.

But at the end of the day, that's all that counted!

```
         Do your best to present yourself to God
                      as one approved,
           a worker who does not need to be ashamed
          and who correctly handles the word of truth.
                     Avoid godless chatter,
                  because those who indulge in it
                  will become more and more ungodly.
             Their teaching will spread like gangrene.
                         2 Timothy 2:15-17
```

CHAPTER 5

Nanoo! Nanoo!

When I was in elementary school, I hung out exclusively with my best friend, Sally. We were inseparable, like conjoined twins fused at the hip. Every recess, we kept an eye on each other to make sure no one was left bruised or bleeding at the playground. We shared packed lunches, toys, crayons, geranium-pink stationeries, doodles, and many other little girly treasures.

To say that our friendship trumped that of Big Bird's and Mr. Snuffleupagus' wouldn't be a hyperbolic fairy tale. Sally and I blended harmoniously like creamy Camembert cheese and Merlot wine. Like vanilla ice cream on sugar cones. Like Fred Flintstone and Barney Rubble. Like hairy King Kong and Ann Darrow ... uhm ... well, maybe not that one.

Sally and I had one thing in common. We both loved to watch this primetime hit series, Mork and Mindy. We enjoyed the comical faces and quirky voices of Robin Williams who played the alien from planet Ork. We both wished to ride inside Mork's cool egg spacecraft. We wanted to follow in the footsteps of Mindy

McConnell, the brunette sweetheart, whose sense of loyalty was top-notch. Above all, we laughed at the way Mork twisted his ears to say goodbye at the conclusion of each program. Wrapped in his red and silver onesie spacesuit, he always bowed with the words, "Nanoo! Nanoo!"

That phrase stuck to us like Velcro. It was so catchy we used it as our dynamic-duo, sign-off code. Each time our parents picked us up at school's end, we folded our ears in similar fashion. We degenerated into giggles all the way to our cars, with "nanoo-nanoo" exploding non-stop from our lips. We were two silly clowns—I could see that now—but, back then, we thought we were adorable.

Sally and I had always hovered on the same wavelength. Towards the end of the school year, however, the predictability of the relationship began to bore me. I wanted to explore other friendships and test the waters for meaningful conversations besides Mork and Mindy. I started playing with other classmates and discovered the joy of non-exclusive interaction.

This spawned jealousy in Sally. She felt betrayed by my abrupt breakaway. To say that she went ballistic is putting it mildly. I never really saw her antagonistic side until the closing of the school year when she threw a bag at my face. In it were all the knick-knacks we shared as well as the gifts I gave her on her birthday, Christmas, and Valentines Day. She returned them all, not just to bury the memories, but because she was spoiling for a fight. She scribbled a spiteful letter that accused me of many things. To add insult to injury, she signed the note "nanoo! nanoo!"

My mom and aunts thought the letter was hilarious. They had such a belly-jiggling hysteria that I thought their dentures would pop off. However, for a child, such name-calling cut deep. "Nanoo, nanoo" was supposed to be our mark of respect, not a sour diatribe. Therefore, the experience was no laughing matter for me. It was my first taste of rejection.

Now who can forgive a person who, without rhyme or reason, mocks you with a nanoo nanoo? How can you forgive a behaviour that is as juvenile as drawing whiskers on your teacher's picture?

I thought I couldn't. But I did ... just before I turned forty. Ha-ha!

Seriously, I had several damaging encounters with people for whom forgiveness was the honourable response, but it was such a bitter-tasting pill I often dispensed halfheartedly.

For how could you not curl your fingers into a fist and disfigure the face of those who took advantage of your kindness? Wouldn't it be justifiable, even natural or human, to respond to defrauders and backstabbers with hate? How do you deal with friends who tarnish your reputation with baseless gossip? Not everyone has the patience of Job. So how can you forgive?

Scripture speaks to us about God, who Himself, is the embodiment of mercy. Daily, He suffers the treachery of His children and yet remains flawless. In so doing, He becomes the perfect benchmark against which we gauge our own actions.

All humanity is misshapen and fickle-minded. We are a people who can't decide if we are for or against God. We are crippled by pride and predisposed to sin. Enslaved by carnal appetites, we throw away modesty and restraint at the slightest exposure of skin. We permit anger to smolder and fester in our hearts. We yield to resentments and blind jealousies, and release them through our fierce speech.

Who forgives such depravity?

God does!

When we corner ourselves into trouble, who gets us off the hook?

God does!

MENU 1: Mercy and Grace

Who wipes the slate clean so we can draw on a blank and start fresh?

God does!

Who strips us of our sin-stained cloaks and drapes on us, instead, a mantle of redemption?

God does!

We are the foul scum that God elevated into His circle of acceptance through forgiveness. We are blemished people, doomed for oblivion, but restored because of God's mercy.

As the Lord says in Isaiah 43,

> "You have not brought me sheep for burnt offerings,
> nor honored me with your sacrifices. I have not
> burdened you with grain offerings nor wearied you
> with demands for incense. You have not bought any
> fragrant calamus for me, or lavished on me the fat
> of your sacrifices. But you have burdened me with
> your sins and wearied me with your offenses. I,
> even I, am he who blots out your transgressions, for
> my own sake, and remembers your sins no more."
> (Isaiah 43: 23–25)

Meditating on what God has done can help us through our personal seasons of unforgiveness. Let us not hold other people's sins against them because God has done the same for us.

It may be true that what we don't know won't hurt. We are clueless and blind when it comes to the judgmental thoughts people harbor. We have no hint on how virulent our co-workers can be when they talk dirty behind locked doors.

But God knows.

He can see the darkest of thoughts.

The filthiest of intentions.

The most indecent secret.

And the malicious words whispered from ear to ear.

He can foresee the evil that men will plot tomorrow. He can see as clear as daylight what foolishness you and I will do years down the road.

And it stabs His heart.

The pain is beyond belief, the sorrow beyond relief.

Yet, God forgives.

Let us, thus, imitate Him who has given us the perfect example of forgiveness.

Chapter 6

Treasures from Out of the Blue

Pajo was a fifteen-month-old hyper-diaper when he discovered a strange form of entertainment. While nobody was looking, he would smuggle whatever his tiny fists could grab and hide them in places no one would care to look. There was a time I couldn't find my house keys. With a mischievous grin, Pajo pointed to the diaper dispenser hanging by his bassinet. With one word—"aysh!"—this playful culprit confessed where he squirreled away the booty.

Once, Colleen hollered from our bedroom, "Mama, I found two spoons! One on the altar and another beside Pajo's potty."

On another night, after Alvin tucked our daughter to sleep, he stepped into the kitchen with a stash of cooking gadgets, an Avent baby bottle, a serving spoon, and a toy recorder.

"You wouldn't believe where I found these," my husband said with a broad smile.

"Where?"

MENU 1: Mercy and Grace

"In the bedroom, behind the headboard!"

Again, one afternoon, Colleen arrived home from school very hungry. As a matter of routine, she wanted to prepare a grilled cheese sandwich before digging into her homework.

"Mama," Colleen peeked into my room. "Did we finish up all the dinner rolls already?"

"No, honey. We have a lot left. They're on the kitchen counter."

"The bag's not there."

"But I just left it there this morning."

Between the rhythmic patter of rubber flip-flops and the mild banging of pantry doors, Colleen busily searched for the missing buns. After five minutes, she announced with a triumphant shout, "Aha! Found it!"

Apparently, the little pirate dragged his plunder of bread into the far corner of the living room, right under the antique chair which nobody would eye with suspicion. That was Pajo's I'll-hide-and-you-go-seek trademark. I bet my last demonetized penny that my son was determined to make the Easter egg hunt tradition a year-round affair.

Now the classic "quest for the lost treasure" that threw us into patches of laughter involved the TV remote. While the family curled up inside Colleen's bedroom for a movie night, the remote was nowhere in sight. We flattened our palms over the duvet and bed sheets, frisked all the plump pillows, and rummaged through drawers. Short of ransacking the building, we tumbled every nook and cranny inside out but didn't find a thing.

All this time, Pajo sat on his sister's bed, an air of innocence plastered on his disarming face. The flurry of activity so excited him; he bounced vigorously on the bed. Just when he did, the TV screen abruptly displayed its menu settings, something that would happen only if you pressed the appropriate button on the remote.

Thinking that Pajo was sitting on the gadget, we lifted the baby and combed through the bed once again.

Nothing.

Tired and a bit puzzled, Colleen plopped herself on the mattress. That bit of movement caused an unexpected switch in channels. Amused by the shift, all of us started wiggling on the bed, pushing the mattress coils to its tensile strength limit. Each time we exerted enough pressure, the TV channels changed.

By then, we all erupted into giggles. What a tough nut to crack! Where could that elusive remote be? The morning rooster didn't yet crow before the riddle was finally solved. The loot, crammed between the iron bed frame and the mattress, had all the tiny fingerprints of a naughty boy.

As I looked back on these hilarious episodes and relived the fun of discovery, I realized how often God also sprinkled my life with amazing finds. The only difference was that I didn't search for the treasure. God made sure the treasure pushed its way to me.

Years ago, I made an early morning trip to the lobby mailbox and found an envelope with no sender name or return address. I assumed it was another invoice demanding immediate payment.

Twenty-five-pound Pajo dangled by my left hip. His left leg was wrapped around my seven-month-pregnant belly while his right foot kicked my butt in steady rhythm. I balanced the bulky parcels with my free hand as I shuffled my heels down the apartment hallway. I was careful not to drop my squirming son as I tussled with the heavy fire doors. With all that heavy cargo, plus the clumsy bearings of an expectant mom, the unmarked envelope slipped through my fingers almost half a dozen times.

MENU 1: MERCY AND GRACE

One elderly lady stood outside her apartment door as I passed through. With the hint of a smile, she kept an eye on this klutzy, graceless figure who constantly bent over to retrieve that mean little envelope. Unable to contain her amusement, she chuckled, "Seems to me you just don't wanna pay that bill! You're trying too hard to get rid of it."

I laughed at my neighbour's candid observation. Nothing could be further from the truth. I really didn't care about what's inside the packet, but I was responsible enough not to leave my clutter on the hallway.

Back inside the house, I threw my mail on the dining table and totally forgot about it until late in the afternoon. When I did get around to opening it, I was pleasantly stunned. Sitting inside the unpretentious envelope was a cheque from our insurance company. Apparently, we overpaid our annual premium for the car, and the honest company gave us a refund! What I feared to be an added expense turned out to be God's blessing, perfectly timed to answer an urgent financial need.

Like Pajo, God must be delighted each time we dredge up His surprises. You see, it is also His trademark to plant treasures in unexpected places—treasures that will jump at you like a Jack-in-a-box precisely when the gray clouds of hopelessness are about to gather.

God often playfully sneaks up from our blind side. Just when we need a little sunbeam in the rain or a welcome smile in a tear-soaked face, His provisions erupt in the flicker of an eye. With impeccable timing, God answers our pressing concerns with gifts far beyond our limited imagination. Therefore, we should always call to mind,

> Every good and perfect gift is from above, coming down from the Father of the heavenly lights, who does not change like shifting shadows. (James 1:17)

Before Pajo was born, I scribbled a list of the basic gears my baby would need. I jotted down only the essentials. I tried with all my sagging muscle to turn my head away from the eye-popping nursery furniture, toys, and other nice-to-have-but-can-do-without baby trappings. Still, my inventory came out only an inch short of an insatiable kid's Santa Claus wish list. With only one man coughing out the payslip, I worried about the huge investment these would require.

My sister-in-law once told me, "When God blesses a husband and wife with a new child, He packs bread along with the baby." She said this in good humour, but I literally took it in prayer and challenged God to send home the bread.

And God came through—in gourmet fashion! Not only did the Lord provide an ordinary white loaf, He also sent Irish cream truffles, chocolate fudge bars, blueberry muffins, banana walnut cakes, pecan tarts, apple turnovers, and all the incredible goodies I never expected to receive.

Like the three wise men of the East who brought presents for the child Jesus, friends rode their modern-day camels and took trips to our home, bearing gifts of car seats, strollers, and playpen. Barely a week after Pajo's birth, we received a great deal more than what we scrawled down on our list—two baby carriers, two bathtubs, a bouncer, loads of clothes, a seven-month supply of Pampers diapers, a dozen cans of infant formula, high chair, and baby swing. You name it; friends gave it.

See how great a God we have! He doesn't hide his loot in hard-to-find corners, beside potty seats, or under thick mattresses. He delivers them to anyone who asks.

MENU 1: MERCY AND GRACE

    Because we are God's family. And to His children, God left this promise:

> Our barns will be filled with every kind of provision. Our sheep will increase by thousands, by tens of thousands in our fields; our oxen will draw heavy loads. There will be no breaching of walls, no going into captivity, no cry of distress in our streets. Blessed is the people of whom this is true; blessed is the people whose God is the Lord. (Psalm 144:13–15)

    Friend, when your vision is narrowly confined and the smoky veil of your problems spoils the view, it is difficult to look far afield—past the present moment—to spot the approaching blessing. Take heart.

    You have a generous God who can crawl on all fours with you if you need to take that uphill climb.

    You won't feel alone because He marches in step, hiking with you through your life's misty, deserted bogs.

    He is ready to trample underfoot any seed of frustration stewing in your heart.

    He drives with you through the foggy road, clearing the windshield as you go, so that you may enjoy the sunrise ahead.

    With amusement, He spices up your journey and blows your mind with dramatic surprises.

    Because God is generous.

    And it is His joy to stagger you breathless with treasures from out of the blue.

FAITH crumbles THE mountains the world SAYS YOU ARE ill-equipped TO CLIMB!!

Chapter 7

The Long Trip Home

"You shall have many children."

This gentle hint repeatedly jumped off the pages of every devotional that landed on my lap for four straight years. With only one child after many years of marriage, the message should have been warm and cuddly comfort. However, my comfort level was no better than that of a carnival clown lounging on a bed of a thousand prickly nails. God's confirmation kept coming like steady clockwork, and I shuddered at hearing it for a hundredth time.

Try as I might, I couldn't filter out what God wanted to say, nor pick only what was sugar-coated. I knew I ought to give pause and mark His words for all the truth they carried because God never breaks promises. He had to speak more periodically than necessary to calm my internal upheavals and melt signs of disbelief.

Needless to say, it wasn't long before the second baby arrived. In the middle of my husband's euphoria, I broke into a cold sweat, and my skittish heart skipped many beats. While he saw promise, I only saw threats.

MENU 2: Faith

Before you wonder why some crazy pregnant woman would leap like a startled gazelle and refuse a heaven-sent blessing, let me rewind a bit and tell you the story.

Many years ago, I held a senior management position in a company where the demands on my rank reeked of hostility. Most of the executives I worked with were too myopic as to value nothing else in life besides the glitz of their profession. High officials were opinionated and apathetic towards the marginal wage-earner. They split hairs over petty issues only to prove whose power had more weight. Needless to say, it was an uphill struggle to work within a culture of conceit, where capricious emotional outbursts kept people on tenterhooks. How then could you expect any woman to survive the rigors of pregnancy amid this intense pressure?

Such was the overriding reason behind my tearful refusal. Surely, I love to have a son. I just dreaded the further strain that my stressful environment would have on the child.

It took time to accept God's plan, but just as soon as hopeful expectation replaced my nail-biting episodes and tension headaches, the bizarre happened. I had a disturbing dream. As crisp as a moonlit reflection on an undisturbed pool, I saw two huge hands carrying a bundle wrapped in crystal beams of light.

A faint voice announced, "Here is your son."

I reached out for the baby whose hair was of the same butter-golden hue as polished brass. His skin felt smoother than fine porcelain. Like the freshness of a vial of lavender oil, the baby gave me his sweetest smile and, upon turning, revealed a beautiful pair of celestial wings. I was thrilled! I realized that the Lord was not only giving me a child; He was appointing His special angel to our home!

When I cradled the cherub in my arms, he immediately snuggled and sucked breast milk. However, I noticed that the more he nursed, the faster he shrunk—like withered, frost-bitten fruit—until he reached a mere inch. To my absolute horror, the baby solidified like glass, burst into a thousand fragments, and blew out like a frivolous sigh.

I woke up with a start with pieces of my dream still lingering in my consciousness. The picture was foggy but unmistakeable, similar to the last mist that has not yet vanished at cock-crowing dawn. I didn't know exactly if what I experienced was a premonition of some sort. I had an ominous feeling that did not subside until that unforgettable day when I began to discharge fresh blood.

Onwards from that point, my condition became very precarious. If I wanted to save the two-month-old baby, the doctor instructed that I strictly avoid work and rest in bed for an indefinite period. However, I had no freedom to take a prolonged leave as this would disrupt pressing assignments in the office. Left with no loophole for escape, I retreated into the same madhouse where physical and mental exertion daily reached its peak.

I was already bleeding profusely for several weeks when the doctor saw the inevitability of my hospital confinement. After a twenty-four-hour, critical-care alert, the specialist wheeled me into the ultrasound section where she administered a more thorough examination.

The baby was alive and well. Sadly though, as nurses transferred me to my private room, I was welcomed by a distressing call from the office. I sensed heavy turbulence on the horizon as my associates juggled through a panic situation. I was very much aware of my baby's borderline health, but the nagging urgency of the moment forced me to act. Left without a back-up, diagnostic plan or an alternate project head, I gathered documents, coordinated with my staff, and finished the time-sensitive business which only I had the jurisdiction to deliver.

I spent two hospital days in my offsite, makeshift office, grieving over my hard luck. Whatever severe contractions I had dropped beneath the radar. More than half of my concentration wasn't on my bodily

MENU 2: Faith

symptoms. Reckless and idiotic, or not, I was bent on proving that I didn't intentionally abandon the ship when the sailing got tough.

Two more days after working on the hospital bed, I started to feel a different kind of pinch—one that I could no longer brush off. This alarmed my husband. Aware of my high pain threshold, he knew I wasn't the type to wince unless the spasm was torturous enough to provoke even the most forbearing martyr. The full wrath of the cramps brought doctors quickly to my side. It didn't take long for them to declare that my son finally died.

Rushed to the delivery room for emergency curettage, I experienced raw pain. The whole building pealed with the melodious wails of newborn babies, the happy groans of tired mothers, and the excited voices of celebrating families. But there I was, crumpled up in tears of remorse and anger, sealing the death of my precious angel.

The anguish didn't easily fade away. Long after I left the hospital, I still tenaciously drummed my head with mad echoes of guilt. I berated myself for not heeding the physical signs, for not listening to my doctor's sound advice, and for allowing work to take precedence over family priorities.

Even after I learned that the fetus was genetically weak to survive, and that no amount of rest or medical attention could stop the premature abortion, I wasn't at peace. I hugged all the blame. Like bent weeping willows, I stooped so low as to avoid my husband's eyes. I flinched at the thought of talking to him because I believed I was outside the range of his forgiveness.

During this period of raging depression, the Lord embraced His beleaguered warrior, smoothed her ruffled brows, and gave comfort.

> My salvation and my honor depend on God; he is my mighty rock, my refuge. Trust in him at all times, you people; pour out your hearts to him, for God is our refuge. (Psalm 62:7–8)

Have you ever grieved the loss of a loved one or experienced a pain so deep that nothing seems to pacify? Maybe your cup of misery right now is overflowing, and no one around you fully understands the picture. Admittedly, it defies logical sequence to trust God when suffering slaps you squarely on the face. It seems callous to believe that a mighty purpose rests beneath the sorrow. Head knowledge of Scripture dictates that all things work for good, but all that hidden victory is easy to ignore when a bitter pill is still stuck in your throat.

It is written in Isaiah 49:13,

> Shout for joy, you heavens; rejoice, you earth; burst into song, you mountains! For the Lord comforts his people and will have compassion on his afflicted ones.

I love how another translation restates the last line,

> ... He has tenderly nursed his beaten-up, beaten-down people. (Isaiah 49:13 The Message)

"Rejoice" is a word that is tough to read in Scripture when you are still bleeding from the nails of your cross. How can you force a smile while you are beaten, pulverized, and squashed down to pulp by the weight of your trial?

And yet, these words in the Bible reveal how the afflicted grip God's compassion. It conjures up images of a Father touching the damp cheeks of a bruised child whose head rests limply on His lap and whose body convulses with every sob. Tenderly He does it. With delicate strokes softly brushing away each sad tear, the Father whispers in our ears, "It's okay. I am here. This may not make sense to you now. But soon it will."

MENU 2: Faith

To the same degree, nothing made sense in my dilemma. Unhinged and fractured by the miscarriage, the Lord answered my "why" by dredging up the past.

As a minor, my daughter, Colleen, suffered successive physical abuse from someone very close to the family. With no patience for the crying child, and in a fit of anger, this fellow often pinched and scalded my daughter's skin, causing nasty bruises all over her frail body. My husband and I were busy working the whole day; we didn't have the foggiest idea what freakish things happened behind our backs. Colleen lost her sense of security, and my absence as a mother pumped up her fears.

All the while, we thought that Colleen's skin discoloration and lumps were symptoms of some blood-related deficiency. Yet, after the doctor conducted tests and results didn't reveal any medical connection, my husband and I suspected foul play. When Colleen displayed abnormal behaviour, I began to gravely contemplate the possibility of our friend's unlawful activity.

I remember how in the middle of the night, horrid, recurrent nightmares disrupted my daughter's sleep. She often roused from bed with wide, clouded eyes. Arms stretched towards the door, she wailed, "Mama, don't leave me!"

Once, she blabbered incoherently and wrestled with me as I shook her awake. It took a stretch of time before Colleen recognized my calming voice, after which she threw her arms tightly around my neck, terrified that I'd let go. I cuddled her quietly until she fell back to sleep, confident that her parents would never walk out nor feed her to the wolves.

These were the memories God flooded into my consciousness. It was His odd response to my question—"Why the miscarriage?" God showed me, in a sorely blunt fashion, how my decision to put my career first hurt the same people I was ordained to love. I was the bonehead who missed the warning signs blinking inches before my face. Thus, I discovered the hard way that my desire to earn a living wasn't worth the loss of my son's life nor the trauma that my daughter sustained.

God wanted me to surrender to motherhood. Not infrequently did He extend the invitation to step into the unknown and bow out of my profession for the sake of a greater good. I argued that life on a single income wouldn't be comfortable so I ignored the call. I was much too entrenched in my views that I lost sight of the miracles faith could accomplish. My pragmatic mind deemed it impossible to throw away a financially rewarding career while the entire country was in the limelight of an economic recession. I felt God was demanding too much when He prompted me to settle back home and retire when I was only an elbow away from tasting power, fame, and fortune.

God assured me that to provide for the material needs of the family was not my burden. It is His business. My mission is not to build an empire of money and lean on my self-sufficiency. God's plan is for me to be a physically and spiritually nurturing wife and mother and to trust that His windfall of loaves and fish, and the many modern alternate forms of manna, can sufficiently fill the need.

I wasn't biased against my parental functions. In fact, the opposite was true. I was more than eager to trade my swanky suits for an apron. However, my worry sprouted from a lack of income alternatives which could tide us over rough-sailing seasons. God gave no guarantees that tomorrow would bring rainbows. He didn't say that the hurdles would be cleared, or the track would be paved. In fact, many thistles and thorny vines fell before me to confuse the path. I could depend on no one else but God to declutter the road.

For one, the fine-print catch in my work contract demanded immediate payment of enormous penalties for all the senior management benefits I enjoyed since the day I set foot in

MENU 2: FAITH

the company. It was a hefty sum of money which I never had the privilege of saving.

The cancellation of my executive car plan not only meant the return of my new Honda, but also the forfeiture of nine months' worth of amortizations I already paid. It was a horrendous barrier which the Finance Director had the option to waive—but didn't—in hopes of dissuading me from leaving.

As though these weren't painful enough, my resignation also triggered the recalculation of my home mortgage. The day I drop out of the corporate hierarchy would be the same day they switch the interest rate from fixed to variable, which at that time was triple the prevailing market level. This translated to more burdensome expenses which my husband's paycheck couldn't shoulder. With no income expectations from my side, I knew we would trap ourselves into an ugly quandary once I say "yes" to God's plan.

Truly, I came face to face with an imposing giant—one which dwarfed my faith and crunched what iota of hope I had remaining.

Have you ever faced your own Goliaths with only a rustic slingshot hanging nervously between your clammy fingers?

Have you ever stretched your neck upwards to stare at the intimidating scowl of a heavily armoured Philistine champion?

The enemy sure looks menacing in stature, and it is no wonder you feel the odds are a hundred and one percent against you. In an effort to ease the threat, you might resort to flexing your muscles and bullying your Goliath with words. Scare tactics don't work, though, especially if a knife is already poised at your throat. Over and above your physical skill, faith is required.

Because faith overrides all fears.

Faith conquers weaknesses and heals.

Faith turns a new leaf so that your impossibility becomes reality.

Faith crumbles the mountains the world says you are ill-equipped to climb.

Faith floods light through your darkest tunnels and brings hope to the depressed.

Faith spins tables around so that you overcome the undertow of failure and rejection and rise as glowing victor.

Faith elevates you to higher ground so that your grief dissolves into laughter and true joy.

Faith breaks down strongholds, pushes you out of the doldrums, and unlocks the doors to success.

Faith runs beyond the limits of reason, defies all human comprehension, and accomplishes so much more than these.

Why?

Because faith moves God's heart.

So when you're stopped dead in your tracks by an impregnable wall or assailed by a foe too ghastly for words, fight back with faith. No Herculean strength is necessary. All you need is the humility to admit your dependence on a Power higher than yours.

These were all the lessons I learned as I battled my personal giant. Even as fears paralyzed me into timidity, God's strong hands nudged me into action. Right after I signified my absolute submission to His will and blindly stepped out in faith, God used His iron fist to break down all the barricades I formerly thought were invincible.

By His wise design, the funds needed to resolve penalties flowed into our pockets from unexpected sources. Together in one huge bulk, my husband received unscheduled bonuses from his workplace. Friends and family pledged their lifetime savings even without security that we could reimburse them on demand.

My brother, an expatriate in Malaysia, who because of geographical distance had been cut adrift from my family, paid us a surprise call. Though he couldn't put a finger on it, he felt something was askew and thus wired money with more digits than I expected. I kept mum about our urgency, but the Lord used him nonetheless as a channel of blessing to make true His promise,

> I will go before you and will level the mountains;
> I will break down gates of bronze and cut through
> bars of iron. I will give you hidden treasures, riches
> stored in secret places, so that you may know that I
> am the LORD, the God of Israel, who summons you
> by name. (Isaiah 45:2–3)

God acted beyond human scepticism or foresight. At day's end, I could only blink with incredulity as we had within our reach staggeringly more than what my employer imposed.

To add to the surplus, the interest rate nose-dived on the exact day my mortgage was recalculated. It plunged to its lowest historical level on the day the loan was booked then spiralled upwards again shortly thereafter. It was a miraculous manipulation God pulled off to quell the worries of His little warrior!

Scripture gives plenty of encouragement for us who often sit in the battle zone with nothing more than broken arrows or antiquated rifles. Keep these words secure in your heart,

> The Lord will fight for you; you need only to be
> still. (Exodus 14:14)

Yes, He fights! He fights as you face disease.

He is your sufficiency when the food pantry is too empty that your kids can play hide and seek in it.

He is the brute force that peels you off the ground when stubborn addictions wrestle you to the floor.

He is the discipline and wisdom that coaxes your wild teenager back into church communion.

He is your tranquility and safe-house when strained relationships raise a racket through your ears.

Yes, the Lord will fight and be the anchor for your savage squalls.

You, who put your faith in the Lord, raise the flag of victory and claim your badge of honour—for God's deliverance is certain!

Let go of your puny swords then and be still. You can't be huffing and puffing the entire fifty yards just to run from your troubles and hide.

It's not worth it!

Wipe the sweat off your brow, and steady your heart. As surely as the Lord said this to King Jehoshaphat at the point of his vulnerability, so too is He telling you—

> "Do not be afraid or discouraged because of this vast army. For the battle is not yours, but God's."
> (2 Chronicles 20:15)

Say it again, but now with conviction.
And own the words ...
This battle is not mine. It is the Lord's!

Chapter 8

Declaration of Dependence

Pajo was only nine years old when he conducted his first scholarly lecture. Stretching to his full height before a one-student grammar class, little genius explained, "Chiara, do you know that the prefix "bi" means "two"? That's why a "bicycle" has two wheels."

Oooh! Impressive! I raised an eyebrow towards my kids' direction and was about to applaud the logic when my son continued, "So when you say 'bye-bye', it means you are saying goodbye two times!"

That made me choke! Hearing my half-gag, half-snort, Pajo turned towards me and said, "Mama! Bok, bok, bok!"

"Huh?" I brushed away a tear that escaped as I laughed myself silly. "What do you mean?"

"I'm HELLOING to you in duck language."

Before I could regain my composure, big sister Colleen interrupted, "Pajo, first of all 'helloing' is NOT a verb ..."

Pausing for theatrics, Colleen interjected, "And 'bok, bok, bok' is for CHICKENS!"

MENU 2: Faith

I tell you! No one in the neighbourhood could hee-haw louder than I did that afternoon! By the sounds of it, even a donkey's bray would be put to shame. If every school was this hysterical and every teacher was a quack, I bet all of us would sign up for class night and day.

Children.

Adults are the life coaches and spiritual mentors of these children. With wisdom of years as qualification, it is our responsibility to broaden the minds of our tiny disciples. This is a fact few people will argue.

I learned from our modest grammar class, though, that roles are reversible. It is sometimes gratifying if parents sit down as students and allow these charming little professors to run the show.

Children, in their simplicity and innocence, model for us the virtues so pleasing to God. If we only pause for a moment, dump our "I'm-the-boss" psychology, and watch with attentiveness, adults can harvest bushels of lessons even from a toddler.

Jesus said, "Let the little children come to me, and do not hinder them, for the kingdom of God belongs to such as these" (Luke 18:16).

What is it about children that gain for them complimentary tickets to heaven? How can you and I evoke God's winning smile and merit the same admission privileges?

For one thing, kids don't hold grudges. There is no unforgiving spirit in these young hearts.

I recall when my eldest daughter was only eight, my maternal radar often spotted her in the act of misdemeanor. The five-minute time-out seat in the living room corner became Colleen's habitual jail cell.

In time, this style of punishment lost its potency since my bubbly mischief-maker learned to cope with the boredom by twiddling her fingers, counting the marks on the walls, swinging her legs, or by singing off-key. The jail sentence eventually became a bit entertaining for Colleen that she no longer minded breaking the house rules in order to slouch in her sweet spot and ditch homework.

And so, the no-nonsense educator in me decided to be more innovative in my behaviour-modification technique. I resorted to books! Instead of the "think-about-what-you-did-wrong" chair, the three-inch-thick Webster dictionary became her prime disciplining tool. When caught in a tantrum, I'd ask her to sit and study two pages of the material, to memorize the spelling and add the fifty or so words to her vocabulary list. Need I say how much she hated this routine?

I didn't want to admit it, but this was an unpopular verdict for me too. Saddled by duty to sit with my daughter, I illustrated every single vocabulary word in ways that Colleen could comprehend. Phew! What a brain stretcher!

The sweat paid off, though. Not only did the task curb the misdeeds; Colleen, in due course, learned to value Mr. Webster— referring to him now as "my best friend".

But I remember the very first time she faced this assignment, the pout and wrinkled expression she flashed on me made her appear worse than crinkled prunes. If there was a point in history when she considered her mother unlovable, it was perhaps that day.

Colleen took an hour to finish studying the dictionary, but she spent half the time whimpering over the inevitable. Later on, I was surprised at how quickly her emotions bounced back.

After an hour, what adults might still consider a fresh sore is, for a child, already a subject buried in ancient archives. One minute, Colleen was throwing dagger looks at me; the next minute, she was clambering all over my body and flinging her arms around my neck in a fierce hug. I don't believe any adult could switch sides in such a snap. Talk about grudges. This child had none!

MENU 2: Faith

God loves children because they are of such a noble spirit that they find it difficult to preserve their anger for long stretches. They are bubbling with spontaneous energy, always eager to forget offensive issues and push forward towards pleasant ground.

Besides their forgiving nature, children have a deep sense of idealism. Out of touch with reality, they think that people journey in a dreamy, Utopian world where problems close with "lived-happily-ever-after". Adults call this immaturity. I wish, instead, to look at their simple optimism as a sign of trust and dependence.

Children look at the human race through rose-colored glasses. Failing to perceive the presence of social evils, they never anticipate harm to pounce from a street corner. They believe life is a romanticized storybook—all poetic and beautiful. Children are convinced you can paint the future with bright-coloured crayons, and it will hold more promise. Snags may hit once in a while, but there is nothing a little cry can't solve.

Why? Because despite their vulnerability, kids accept in faith that they can depend on the competence and protection of adults far stronger than themselves. They have no illusions of their own power. They only know how to run towards the defending arms of trustworthy people—people who can hold them up with stability and make the pain go away. If you ask a child to scribble down his statement of principles, he will probably write five short words, "When in doubt, ask Daddy!"

This is exactly how God wants you to behave. He wants you to quit worrying. He wants you to push away all negativity even when trouble clouds your mind. He wants you to swap your inhibitions with faith and, like a child, be quick to crawl under God's protective custody.

Such idealism is not an offshoot of naïveté. It springs from an awareness of our helpless state and a declaration of dependence on One higher than our circumstance.

Be honest then. Confess that you do not always have a grip. God sometimes strips you of your defenses so that you'll finally admit you can't be in control. You can't hog the steering wheel, burn a hole through the driver's seat, and race until the odometer reads "Death's Door". Stand up from the Commander's spot and learn how to be a quiet passenger for once! Give God the latitude and you'll be amazed at what He can do without the interference of your stubborn self-will.

One afternoon, eight-year-old Chiara rushed towards me with an expression so forlorn that I thought the world was about to end. Obviously sick at heart, she knew that her mother would be the only one to solve her problem. Despite my earnest pleadings that the kids stay quiet so that I could focus on my writing, Chiara still persistently disturbed me that day. Confident that her mother always had a welcome reception in store for her, Chiara wailed as she held up to my face a cute undergarment.

"Mama, what will I do? I want to use my jellybean underwear so it matches my penguin pajamas. But look! There's a hole!"

To prove that her situation was a real toughie, she pushed a finger through the damage on her favourite undershorts.

I acknowledged that she was indeed in a pretty pickle. Although momentarily tempted, I didn't chase Chiara out with a quick temper or a bored yawn. It was easy to say, "Stop fussing! Don't disturb me with panties. Just get rid of it!" Instead, I gave her my undivided attention. I allowed her the freedom to croak and boo-hoo-hoo until she felt relieved.

Chiara acted as if her interest was of high priority, it was worth the intrusion. Children are like this. Every trifle seems so valuable that they are brimming with courage to break the silence and take the podium. They want to unbridle their hearts, to speak unhampered, certain that even foolishness wouldn't be grounds for rejection.

Scripture says,

> See what great love the Father has lavished on us,
> that we should be called children of God! And that
> is what we are! (1 John 3:1)

We are children of God! Repeat after me ... I am a child of God!

How beautiful it is then for you to learn such trait—

To disturb God with your silliness and to confide in Him with the same spontaneity,

With the same sparkle and spirit,

With the same genuine excitement that children muster when they run to adults.

Don't be afraid. There is nothing irrelevant in what you want to breathe in God's ear. It is alright to stammer. Nasal or throaty, off-pitched or baritone, your voice sounds all the same to Him. It is joyful melody!

Don't be afraid. You will never be brushed aside. God does not have a "do not disturb" sign hanging on His office doorknob. He has a humongous "welcome" mat. He doesn't have the same brand of stiff leather chair you find in psychiatrist's clinics. To get rid of any suspicion of aloofness, He lets you sit comfortably on His lap for a heart-to-heart exchange.

Mull over this!

Jesus didn't say that the Kingdom of God belongs to little children just to impress their parents or to keep the meddlesome disciples at bay. There is a reason He judges them so special. Thinking along these lines then, if you want reserved seats in God's heavenly Kingdom, discard your self-sufficiency and imitate the little ones.

And to God make your own declaration of dependence.

He took a little child whom he placed among them.
Taking the child in his arms, he said to them,
"Whoever welcomes one of these little children
in my name welcomes me;
and whoever welcomes me does not welcome me
but the one who sent me."
Mark 9:36-37

Chapter 9

Unshaken Faith

"Wake up! Wake up!"

It was a muffled whisper, but I sensed the urgency in the voice.

Through a ray of moonlight streaming from the windows, I peered at my watch. It was only 2:10 a.m., and the whole house was asleep. It was a faint nudge that roused me, but I didn't know who could have done so.

Strange.

All remnants of sleep flushed out of my body within seconds of opening my eyes. That, too, was strange.

And then the unthinkable happened. The whole house started to shake violently. Oh snap!

EARTHQUAKE!

Without wasting a moment, I dashed towards my daughter's bedroom and scooped her semi-conscious deadweight onto my arms. Pumped up adrenaline made me strangely Samsonian. Scurrying

MENU 2: Faith

out the hallway while mouthing a litany of prayers, I met my husband who was also awakened by the tremors.

"This one's strong," he panted as we escaped down the oscillating concrete stairway towards the front door.

Against my daughter's dozing frame, I could feel my heart pounding. Although it raced murderously, I still adhered to hope that the Lord would spare us. I presumed, since His angels woke me up a minute before the earthquake started, He must have planned for us to ride out the temblor but cheat death.

Nine years prior to this event, back in 1990, we also experienced a horrific quake. On a national scale, casualties and property damages were cataclysmic in proportions. Even so, my husband and I walked out of wildly swinging mid-rise buildings in one solid piece. It was broad daylight then, and despite the mayhem, our spirits held peace.

After momentarily struggling with the door locks, the family rushed to the front yard where we awaited the outcome with bated breaths. Dogs in the neighbourhood barked furiously. Lights in adjacent houses flooded the streets in rapid succession. Nervous voices thundered like a wave. The tranquility of the night was disrupted. The intensity six tremor lasted for only twenty-six seconds, but our fear seemed to stretch it forever and a day.

News of the recent seismic activity in Taiwan filtered into memory. One Chinese victim, rescued from the rubble after five days, toughed it out because he fell beside a collapsed fridge. We had no emergency kit prepared, no crude disaster plan. Recalling the Chinese survivor, I only thought of hauling food with us in case events turned nasty.

Convinced that the vibrations ended, my husband scooted back into the house and threw into a bag some canned goods, a battery-operated radio, and flashlight. We took temporary shelter inside the car and waited for aftershocks, which seismologists warned would definitely come.

By this time, my daughter's eyes stirred open, and she wondered what we were all doing outdoors in the dead of night.

"There was an earthquake, honey," I told her calmly.

"Was it strong, Mama?" Colleen echoed maturity even at age five. She already saw from TV news footages what awful wreckage an earthquake could whip up.

"Yes, it was."

Mindful of my daughter's emotional sensitivity, I tried to downplay the urgency of the situation.

"Mama, let's pray to Papa Jesus so He'll take care of us."

I was surprised that the suggestion spilled from her. Although she was still very drowsy and probably too spaced out to grasp the full radius of events, Colleen's first response was to hide in God's sanctuary.

My daughter's reaction was a knocking reminder. Yes, our God is a mighty fortress. When unnerved by a test, why didn't I hug this truth as tightly as a barnacle would cling to a rock? Why didn't my adult brain have the sharpness to consider prayer when fear hit me dead center?

With Colleen at the helm, the family prayed. Head on my lap, she squeezed out a tired yawn, shut her eyes again, and whispered, "Will Jesus hear our prayers, Mama?"

"Yes, honey. I'm sure He's watching us right now."

"Okay." Colleen settled back to a perfectly relaxed sleep. Her glistening smile was a kiss of faith on God's face. This little girl didn't need further reassurances from her earthly parents. She believed straight away that because she prayed, the big Dad would restore order.

On what basis did Colleen keep that faith? It's the fact that God is so dependable; He is fail-safe. Devoid of the complications

MENU 2: FAITH

of adult logic, Colleen trusted that God would handle the earthquake jitters and vouch for her safety. She could close her eyes, confident that danger wouldn't trap her while asleep.

I guess I needed to learn a load of lessons from this little angel. Her optimism was in stiff contrast to my paranoia. Her faith was so untarnished; she didn't need to see to believe.

How I wish I abandoned my apprehensions to God in the same carefree way. True, I verbalized my petitions, but I did so only because the calamity was out of my league. The problem was beyond my province of control. I'm sure that if we weren't up against nature's rage, I would have leaned solely on my own competence. Tapping into the supernatural muscle of God wouldn't be an option.

The tragic part was that after I tapped on heaven's door, I still bothered God with my pessimism. I must have blocked the calming effects of prayer with mental images of homeless children, grieving families, and disruptive aftershocks. Instead of returning to our cozy bedroom and resting my life on the hands of a trustworthy Father, I chose to suffer the lumpy car upholstery. I scanned the radio waves until sunlight invaded the skies.

At the crack of dawn, my heroic patrolling brought me nothing but dark raccoon eyes. My extremities and ligaments were tortured by a thousand pins and needles. A throbbing migraine crippled me throughout the day.

The eight recorded aftershocks weren't violent enough to harm a flea. Not a single building or house flattened to a pancake. Reported damages in the entire northern region were minimal. It gave the population of survivors much reason to celebrate.

Friend, periodically, God gives us spiritual wake-up calls to expose the backbone of our faith. Mine was an earthquake. Yours might be a prolonged illness, a suffocating marriage, career decisions gone drastically wrong, or a prayer that hasn't been answered for years. God tests the toughness of your faith to see that you don't easily collapse under the pressure of affliction.

There is one golden lesson I learned from my five-year-old that day. It doesn't require much effort to make God act. If you think God can, then believe God will. Such healthy faith budding from a child is a far cry from adults' I-know-you-can-but-what-if. Sadly, for most of us, faith lacks depth.

When our carefully laid-out plans, God doesn't follow,
And life cooks up bitter tests we can't swallow,
Our visions for the future narrow,
Loyalty to God turns shallow,
Trust caves in to fear ... because faith is hollow.

Brother, does your pragmatic mind encase the Lord's power in such a tight boundary that it assumes no impossibilities? Remind yourself that there is nothing too grand or too great for your God.

Sister, is your faith losing strength because you can't see where your life is headed?

Is your heart bleeding because you have waited too long, and the answer to your yearnings remains out of reach?

Are you tired of sitting in the valley, wondering when you can move out of the lows to taste the peak of your dreams?

Are you starting to think that your faith is leading you nowhere, that you've wasted enough time clinging to a God who seems inert and wimpy to do anything?

Do not despair, dear friend. His answer to prayer will surprise you, and it will jump forth in your face like a serendipitous encounter. Meanwhile, the valley is the perfect place to wait for the showers of God's nourishment. Soon, rain will pour like the freshness of spring. Soon, His blessings will drench you as a reward for your faithful endurance. Like a basin that catches the outpour,

MENU 2: FAITH

you who are in the valley will be soaked—flooded with blessings to the point of overspill.

Do not envy those who perch on the mountaintop, reigning arrogant and tipsy with success. The Lord's effusions of blessings upon the mountains swiftly slide down its slopes, useless and unnoticed. For the egotistic man who sits on the mountaintop for too long forgets Him who brought his feet there. And the Lord of provisions is discredited, bumped off by blind self-reliance and selfish pride.

Therefore, rest in the valley of your affliction. Be intentional in humility while keeping faith. Give God the space He needs to bathe you with blessings and to save you from your personal upheavals.

The season of showers is drawing near.

Soon, the Lord will make all things new for you ... as long as your faith in Him is unshaken.

Now faith is confidence in what we hope for and assurance about what we do not see.
Hebrews 11:1

Chapter 10

Big God in a Candy Wrap

A quarter fell out of a denim pocket while I was finishing the laundry one afternoon.

"Honey, can you please slip this coin inside my wallet?" I asked my daughter, Colleen.

"Where's your wallet, Mama?"

"In my beige bag," I answered.

"Where did you put your bag?"

"I hung it on the foot of the bed."

"And where's the bed?" At this point, I realized Colleen was horsing around so I just played along.

"In our bedroom, of course."

"And where's your bedroom?"

"In Suite 502."

"Where is Suite 502?"

"In Harrington Oaks Pointe."

"Where is Harrington Oaks Pointe?"

"In Miller Road."

MENU 2: FAITH

"Where's Miller Road?" Colleen caved in to cute, silly giggles. I doubted this lengthy recital would end shortly.

"In Canada."

"Where is Canada?" was the predictable reply.

"In North America."

"Where is North America?"

"On Earth." I could see where the litany was headed and I knew I would run out of answers pretty soon.

"Where is Earth?" Colleen still persisted. I began to wonder if my coin would ever land inside the wallet.

"In the solar system."

"Where is the solar system?"

"In the Milky Way."

"Where's the Milky Way?"

I was definitely stumped. I had none left. No complex and scholarly answers. No daffy jokes. No witty remarks. My mind went kaput! So I bolted towards the nearest escape route. Thinking of the milk chocolate bar I used to eat as a kid, I just spilled out a moronic reply—

"In Superstore."

"What?!" Colleen gaped at me with a shade of amusement lining her brows.

"If not there, I'm sure you could grab one at Wal-Mart."

That sealed the exhaustive cross-examination for a couple of minutes. Whew! I was glad that was over.

Just when I thought Colleen was fully appeased, she blurted out, "Mama, you're wrong! The Milky Way is not in Superstore. It's in God's hands!"

The meaty remark was like a shrill smoke alarm that screamed in my head in the days that followed. Rarely does a light-hearted wordplay with a nine-year-old force down a dimple in my brain. But that afternoon, by a fluke, Colleen awakened some valuable insights on how incredibly big God is.

Sometimes, it is good exercise to remind ourselves of the grandeur of God. Think about it! God's dimensions defy calculations. His existence breaches the boundaries of time and space. His sphere of influence and miracles overtake our most outrageous dreams.

Therefore, when we're up in arms against a boulder of misfortune, it is wise to recall that He who carries the entire Galaxy in a single palm has enough sinews to haul that stone.

Sadly, though, crisis tends to make people shrink God down to the size of a mini chocolate bar. Like me, they swaddle an omniscient God in a bite-size Milky Way wrapper that hides His true power.

Burdens look more titanic.

The chink in the armor looks more like a cavernous hole.

The crown of thorns gives the same nauseating impression as the ten-foot waves in a tempestuous sea.

Problems tower as high as Gulliver, and we treat God like a six-inch resident of Lilliput.

We shrivel God to a fragment so tiny and negligible that whenever we dig into our personal tool box for the right device to solve our problems, we easily ignore Him. We only search for God when we are pinned against a brick wall. We pray only after we have exhausted all our neurons and grey matter, and we don't know where else to turn. However, like a mechanic with a troubleshooter's apparatus in a tow truck, God stands ready to help. We just have to humbly ask.

I remember when I was still working in an offshore investment firm, I got entangled in a sticky situation that made

MENU 2: FAITH

me break out in a cold sweat. One of the departments I formerly managed used to draw up a monthly profile of the company's in-house exposure to its directors and officers. The total outlay to these recipients should never exceed the government-prescribed limit. Any infringement would set in motion a string of painful sanctions.

The signature I affixed on this report was like a stamp of approval that certified the accuracy of the information. The document was passed on to the President and Comptroller who, in turn, spelled out the details to the Board of Directors.

I don't want to plunge into the technicalities of the issue. Suffice it to say that a mix-up in the monitoring structure resulted in an infraction of the ceiling. On the basis of an erroneous report, the company advanced huge funds to a Director, unaware that the amount would violate the law.

The ramification of this ill-advised decision was horrifying. On that note, it wasn't hard to imagine how the temperature rose in the President's office. His sweltering rage hunted for a sitting duck on whom to pin the blame.

Lucky for him, my name broke the surface. Though I wasn't the one who physically drafted the report, my signature was glaring testament to my share in the fiasco. By virtue of command responsibility, I had to take the flogging for the oversight of my staff.

That was the day I wished the earth would crack open to swallow me whole. As I took skittish strides towards the Executive Office, morbid thoughts of death by guillotine crossed my mind. Maybe, if my head was served on a platter and offered as a peace sacrifice to the senior management, the hysteria would fade.

But such was not the story. I had to confront an irate sea of humanity. Not only was the President piqued; so were the Comptroller, the Board of Directors, the Vice President of the Accounting Division, and the lawyer who co-signed the document in question. I guess the only person who could breathe calmly that morning was the employee whose backside I was trying to cushion.

In the thick of the confusion, I mechanically put the thought of God behind me. My nerves were so worked-up that I could easily jump out of my skin at the slightest goad. I bumped God off the picture as the formidable image of my bosses floated in the giant screen of my head. I forgot that God was larger than my affliction—that the whole Milky Way, in fact, sat on His hands.

Have you ever been in a situation so insane that it also put you out of joint?

Have you been so distraught over an impasse that you didn't notice God who was holding the key to the exit door?

Did somebody bark the bad news like it was a malevolent battle cry, and you lost track of whose side you were on?

No doubt, you must have been like the lanky schoolboy who was elbowed by a party of notorious thugs. When provoked into a fist fight, he took a cursory glance at his undeveloped physique and instantly had cold feet. He realized that the muscled tyrants could crush his frail bones with a single blow.

The brewing clash of arms would give him more than just a nosebleed. The thought so intimidated him that he temporarily forgot his identity. He, in fact, was the son of a martial artist who was well-trained in stunts and aerial tricks as the legendary Jackie Chan himself. He only needed to holler, and his dad would swiftly run to his defense.

Sometimes, we are inclined to react like this young boy. You and I also forget that we have the resources to ward off any assailant. Our heavenly Father has more than the combined talents of Jackie Chan and Bruce Lee. His devices make our

MENU 2: FAITH

state-of-the-art technologies and futuristic thingumajiggers look medieval in comparison.

His power and genius are far more superior to the gifts of all the *X-Men* mutants fused together. At the risk of sounding like a blockbuster movie aficionado, let me add that God existed even before Reed, Ben, Susan, and Johnny discovered the *Fantastic Four* superpowers in them.

Really, God is bigger than all of the *Marvel* superheroes we've known from birth. He does not have the faculties and strength of dwarfish measure. He is not a miniature God who is of the same stature as Arrietty and the *Borrowers* who live under the floorboards of people's houses.

God is the chief engineer who makes the solar system run through a non-collision course. You must be in the major league to be able to do something as mammoth as that!

God is perfectly indestructible. No powers of the underworld can ever subdue Him. He can frustrate or out-maneuver any attack with the whisper of a single word.

Knowing this to be true, why then should an ordeal twist our stomachs into a clump of nerves?

> If God is for us, who can be against us? He who did not spare his own Son, but gave him up for us all—how will he not also, along with him, graciously give us all things? (Romans 8:31–32)

Go ahead. Read that verse again. Highlight it in shocking neon pink, if you will.

"If God is for us, who can be against us?" If you are on God's squad, of whom should you be afraid?

I love how another Bible translation brings out the meaning of this verse.

> With God on our side like this, how can we lose? If God didn't hesitate to put everything on the line for us, embracing our condition and exposing himself to the worst by sending his own Son, is there anything else he wouldn't gladly and freely do for us? (Romans 8:31–32 The Message)

The next time a disquieting problem of Goliath proportions tests your grit and makes your blood run cold, just think again—nothing is too extreme for God. He already accomplished the unthinkable when He gave up His Son. Therefore, none of your troubles are too circuitous or cryptic as to intimidate Him further.

If He can carry the limitless Milky Way in His hands, surely, He can easily carry your headaches and heartaches too!

Chapter 11

The Armor of God

> Be alert and of sober mind.
> Your enemy the devil prowls around
> like a roaring lion
> looking for someone to devour.
> 1 Peter 5:8

June 24, 1994. Twelve midnight.

I had the most mystifying nightmare. I saw myself driving along a very narrow, winding alley. It was very dark, and the initial drabness was swiftly replaced by a feeling of imminent danger as the path revealed deep trenches on both sides. The end of the road led to an ominous cavern with troll-like creatures of varying heights—some gigantic, others short but equally domineering. I found myself in a room amid such beasts, several of them gleefully shrieking because of some corrupted pleasure.

At close range, I noticed that they sported so much hair and slime on their bodies. Others had hideous-looking boils on their skin and dislocated bones protruding from various parts, giving them a totally grotesque and wicked appearance.

MENU 2: FAITH

"Who are you?" I asked.

"You guess," he taunted. A mysterious chill crept from under my skin. A terror-breeding sensation of evil began to pierce the foggy air. Suddenly, out of nowhere, a hand grabbed my arm. I jerked out of fright.

"Don't be afraid," a man said.

At this, he handed me a flat piece of smoked glass. I peered at it and saw a celestial vision of a beautiful lady in flowing white garments, the wind delicately sweeping beneath her feet. It was Mary walking towards the cross where her Son, Jesus, was nailed. With a graceful wave of the hand, she beckoned me to join her. Totally overwhelmed by the magnificence of the scene before me, I succumbed to tears.

Fleetingly, the apparition withered into blackness. As quickly as it did, my eyes were opened; I discerned where I stood. The gargoyles which circled me were actually demons! This impression hit me like lightning and brought back an indescribable surge of foreboding. The beasts watched my cold shivers and knew that I recognized them. Together, they closed in on me until their huge frames muted my screams.

The shrillness of my dream-state shouts turned out to be mere groans in reality. Nonetheless, these were discernible for Alvin, who coincidentally, woke up at 12:15 a.m. He gently slapped my face several times to rock me out of my torture.

When I stirred awake, sinister shadows besieged us, and I had a vanishing intuition of demons still prowling in our room. The nefarious specter was so petrifying; I thought I got drained of every bit of sanity. What I witnessed was no longer an illusion. The surreal elements of my nightmare took realistic form and invaded our space while my eyes were wide open!

I described to my husband every fraction of the outlandish vision. He then rose from bed, secured the vial of blessed holy water, and sprinkled it all over the room in accordance with our Christian tradition for purification. While doing so, goosebumps covered my body as I sensed the evil spirits' physical presence. I felt them scampering as Alvin blessed our house. With hands locked together in a tight grip and with a depth of devotion we never knew we had, Alvin and I prayed.

EPHESIANS 6

This experience was a vivid portrayal of the spiritual warfare Paul warned us about in Ephesians 6. It was an assault that angled my perspective from this finite physical world to the domain of the impalpable.

Though this spiritual territory cannot be perceived by human eyes, no one can fully dispute its existence.

> Put on the full armor of God, so that you can take your stand against the devil's schemes. For our struggle is not against flesh and blood, but against the rulers, against the authorities, against the powers of this dark world and against the spiritual forces of evil in the heavenly realms. (Ephesians 6:11–12)

There's more to the struggle we face day to day than most people care to admit. There is a raging war, and it is far more ferocious than the ones sparked off by nations. It is not a war to be won by heat-sensitive missiles, destructive chemicals or highly-trained armies. It is not a conflict paid for by the blood of soldiers.

MENU 2: FAITH

What we face is an intangible battle fought by faith, not by sight. It is a war where the consequences of indecision and idle complacency reach far into eternity. A war where the apathetic becomes easy prey of the devouring enemy. A war that can be won not by sheer muscle but through the power and grace that God provides.

Scripture gives us a clear perspective of where this hostility is headed.

> Then war broke out in heaven. Michael and his angels fought against the dragon, and the dragon and his angels fought back. But he was not strong enough, and they lost their place in heaven. The great dragon was hurled down—that ancient serpent called the devil, or Satan, who leads the whole world astray. He was hurled to the earth, and his angels with him. (Revelation 12:7–9)

The story proceeds to give us fair warning.

> But woe to the earth and the sea, because the devil has gone down to you! He is filled with fury, because he knows that his time is short. (Revelation 12:12)

People tend to belittle the influence of demons and reduce this warfare to a mere rock-paper-scissors match. Let us not be deceived. Satan has more cunning than we give him credit for. He may not often be launching a frontal attack, but his subtle treachery has caused the downfall of many.

Christian warriors may not engage in hand-to-hand combat, but they may still be badly beaten by camouflaged snipers, minefields, and booby traps. Such are the tactics employed by the devil.

He doesn't have to brusquely pull you out from giving charitably to the Church. He only needs to tempt you with a spur-of-the-moment shopping whim to drain your resources.

He doesn't directly stop you from praying. He skillfully beguiles you with overcommitments to blind your mind with the urgency of deadlines.

He doesn't force an innocent teenager into juvenile delinquency. He just sprinkles a pinch of curiosity into his head. If this drifts the child into drugs and pornography, then the devil washes his hands clean of all liability.

He doesn't outwardly break marriages apart. He simply whispers a seed of doubt in one spouse's head and allows the suspicion to gravitate towards its own ignominious direction.

He doesn't twist a husband's arm so that he'll divorce his wife. He just makes his eyes wander.

We may have lofty goals and kind thoughts, but if we permit the devil to hoodwink us into shelving our acts of charity, the blame weighs upon our shoulders. By allowing our good intentions to fizzle out into indifference, the devil has completed his job with great profits.

Perhaps we have plans of interceding for a terminally-ill friend. Perhaps we have entertained thoughts of buying flowers for a single mother who is beset by depression, or we may have considered apologizing to a wife we disgraced with cruel words. If we never lifted a finger to make things happen, then the enemy wins the point in this tricky push-and-pull game.

The devil bluffs his way into waywardness and rebellion by using our busyness or tendency to procrastinate. It is a wise man who sees through his notoriety.

MENU 2: FAITH

Satan cannot easily be duped. This is why God instructed us to wear His armor at all times. We may never predict when we'll come under heavy fire, but it always pays to be prepared with the weapons in God's arsenal.

Ephesians 6 gives an account of the Christian's impenetrable artillery. Our spiritual ammunition enables us to march confidently into the battle zone.

> Stand firm then, with the belt of truth buckled around your waist, with the breastplate of righteousness in place, and with your feet fitted with the readiness that comes from the gospel of peace. In addition to all this, take up the shield of faith, with which you can extinguish all the flaming arrows of the evil one. Take the helmet of salvation and the sword of the Spirit, which is the word of God. (Ephesians 6:14–17)

Read through the verses again. Do you see what disarms the devil?
Truth.
Faith.
Righteousness.
Carry the Word of God faithfully in your heart, and you despoil the devil and expose to light his encroachment.

Many years prior to the 1994 demonic encounter, I had a similar bizarre dream. I saw a woman with long, shiny hair, an unblemished complexion, and a searing magnetism that immediately drew my emotions close. We moved absentmindedly together like little children and took pleasure in each other's company.

Our casual friendship lasted for a brief moment. In a blink, her features switched from a spellbinding beauty to a blistered, misshapen figure that revealed to me the real creature that she was. The charisma that hypnotically enraptured me dissolved so rapidly. I felt numb. I became keenly aware that I was exchanging pleasantries with the devil who used an attractive, civilized human form as smoke screen.

Before I had the chance to regain my composure, I felt the demon's rough, scaly talons fiercely throttling my neck. I choked and coughed so violently as I attempted to disentangle her strapping grip.

I mustered the courage to scream; no sound left my throat. For so long, I thrashed about in vain. I thought I would die. My mind was fully awake by then. I had a clear sense of the room where I was sprawled. But I couldn't open my eyes.

I remember thinking, "Stand, Ginger! Stand up now!"

But nothing happened apart from the continuing torment of the sinister presence.

In desperation, I prayed, "I believe in God, the Father Almighty!"

To my surprise, the demon disappeared.

Just like that!

There was no puff of smoke. No dramatic evacuation of the dark forces. Nothing.

But I was abruptly in control of my limbs. And I was able to breathe again. I was panting in my bed; sweat beaded on my forehead.

Whether or not I survived an actual confrontation, I didn't have any conclusive proof. Everything seemed so real. Half my no-nonsense, levelheaded logic knew that there were more underlying complications to this nightmare than met the eyes.

MENU 2: FAITH

This experience impressed upon me the consuming desire of Satan to conquer men's souls and force them to renounce their submission to God. His ruthless mission is to blind us with the world and to deflect our attention from the light of Christ's Gospel.

The onslaught we now face is real!

Our inability to perceive it doesn't make the spiritual war less potent. It just pushes us to the precipice so that we become eager victims of the roaring lion of wickedness.

Our generation has reached a crucial point where a solid choice must be made.

This war is about taking sides.

There is no middle ground.

There is no soft spot for the lukewarm in heart—no room for timidity and vacillation of spirit.

For if we resolve to be indifferent, if we fail to engage in spiritual warfare, we are really losing the war.

On whose side do we then fall in line?

Do we cling to God whose victory was already gained on the cross of Calvary? Or must we cavort with the evil principalities of this world whose entrapment in the eternal abyss is assured at the Lord's Second Coming?

Now is the time to decide.

We already know the scores even before the match ends. We already know the conclusion even before the plot thickens. We need not peek at the back pages of the book to know who will prevail— the scoundrel or the hero. God has already hoisted Christ's cross of conquest for humanity to see.

The question then is not "who will win?" but "shall we dwell on the side of the Champion?" Shall we faithfully run the race and stand triumphant with Christ?

The battle line has already been drawn. Now is the time to take sides. We want to close ranks with God. We want to be His allies, not Satan's conspirators. And with this admission comes our duty to wear the Lord's coat of mail.

And gird ourselves with the full armor of righteousness.

The armor of God.

```
... I want you to be wise about what is good,
      and innocent about what is evil.
     The God of peace will soon crush
          Satan under your feet ...
            Romans 16:19-20
```

Chapter 12

Snapshots of Eternity

```
Teach us to number our days,
that we may gain a heart of wisdom.
            Psalm 90:12
```

July 19, 1989. Walking through the front door, I was surprised when my mom welcomed me with a crushed expression on her face.

"I was just on the phone. You have to call back Bennett right away," she said. Bennett was a close buddy from university.

"Why? Was it about the job opening? Am I hired?" I asked expectantly.

My mom shook her head. I wondered why she was trying to choke back tears. There was a minute of silence after which she sighed heavily and spilled the news, "Gabrielle was burned."

"Huh? What?" Arriving home from a party, my mind still afloat with happy thoughts, I was momentarily confused. Did my mom perhaps mean Gabrielle burned her fingers while cooking? But why would that be upsetting news? No, something was off!

Not wanting to keep me suspended, my mom recapped Bennett's phone message. Almost painfully, she narrated how

MENU 2: FAITH

tongues of fire razed Gabrielle's house in the late evening of the eighteenth.

"Where is she now?" I interrupted. "Which hospital?" My muscles quivered wildly at the shocking news, but deep inside was a sliver of hope. I wanted so badly to believe my friend was okay. I clipped my imagination, forbidding it from running amok with worst-case scenarios.

"No," my mom said softly. Her eyes conveyed the message which she agonized to put into words. I understood instinctively that she was about to break some dreadful news. "Gabrielle didn't make it."

My mom managed to unload, but I wasn't prepared to handle the truth. It numbed me. I visited Gabrielle just a week ago, at work, and she was all smiles—alive and perky, as any breathing being should be. It wouldn't make sense for her to be dead now, right? And charred to ashes at that!

Not wasting a second, I phoned Bennett, wishing that she'd take back her words and prove the rumor false—but there was no mistake about it. Gabrielle confronted the worst nightmare in her life and came to be with the Lord.

The library was the first to go up in flames. Fire spread rapidly throughout the second floor, blocking the stairway and all other escape passages. Gabrielle was trapped in her upstairs bedroom. Two housekeepers, the only other people in the house that evening, barely survived. One housekeeper, who lost consciousness because of excessive smoke inhalation, had to be dragged out, inch by inch, by her wounded coworker.

Once outside, the injured housekeeper, hardly lucid herself due to panic, instructed Gabrielle to shatter the windowpane and jump from the second floor. Gabrielle fumbled around the smoky interior for a hard object with which to smash the glass. Paralyzed by horror, her attempts did little to set herself free.

Firefighters arrived much too late. Gabrielle was already dead—devoured by the unforgiving conflagration, reduced to an unrecognizable state. She was found huddled in the bathroom, fenced in while waiting for help. Indeed, for someone as soft-hearted and good-humored as Gabrielle, it was a cruel way to die.

Death has a peculiar way of slowing people down. Grief pressures us to review life's priorities. Matters of urgency seem puny when set against a backdrop of mortality.

Rushing through traffic, beating report deadlines, catching delivery schedules, meeting business profit objectives—all of these become mediocre targets when the certainty of death beclouds the panorama.

This is what I learned from Gabrielle's tragic engagement. Her twenty-two years on the grand theater of life had been too brief. Her concluding scene caught her off-balance. The Master Playwright altered the last act, and death didn't grant her the benefit of curtain calls. I wonder if she exited the stage with any unfinished business.

Was her life still a work in progress?

Did she yearn for an encore, a second chance to give her past regretful actions a face-lift?

Were there morose dialogues written for her like, "If only I had more time. I wish I didn't do that. I could have done this instead"?

Time is a paradoxical resource. The more you need, the less you seem to have.

Time drifts in a boundless continuum. And yet for us, it has a definite end.

Time is ageless, and yet it matures.

MENU 2: Faith

It marches in steady cadence, yet advances too slowly in the eyes of one who waits.

Time is invaluable, beyond the price of the rarest diamonds, yet we waste it like we have whopping volumes to spare.

Time, once consumed, is irretrievable. Once misappropriated, it is irreplaceable. The consequences of its misuse is irreversible.

Regretting over the wastage cannot change the outcome. Remorse can only modify future decisions ... if there is still a future to hope for.

Every so often, God gives us snapshots of eternity to press us forward on the right footpath. Bereavement challenges us to face an internal audit of our life. When caught dead in our tracks, when the unannounced inventory check finds us lacking, when the character appraisal uncovers a wider room for personal growth, then we know it is time to take stock.

Brushes with death bring to light our rotten attitudes and crooked morality. It magnifies the barrenness of our ideals. But why wait for such episodes to weigh up? We can evaluate our timesheets and shift our priorities starting today.

Remember, using eternity as a frame of reference, we are like mayflies that exist only for a day. Life is fragile. Ephemeral. Therefore, let us walk through it with prudence.

The psalmist captured this thought from a better angle when he wrote:

> Show me, Lord, my life's end and the number of my days; let me know how fleeting my life is. You have made my days a mere handbreadth; the span of my years is as nothing before you. Everyone is but a breath, even those who seem secure. Surely everyone goes around like a mere phantom; in

> vain they rush about, heaping up wealth without
> knowing whose it will finally be. (Psalm 39:4–6)

God brought the full impact of this message closer to home through a gut-wrenching event that gave me pause. At the midpoint of this crisis, God taught me what it means to "number our days".

Years ago, at around two in the morning, I was stirred from sleep by a family emergency. With his face and neck cranberry red, my grandfather complained of excruciating pain in the nape and heaviness on his chest. With our emergency home kit pulled out of the drawer, I quickly checked his blood pressure and was stunned by the 190/120 reading. Papa's blood pressure had never before escalated to this level. I feared that the spasms were symptomatic of a looming heart attack.

At my neighbour's insistence, I called 9-1-1 despite my grandpa's protests. The man who answered the line had a slightly slurred speech; I wondered if my badly timed call disrupted his nap. Though my whole body was visibly shaking with alarm, I tried to keep my voice under control because I didn't want to build up Papa's stress and indirectly trigger a further rise in his blood pressure.

Because of my forced calmness, the 9-1-1 aide presumed I myself was capable of bringing Papa to the hospital. He refused to dispatch an ambulance to our apartment saying, "You can drive him yourself. This isn't such an emergency anyway!"

How he jumped to the conclusion that I knew how to drive was beyond me. If he was fortunate enough to guess correctly, how could he judge that a panicky woman could safely transport an unstable patient? Left with no choice, and with no professional help available, I grabbed the car keys and drove to the hospital.

With no consciousness of the speed limit, I floored the gas, sneaking periodic glances at Papa whose eyes were shut through most of the trip. Blinded by the flashing lights of a police car that

MENU 2: Faith

tracked my rear out of nowhere, I realized my speedometer gauge already pointed twenty kilometers past the maximum road limit.

The police officer's intimidating presence served only to spike up my anxiety. For several minutes, he tagged along, his siren not yet screaming my doom. But I didn't pull over for fear that Papa couldn't sit tight a minute longer. While only a few blocks away from the hospital, the officer gave up the chase and left me alone, realizing at last that I was headed towards the ER.

I thought that the sight of the empty emergency room would soothe my palpitations. Since the place wasn't crammed, I guessed the wait wouldn't last an hour. I thought that leaving my gramps in the care of qualified professionals would untie the knot in my stomach. Little did I know that they'd amplify my fears because of poor bedside manners.

Though Papa was the third patient in line, we waited for hours before the physician on duty took a look at him—and what a cursory look that was! In all the five minutes he spent inside the examination room, he was instructed to down five Tylenol tablets for the headache!

I was horrified at such reckless prescription. Without batting an eyelash, I stared the triage nurse in the eye and inquired, "Will they not give him anything to stabilize his blood pressure?"

"There's nothing more we can do for him here," the nurse answered tersely then went back to read her chart. "Just go home and let him sleep off the pain."

"But my grandpa's BP is still so high," I interjected, my tone a mixture of desperate pleading and crankiness. "Can't you at least give him a relaxant or an emergency drip?"

Obviously peeved that I had the audacity to dictate to them what to do, the nurse snapped, "We don't do that here! Just bring him to your family doctor tomorrow."

The overbearing attendant hastily stood from the swivel chair and marched away from the admitting counter where I stood nonplussed. I couldn't even bring myself to mouth the words that flashed across my mind like a neon sign—

"What if my Papa gets a heart attack now and couldn't live through tomorrow?"

The lady ushered us to leave, but my gut feeling dictated we linger awhile. I didn't want to travel, knowing that my passenger's blood pressure didn't budge from the 190/120 band.

I had no doubt it was the Holy Spirit's prompting that we stayed. In the meantime, our best friend, Billy, whom I phoned earlier to ask for prayers, decided to travel across cities, from his outlying residence to the hospital. A truly faithful brother who believed in the power of presence, Billy was a warm body who comforted us in our crisis. What an inspiring twist of providence that our cars met in the empty intersection outside the hospital!

We were unaware that Billy defied sleep to be with us at close to 4 a.m. I had a nagging sense that God wouldn't leave us cold and vulnerable; but since the sassy nurse in the ER considered it unwise for us to warm their lounge chairs a second longer, we had to leave. At the precise moment my hope withered, Billy turned from the highway, his hand waving frenziedly out the window to capture our attention.

It was at this point that my tears of relief finally cascaded without embarrassment. I was no longer alone. I had a brother who sacrificed all comfort to show evidence of his faith in action. It didn't matter to him that he had a certification exam the following day for which sleep deprivation was not the ideal form of preparation.

Here was a man with an authentic understanding of the brevity of life and who, therefore, invested his time on matters

MENU 2: Faith

with eternal weight. In this man's life was concretely displayed the psalmist's words,

> Teach us to number our days, that we may gain a
> heart of wisdom. (Psalm 90:12)

Faith more than compensated for the emergency personnels' deficiencies. In the end, God pulled my grandfather from the brink of threat through prayers. However, more than the healing, this experience sharpened our perception of the brittleness of life.

Friend, everything is perishable. Our bodies decay even as we breathe. Much of what the world exalts is vanity in the eyes of the eternal. It is a wise man who measures his life against the horizon of death, knowing that he will soon give an account before the judgment seat of the Lord.

As Ecclesiastes 12:14 reminds us,

> For God will bring every deed into judgment,
> including every hidden thing, whether it is good or
> evil.

As with finances or any other resource, God demands faithful stewardship of the time He entrusts. Brother, inasmuch as you don't know whether you'll live for a few decades or a century, do not be wasteful. Numbering your days properly doesn't mean you stuff your schedule with activities and goad yourself to the verge of collapse.

Sister, your importance isn't gauged by how brightly you shine in the world because of your profitability. Life is not so much about badges and accomplishments as it is about breeding loving relationships with people.

Building a fancy title for yourself is not what should typify life's race. Instead, stewardship demands that you work with vigilance, each day, to put your identity under Christ.

Be purposeful in impressing the Lord. Be strong-willed in obtaining His approval, for this is what it truly means to "number our days".

Think about this.

In point of fact, it's easier to move the Lord's heart because He can see even what's hidden from the public lens. You don't need to make a huge splash to flag His attention. There's no urgency to publish promotional materials or newpaper headlines to advertise your good intentions. You do not need to push your weight around to be conspicuous.

Press releases are worthless because God sees the love in your heart even when no one else cares. He discerns every gear and spring that makes your life's clock tick. He sifts and audits every evidence that proves how your enthusiasm blessed others.

Do not wait for a calamity or sickness to happen before you recognize the fragility of life. Don't wait for God's wake-up call before you redeem the time. This message isn't reserved for the deathbed.

Life is too short to spend on anger, unforgiveness, or egocentric fanfares. It is too precious to waste on what won't reap a harvest of heaven. Therefore, manage time as God desires. Don't create an archive of memories that are too shameful to expose.

Instead, cultivate life stories which future generations will consider golden to treasure and worthwhile to retell.

Friend, now is the time to chase after your days to make every wink and breath count. Now is the time to gain wisdom of heart.

Pray that when you reach the end of your road, God will pay you a triumphant tribute.

MENU 2: Faith

And with a standing ovation applaud, "Well done my faithful servant. Yours was a life well lived ... and time well spent."

```
            Now listen, you who say,
   "Today or tomorrow we will go to this or that city,
              spend a year there,
          carry on business and make money."
   Why, you do not even know what will happen tomorrow.
              What is your life?
    You are a mist that appears for a little while
                and then vanishes.
                  James 4:13-14
```

Survey the panorama of positive possibilities & believe that GOD will bring YOU → THERE

Chapter 13

Soar Like an Eagle

The walls cast gloomy shadows on the sparsely-lit room. The carpet, tattered and faded with age, added to the aura of melancholy on many bitter cold days. Christmas was forthcoming, the very first one we would celebrate thousands of miles away from home.

Maybe "celebrate" wasn't even a suitable label, for there was not a single soul in the house who had the wild craze to cry "whoopee" and indulge in a confetti blow-out. There we stood in a totally strange territory, swallowing our first taste of winter, with nothing but the thin, scrimpy clothes our luggages carried.

This was supposedly my personal "Promised Land"—a God-ordained sweet spot crawling with valleys and streams, snow-capped mountains and fertile landscapes of multi-colored flora. A land with organic harvests of grapes, plums, peaches, and cranberries.

For some reason, I felt that this promise wasn't worth the painful separation from the country of our birth.

MENU 2: Faith

To describe our adjustment to the North American lifestyle as tough was an understatement. Jobs were elusive. Our unfurnished room was uncomfortable and awkward. The dropping temperature, which was a far cry from the humidity of the equatorial region we grew up in, made our wool sweaters feel like thin nylon pantyhose. Our dropping finances excavated worry lines on our foreheads, and the memories of bygone luxuries pushed tears of regret down our cheeks.

For a whole month, our family tried to settle in a ghetto-esque hole, sleeping on the floor on top of collapsed cardboard boxes. Three of us huddled together to keep warm, playing tug-o-war with the single fleece blanket we had.

When snow and hail hammered lightly on the windows, it felt like we were swimming stark-naked with the Emperor penguins in Antarctica. Through those lonely nights, I asked myself a thousand times, "Is this it?! Is this what we came here for?"

We didn't own a car during the first two years of our residence in Canada. And so when time came for us to buy groceries, we took great pains transporting everything by transit. We had a small, two-wheeled buggy which lightened the load somewhat; but pulling that handcart was a real chore, especially in wintertime, since we ended up shovelling all the snow from the pavement. The wheels dragged slush, which added to the trolley weight as we walked uphill from the bus stop to the apartment building.

To itch for the same managerial professions as before was wishful thinking. To imagine the same wallpapered cubicle and metal-engraved nameplate was delusional. Canadian education. Canadian experience. Canadian references. Such were encumbering requirements for newly-landed immigrants that easily bumped us off the qualified candidates list.

This is Canada. We had to step out of the gateway of our fantasy cycles. We had to stop being dreamy. The explosion of reality hit our faces like a spattering of Arctic water—it was time to scratch out a living! We had to gulp down the sharp-tasting pill of pride, forget about the white-collared jobs we were accustomed to, and humbly engage the first available casual work.

Life on foreign soil had been challenging. The absence of sympathetic family and life-long friends stoked the fire of vulnerability and isolation which we felt most severely during holidays.

On the calendar, Christmas was just a stone's throw away. Compared to the city of our birth, Vancouver's brand of celebrations paled miserably.

We used to live in a country where festive Christmas lights and hand-crafted ornaments peppered every street, house, and commercial structure long before Halloween. Old-time carols tirelessly invaded the airwaves and added to the joy of the season. Reunited families gathered for weekly banquets and paraded their best home-made gastronomic inventions. Revelers slapped party invitations left and right, night after night. It was a nation where selfless gift-giving was visible at every turn.

However, back here, inside our poorly-lit suite, Alvin, Colleen, and I had no Christmas tree, no embellishments to hang on the walls, no scrumptious feasts to share. We only had each other, and that was more than sufficient.

We had faith enough to thank the Lord for our safe passage into this country—this land which He promised would soon overflow with "milk" and "honey" for our small family.

One December afternoon, seven-year-old Colleen tugged at his father's sleeves, coaxing him to carry her up in his arms. Alvin obliged and lifted her giggling daughter, belly and face down, with

MENU 2: FAITH

limbs stretched. He then twirled her round and round while Colleen pretended to be airborne, soaring in the fashion of a true superhero.

"Mama! Come and watch me!" Colleen shrieked gaily. I skipped out of the bedroom to see what the rumpus was about.

"See, Mama," Colleen said. "I'm flying like an eagle."

Immediately, I felt God speak to me as the lines of a familiar verse drifted through my memory.

> But those who hope in the Lord will renew their strength. They will soar on wings like eagles; they will run and not grow weary, they will walk and not be faint. (Isaiah 40:31)

Tears escaped from my eyes as I watched father and daughter in this carefree pose. For a brief moment, I imagined myself as the unflustered child, contentedly resting on the arms of our Heavenly Father, soaring like the eagle and rising above our present troubles.

Just then, I knew everything would be okay.

God was near.

He left that promise for us to read in the book of Habakkuk.

> Though the fig tree does not bud and there are no grapes on the vines, though the olive crop fails and the fields produce no food, though there are no sheep in the pen and no cattle in the stalls, yet I will rejoice in the Lord, I will be joyful in God my Savior. The Sovereign Lord is my strength; he makes my feet like the feet of a deer, he enables me to tread on the heights. (Habakkuk 3:17–19)

Have you ever been to that sheep pen of nothingness?

Have you ever felt the stab of heartbreak and the jitters of an insecure future? Mark down the words of Habakkuk.

The Lord is your strength.

Let His hands steady your footing. At the moment of His choosing, He can lift you above ground and displace your weaknesses with His adequacy.

Whether they're empty barns or empty grocery carts, withered wheat fields or withered paychecks, fruitless grape vines or fruitless attempts—nothing can choke God's power to intervene.

Let God prove His doting concern for your welfare. Wait. He'll eventually plant visible evidence that will bring back the sparkle of enthusiasm in your eyes. Rejoice in the Lord and trust that the barren desert will sprout new buds.

Back in those dark, winter days, God steered our family into the company of people who softened the blow of our transition by their generosity. One couple handed down a spare dining set and from then on, we didn't have to eat by the kitchen sink. Several other families arranged regular car pool schedules so we could do errands without much stress.

Another Jamaican lady, who was positively adamant that "nobody can survive in North America without a microwave oven", buzzed our door one afternoon.

"Alvin, can you help me with something in the car, please?"

Thinking that our friend, Alfreda, faced some sort of engine failure or flat tire, Alvin hastened to the driveway. Minutes later, he shuffled back, bearing a brand new 1100-watt microwave. I stood totally speechless, my jaw dropped as wide as the doorway, and my heart pounded with gratitude.

MENU 2: Faith

"Just an early Christmas present," Alfreda said nonchalantly, as if the pricey appliance was the most ordinary souvenir anyone could give a newcomer in Canada.

"How could this woman be so generous?" I thought to myself. "She barely knows me!"

But such was the hand of God, throwing miracles that would patch-up dispirited hearts. He wants to take people by surprise, if only to break the pattern of hopelessness and bring about an emotional "renovation"—a renewal of faith.

The point where genuine faith starts is the point where the mockery of worry fizzles out. Matthew counsels us,

> Therefore I tell you, do not worry about your life, what you will eat or drink; or about your body, what you will wear. Is not life more than food, and the body more than clothes? Look at the birds of the air; they do not sow or reap or store away in barns, and yet your heavenly Father feeds them. Are you not much more valuable than they? (Matthew 6:25–26)

Highlight that line.
Scribble it front and center in your journal.
Make sure you don't miss it.
It says, "Do not worry."

God inserted those three compelling words in Scripture because He understands how quickly anxiety gnaws at us. He knows that even the most faith-driven saint has battled with tension and has felt the stab of human misery.

Today, you may be weighed down by a health crisis. Perhaps pressing mortgage payments in the face of an unexpected job loss keep you restlessly tossing and turning at night.

Maybe, as a well-meaning parent, your intentions are misunderstood by a fiercely self-willed, back-talking teenaged son.

Be freshly recharged by God's promise. You are more treasured than the wildflowers in the meadows and the sparrows He feeds. What is important to you matters to Him.

Friend, your hope was not blighted. God didn't pound it to a wreckage nor wither it to extinction. Therefore, do not feel miserable. Lift your chin and carry a smile. Erase the disillusionment.

Your hope was not ruined.

It was simply deferred.

Are you on the waiting list, with the response to your prayers still pending?

Is the Lord too quiet that you wonder if He's within earshot?

Know that God's silence doesn't spell weakness! He isn't tongue-tied, nor is He trying to skirt detection. He has worked out a solution for you but it isn't yet ripe for delivery. Believe then that God's delays are perfectly timed.

If the answer to prayer hasn't come, do not assume that He is weighing your troubles in the scale of pros and cons. God isn't arbitrarily flipping heads or tails to gauge whether or not you deserve His focus.

If the answer never comes, it can be that the goals you set, not befitting His grand design for your life, will trip you over sinful seductions and curse your soul to an infernal pit.

If the answer to prayer hasn't come, neither should you believe God's storehouse faced bankruptcy and provisions are on ration. You're never going to lick crumbs.

God's help is near.

And your barns will be well-stocked with His blessings when the hour chimes!

MENU 2: FAITH

As you wait, tuck in your worries. When it seems like your heart is losing buoyancy and grey clouds are threatening your fragile hope, dig into the Book of Lamentations. Use these words as a brace to shore up your spirits.

> I remember my affliction and my wandering,
> > the bitterness and the gall.
> I well remember them,
> > and my soul is downcast within me.
> Yet this I call to mind and therefore I have hope:
> Because of the Lord's great love we are not
> > consumed,
> > for his compassions never fail.
> They are new every morning;
> > great is your faithfulness.
> I say to myself, "The Lord is my portion;
> > therefore I will wait for him."
> The Lord is good to those whose hope is in him,
> > to the one who seeks him;
> > it is good to wait quietly
> for the salvation of the Lord. (Lamentations 3:19–26)

It is possible your circumstances hardly changed throughout your faith journey. You still live in an urban rathole and your tough questions hang in mid-sentence ... still ambiguous ... unsolved. For months, your career has been in a deadlock, and your legs have numbed as you waited at the unemployment line. You continue to feel the pinch of a strained family relationship, and your crumbling health still henpecks like a nagging wife. Money may still be a perilously dwindling reserve.

But surprisingly, your posture and demeanor changes. Your doomsday perspective submits itself to a total make-over.

For now you approach life with hope.

Now, you pull yourself together with all your doubts buttoned down and malignant thoughts locked away. Now, you survey the panorama of positive possibilites, and believe that God will bring you there.

Remember, you have a God whose arms are wrapped around you in a fatherly squeeze. Friends may desert you in the peak of your desperation, but God never leaves His children in a lurch.

Put your hope in this. And in your heart believe ...

The Lord has power to bear you in flight.

Just like the majestic eagle.

Chapter 14

Of Burps, ABC's, & Ladybug Eyelashes

Clunk ... Clunk ... Clunk ...

The rhythmic metallic grind of an approaching shopping cart didn't draw my attention away from the package label I was reading. Every aisle in the local grocery store had one of those old, rusty types. I was too focused on the nutrition facts until a loud-mouthed lady suddenly made a fuss.

Tilting my head an inch, a saw to my alarm that the lady was about to run me over! The rickety buggy was within a whisker away from grazing my legs. On the pushcart sat a blonde pigtailed girl of about four years old. On either side walked two young siblings.

"Just push your way forward," the mother instructed her sons with a tone so gruff and deep that I thought a bullfrog croaked. "That's the only way these people will move."

MENU 3: HOLINESS IN RELATIONSHIPS

What?! Is this woman training bullies? I fixed my wide-eyed gaze on the little band of shoppers then took a quick mental note, "Okay, the kids are sheep, but the mom's a total goat!"

Remembering the story in the book of Matthew about the sorting of sheep from goats on Judgment Day, I wanted to retaliate, "Keep that attitude and let's see you wicked goat fall on God's left side."

For a brief second, I allowed the lady's crass remark to prick my nerves and steal my patience. The aisle wasn't narrow, and my buggy, neatly parked on one side, didn't block the entire way. The two-lane path had plenty of room to maneuver. Even a break dancer could headspin and twirl windmills without touching the shelves.

In a fit of insanity, my first impulse was to raise a counter-attack. With all the nerve I had in me, I wanted to kick her sweet bum into a fiery furnace—with no Shadrach, Meshach, or Abednego to keep it cool.

However, I realized that if I was to teach this mother a civilized way of handling the situation, I must be civil myself. Besides, these impressionable children needed to see the flipside and learn social courtesies even though it was modelled by a complete stranger.

Sarcasm and flippancy aside, I called out over my shoulder, "You know you could say, 'excuse me'."

My statement had so little impact; I wondered if I said it all in a whisper. The lady chose to ignore my remark as she squeezed past, nearly knocking me off-balance again. She really was more annoying than the gum stuck on the sole of my sneakers. Not even a blink of guilt pinched her conscience.

As I reflect on this incident, I wonder how many more kids out there have a conviction so loose that their sense of right or wrong floats wherever the wind blows. So many minors act like fools with no moral direction. So many behave like thick-skulled mules who

[114]

refuse correction—all because parents, who don't know any better, thrust them towards fallacious, vice-prone trajectories.

The Lord beckons us parents to take our role as teachers earnestly. We should be deliberate, Christ-rooted in intention, always afire in the pursuit of our mission. It is the peak of ineptitude to allow our children's peers to influence their growth while we lazily sit in the sidelines without a nudge of caution.

It is a reckless decision to allow media and technology to shape our children's values. We can't hand over our spot as role models to skimpily-clad Hollywood stars only because they are more current and relevant while we are "out-of-style". We can't be impassive while our kids test boundaries and push them to where sin thrives.

True. Kids still need to be street-smart. Yes, we can't underestimate the fruits gained from the school of hard knocks. Negative experiences and disappointments give birth to wisdom. And only the university, we call "Life", offer that curriculum.

Nonetheless, as parents, it is our duty to provide positive guidance as our children advance in years. Whether in terms of intellectual health or moral decency, behavioural discipline or spiritual formation—it is central to our vocation to be involved—

With deep passion.

With commitment.

And propelled by our love for God.

Let the powerful words in Deuteronomy serve as a reminder.

> Love the Lord your God with all your heart and with all your soul and with all your strength. These commandments that I give you today are to be on your hearts. <u>Impress them on your children. Talk about them when you sit at home and when you walk along the road, when you lie down and when</u>

MENU 3: Holiness in Relationships

<u>you get up.</u> Tie them as symbols on your hands
and bind them on your foreheads. Write them on
the doorframes of your houses and on your gates.
(Deuteronomy 6:5–9 emphasis added)

In everything we do—in and out of the home—we are to drum into our children's hearts a deep, reverential love for God. We don't just instruct with words. We sincerely adopt it in our lives.

As we talk, as we walk, as we push buggies along shopping aisles, we persist in this love. While we idle in traffic under the scorching summer sun, or queue up endlessly at the grocery checkout counter, we tough it out and prevail in love. For at the same moment we quit the frowns and pacify our temper, we grind into our kids' memories that patience reveals love.

This is how we become authentic teachers. We pursue, not just with words, but with our lives.

When we soak in God, we breathe love in.

In the end, everything that pours out of us becomes credible witness to our children.

One morning, over at the breakfast table, I overhead the most outlandish advice from three-year-old Chiara.

"Pajo, don't eat your food while it is hot or you'll have hot wee-wee when you go to the potty!"

A year later, on the same breakfast table, Pajo warned, "I need to burp."

After a few seconds of complete silence, Chiara observed, "I think your burpness is gone."

"Honey, there's no such word as 'burpness'," I intruded.

Apologetic about the blooper, Chiara self-corrected her statement with a sheepish smile. "Oh! Sorry, Mama. I meant 'burpingness'!"

I'm not quite sure what initially motivated me to homeschool my children. I just knew at that point that I couldn't let them walk around in public saying, "Excuse me for my burpingness" or go on believing that the thermal reading of their soup has a direct link to the temperature of their pee!

Even before my son Pajo turned six, his imagination stretched across many landscapes. He fired on all cylinders— nothing stopped his inquisitiveness.

"Mama, do ladybugs have eyelashes? What goes on inside a cement mixer? Why do pine trees stay green during winter? Up to how many miles away can an opossum smell? If a spider has eight legs, how many bodies does it have? Can a new tooth wiggle? Why does the Burnaby museum have paintings of people without clothes? Isn't that inappropriate?"

The battery of questions exploded from a vocal bazooka towards any Tom, Dick, and Harry who had ears to listen. I didn't have Galileo's braincells so I embarrassed myself by giving dummy answers. But although I wasn't a minefield of information, I realized Pajo's every question was a learning opportunity. I knew I had to reach outside of my limited capabilities and teach.

I had no credentials on which to lean. I wasn't a multi-medaled, corporate chart-buster, nor was I a conquistador on the hot trails of discovery. I didn't have the mental faculties it took to be successful. All I had was a calling from the Lord and a nutty, crazy fondness for my children. All I had was the ability to restrain my facial muscles and keep a straight face. You wouldn't believe how I elevated that skill into an art form because I had to use it often!

For how could you not laugh after a four-year-old girl enthusiastically waved her hand during comparative adjectives

MENU 3: HOLINESS IN RELATIONSHIPS

discussions, then volunteered her two-cents-worth "good, gooder, and great" or "beautiful, beautifuler, and pretty"!

Also, due to a five-year-old boy's cross-curricular confusion during Science classes, he insisted that "lioness" was the superlative of "lion". What?! Lion. Lioner. Lionest?!

How could you suppress a smile when a cute little horror declared on disaster prevention week that the ABCs of fire extinguishers stood for "aim, blow, and cough!" (or "cry" if you can't find your mommy) and that CIBC didn't stand for *Canadian Imperial Bank of Commerce* but "can I bite Chiara".

Homeschooling seemed formidable at first. But after I hurdled the teething troubles, I had such a field day listening to my son reinvent Webster with grammatical monstrosities like, "I'm security guarding you!" or "Teacher, I brang my crayons."

Conversations with little children could get mildly intoxicating especially when an eloquent kindergartner observed right after a thematic study on the environment, "Mama! Papa! You're old. You will be recycled!"

My teaching career may not be as brilliant as that of Harvard professors. Many may even argue against the effectiveness of demonstrating buoyancy on the kitchen sink or teaching precipitation while standing on the patio, catching bean-sized hail with a bowl. These teaching strategies may be a little off the beaten path. But through time, I discovered how I genuinely love teaching.

These children are breathing, expanding craniums who today may assume medicine droppers can travel far inside the ears or that paper towels taste saltier than cheese. Lead them well, and tomorrow, they can be the pillars of influence in our society—a modern-day Moses, Joshua, Esther, or Paul.

Even as we nurture our children, we must realize that we, too, receive education from our Great Professor. God mentors us with a lot of forethought; with diligence He enforces discipline.

He is the Teacher like no other.

With a steady hand, He cautions and steers so that none of His beloved may drift off the set course. So that we may not miss the bend, He assembles a signpost as we approach critical crossroads in our lives. With the road map on hand, we can trust that He knows the way.

In the Book of Isaiah, it says,

> "I am the Lord your God, who teaches you what is best for you, who directs you in the way you should go." (Isaiah 48:17)

The Lord further warns,

> My son, do not forget my teaching, but keep my commands in your heart, for they will prolong your life many years and bring you peace and prosperity. Let love and faithfulness never leave you; bind them around your neck, write them on the tablet of your heart. Then you will win favor and a good name in the sight of God and man. (Proverbs 3:1–4)

Unlike the sassy lady I met at the grocery aisle, the Great Professor, doesn't say, "Just push your way forward, and crush anyone who blocks your path." Instead, He teaches us to wear the cloak of humility.

Let us then take the high road, and step back so that others may be first. Even if we feel wronged, may we not blacken our souls by holding grudges or by stinging others using our tongues as deadly swords. Resentment is a venom that embitters the heart and ruins grace. At every turn, let us follow our Teacher's example on how to show mercy. Let us restore our hidden luster by reflecting God's light.

MENU 3: HOLINESS IN RELATIONSHIPS

Ultimately, we live the gospel if those we touch can honestly say of us, "This must be how it feels like to be in the presence of a saint!"

If, however, all calmness flees when we enter a room and people feel cramped or tortured in our company, then what a weak evidence of faith we must have shown!

The Lord, like a wise teacher, gives us choices. For every choice, He reveals the consequences. Our understanding is too narrow and linear; it often leads us to pick for ourselves what is not truly "good, gooder, and great".

But with our Professor's judgment, we gain clarity on alternatives that are "pretty, prettier, or pretty harmful"!

Let us then submit to the direction of the Lord who knows the way, acts with love, and teaches us with polished, infallible wisdom.

```
Trust in the Lord with all your heart
and lean not on your own understanding;
    in all your ways submit to him,
  and he will make your paths straight.
              Proverbs 3:5-6
```

Chapter 15

Who Wins?

My husband and I picked up some newly-developed photo prints at the mall and were about to rush to another errand when we decided to pop by the apartment for a brief pit stop.

While still a few blocks away from home, I suggested, "Just park out front."

"No, I'll park in the basement," Alvin said. The smell of thunder wafted in the air, and scant rain was already drumming the windshield. Alvin didn't appreciate an ill-timed cold shower.

"But we'll just be a few minutes," I reasoned. "I want to take a look at these pictures and it's too dark inside."

"Look at them later." The snappish inflection and the high-voltage stare peeved me.

I knew I was skating on thin ice when I pushed the issue further. "But why should I wait later when I can look at the pictures now while I'm waiting for you in the car?"

"Later, I said." The curt don't-you-dare-oppose-me tone droned in my ear like a mosquito's maddening buzz.

Menu 3: Holiness in Relationships

The mood inside the car turned sour, tempers swelled, and the temperature began to surge.

"Why are we arguing over such a petty thing as parking?" I asked.

"Exactly! It's senseless so why don't you just let me decide. Just follow what I say. I'm the one driving anyway."

"Well that's the problem!" I felt blood rise into my face. "You want to be in control all the time. It's always about what you want. It's never about me."

My emotional outburst piqued him. The purplish veins on his neck bulged in anger but Alvin remained impassive. It is his nature to withdraw when in the heat of an argument. My husband then steered into the driveway and clicked the remote that opened the basement gate.

"Of course you win." My tongue was dripping with contempt. "You always win."

There was no triumphant smirk on Alvin's face but his dry expression entangled my stomach in writhing knots. Freezing icicles pierced my heart, and I became a hurricane-tossed wreck.

The rest of the afternoon drifted by in quiet hostility. For many muscle-stiffening hours, the friction in the air was so thick; you could chop it with a cleaver. We gave each other the cold shoulder, and neither one dared to break the silence. For all the pain I felt, I could have been better off if I just scraped my knuckles against a cheese grater.

I didn't know what was running through Alvin's head, but I was steaming. The conflict wasn't so much about the photos as it was about the control issue. I felt that my husband pressed me into submission pointlessly.

While I was blistering in the heat of my annoyance, Alvin was lost in deep reflection. He had long surrendered his ill temper and had sought God's grace to mend the relationship. He didn't wait for me to own up to my share of the blame. With a posture of meekness, he made the first move.

"Please forgive me," he said. "It's not my intention to always win. I find no joy in that. Remember that God made us one. You and I are one. So if you lose, then I lose too. If you're hurting, I hurt as well. Your gain is my gain. Your defeat is also my loss."

Alvin's warm and tender hug chased all bitterness away. His deep insight made me realize one element of Christian life so valuable to God. Unity.

> As a prisoner for the Lord, then, I urge you to live a life worthy of the calling you have received. Be completely humble and gentle; be patient, bearing with one another in love. Make every effort to keep the unity of the Spirit through the bond of peace. (Ephesians 4:1–3)

Although fashioned by the same Creative Hand and borne of one Father, each man is as unique as his fingerprint. Our personalities are as multifarious as the cloud impressions constantly disturbed by shifting winds. Your genes may have the timidity of a lamb while another is imprinted with the ferocity of a lion. Yet, God desires that we embrace the contrasts, and all may blend like a sweet bowl of potpourri, to serve and love in unity.

Unity is so important to God because we are one family, bound together as one body in Christ. We all have His Spirit breathing within us, with each of our names rubber-stamped on the same nail-scarred palm.

> Therefore, as God's chosen people, holy and dearly loved, clothe yourselves with compassion, kindness, humility, gentleness and patience. Bear with each other and forgive one another if any of you has a

MENU 3: HOLINESS IN RELATIONSHIPS

> grievance against someone. Forgive as the Lord
> forgave you. And over all these virtues put on love,
> which binds them all together in perfect unity.
> (Colossians 3:12–14)

One afternoon, my twenty-year-old daughter wanted to snack on a banana. While trying to slice it in half using a butter knife, she barely scratched the thick peel.

"Mama, this isn't working," Colleen observed.

"Of course it wouldn't work! That knife has no teeth." Then emphatically stating the obvious, I continued, "It's called a BUTTER knife for a reason."

Eight-year-old Chiara, who was within earshot, raised an eyebrow and said matter-of-factly, "Yeah! It's for CHEESE!"

Two people stared at the same picture but raised conflicting opinions. And yet, they challenged a point without sounding disagreeable. You, too, can oppose without being repugnant—contradict without being irreconcilable.

Remember! You're not an Egyptian Pharaoh. You don't have a dynasty to build, and your words are not the law. There's no need to be hard-core and pompous like a stuffed shirt. Nor are you a Jurassic dinosaur of the primeval era. You need not be bloodthirsty and create chaos at the slightest injury.

As God's people, we are called to be prudent in speech.

Far-reaching in patience.

Harmonious in love.

And humbly embracing our diversity.

Don't be inflexible as tombstones. Do not choke your relationships in a bed of thorns and brambles. Your neighbour or your spouse is not Aladdin's lamp that you should be rubbing the wrong way. Instead,

Let your gentleness be evident to all ... And the peace of God, which transcends all understanding, will guard your hearts and your minds in Christ Jesus. Finally, brothers and sisters, whatever is true, whatever is noble, whatever is right, whatever is pure, whatever is lovely, whatever is admirable—if anything is excellent or praiseworthy—think about such things. (Philippians 4:5, 7–8)

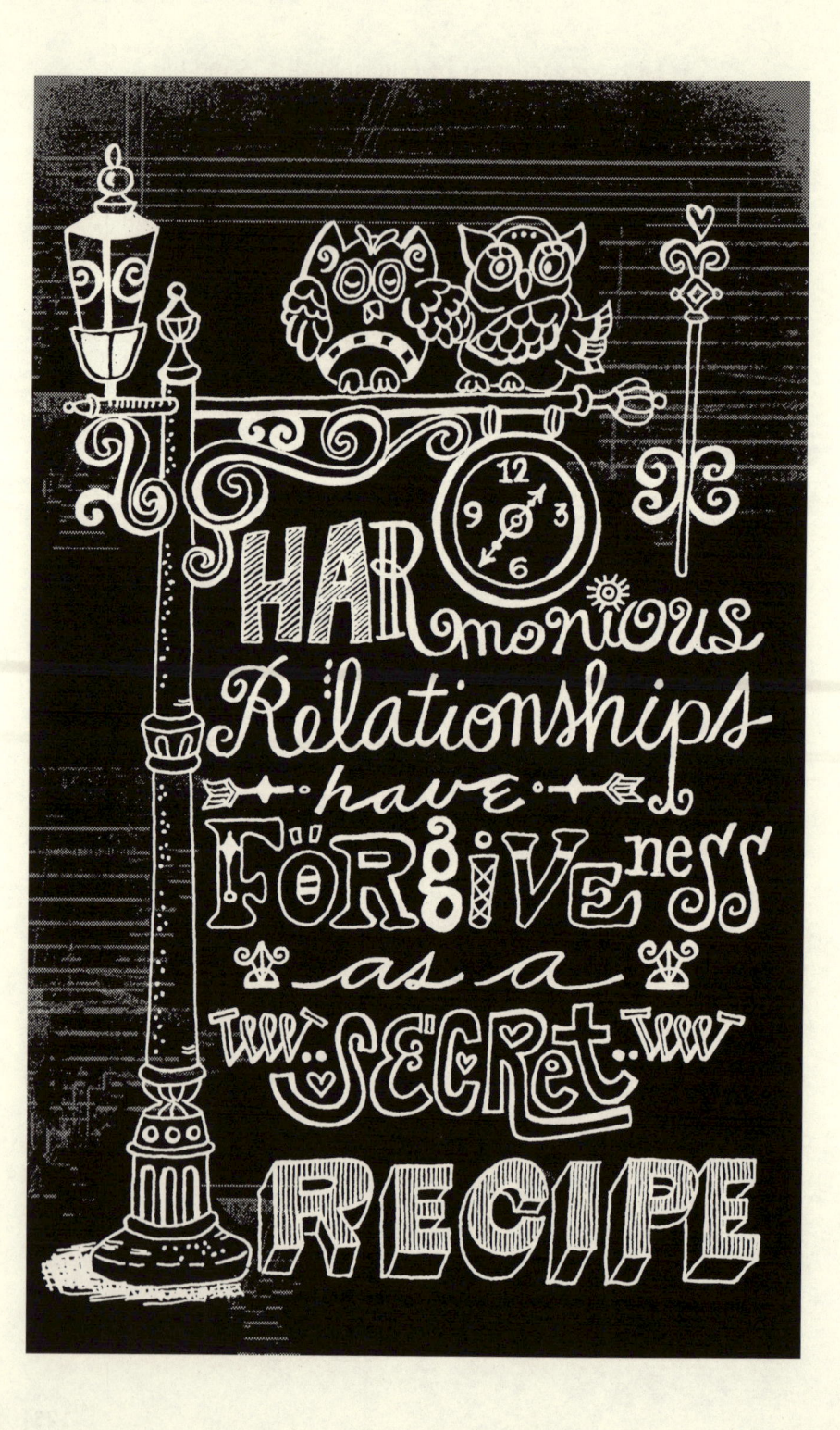

Harmonious Relationships have Forgiveness as a Secret Recipe

Chapter 16

Tongue under Lockdown

While driving along Vancouver's slightly potholed Fleming Street, my then four-year-old son observed, "Mama, why is the road so bumpy?"

"It's not yet fixed." I looked at the road, and there seemed to be no sign that construction would be underway.

Probing further, Pajo asked, "Why don't people fix it?"

"Maybe because they don't have money."

Not fully satisfied with my whys and wherefores, Pajo pumped my brain for more information. "Why do you need money?"

"Before you can fix roads, people need money to buy materials. They probably don't have MATERIALS."

At this, the soft voice of my two-year-old princess chimed in. "CEREALS? Mama, we do have cereals. We can give them some."

The twist of tongues had our wires of communication criss-crossed that night. The mere thought of paving the road with

MENU 3: HOLINESS IN RELATIONSHIPS

frosted cornflakes that crackled under the pressure of rubber tires brought our family down into convulsions. While my son's mind typically dwells on the mechanical hows and whys of science, Chiara's thoughts always linger around food. It was no wonder then that she easily fell into a materials-cereals rhyme trap.

This incident with my kids sparked memories of the times my husband and I had our own communication gaps. Men and women normally process thoughts and display emotions differently. Understanding each other's intentions can be as tough as decoding an Aesopian language or an archaic crytogram. Alvin and I were no different, and so repeatedly exchanged mixed signals that ended in bickering. We got into he-says-she-says power struggles that were nowhere as cute as my kids' rhyming mismatches.

Years ago, I was a fence-sitter who silently observed Pajo and Chiara as they tackled their own toddler business. Chiara scrambled towards the nearest bar chair, hysterically screaming, "No, Pajo. No!"

My naughty son growled like a ferocious grizzly and ran after her beet-red, teary-eyed sister. Although our dining set was a bit more elevated than standard furniture, Pajo was tall enough to reach Chiara, who sought protection and height by kneeling on the seat.

For a fraction of a heartbeat, I didn't understand what the loud-mouthed brouhaha was about. But picture this scene. As the four-year-old boy curled his fingers to mimic sharp bear claws, Chiara recoiled inches away from him. With a roar, Pajo banged his head on the little girl's fat tooshie—not just once, but many times over.

With no regard to Chiara's pleas, Pajo continued headbutting. Curiously, the snarls were replaced by audible slurping sounds. It was only after Chiara yelled that I understood what set the goofy riot in motion.

With tears flowing in pail-loads, my panic-stricken daughter cried, "Paaaaa – jooooo! Stop licking me! I AM NOT ICE CREAM!"

I scooped my delectable gelato-baby in my arms, away from the slobbering tongue of her big brother. Tears welled up in my eyes too ... neither in sympathy nor anger but in uproarious laughter.

Later, I realized that there is a serious lesson to this side-splitting nuttiness. Much of the fights we have in marriage are this petty—not half as comical, but every inch as trivial.

People pick fights over absurd issues that do not deserve a drop of sweat. Either because of inflated egos or a burning itch to prove we are always right, we carp at even the minor errors our family members make. We become experts at throwing peevish complaints. In so doing, we bring ill-natured undercurrents into our relationships. We give affection with overtones of cynicism. This is love watered-down.

There was one nugget of truth I learned years ago that I carry with me like a treasure through marriage. No matter what happens, never argue with a husband who is tired or hungry. Even if you're pushed against the wall, don't do it. Even if you're boiling over in rage, bite your tongue. Sleep over your argumentative pitches, and leave them up for discussion over a warm cup of latte and a platter of stacked flapjacks at the breakfast table. You will be surprised to see that your husband is less the hostile critter he was the night before.

Choose your skirmishes. Always go down to the very meat and potatoes of your problem. What is the soul of the matter? What are the pivotal concerns in your relationship that need your focus? This is where you should invest your energies—not on frivolous, often juvenile nitpicking. Forget about who left the trash out for the bear scavengers. Don't arm-wrestle over the TV remote or who

MENU 3: HOLINESS IN RELATIONSHIPS

takes a turn with the dishes. It's not worth jumping into the boxing ring over cases that have no substance.

And while the dispute is on, don't keep score. Never keep mental track of your spouse's past mistakes only so you may have ammunition to use for future debates. Remember, harmonious relationships have forgiveness as a secret recipe.

As people who have been redeemed by Christ,

> ...you must also rid yourselves of all such things as these: anger, rage, malice, slander, and filthy language from your lips. Do not lie to each other, since you have taken off your old self with its practices and have put on the new self, which is being renewed in knowledge in the image of its Creator. (Colossians 3:8–10)

Beyond question, you were chosen by God to live in holiness and kindness. Therefore, as one created in His image, do not allow irritability to overstep boundaries and make painful inroads into your gentle, even-tempered posture. Remember what a powerful weapon your tongue can be; pick your words wisely. Do not hesitate to keep your tongue under lockdown when the temptation is strong to wield it in a malicious way. Count up to ten before you open your mouth again. If that doesn't work, count up a hundred times more!

Let us wisely heed the warning in Scripture,

> With the tongue we praise our Lord and Father, and with it we curse human beings, who have been made in God's likeness. Out of the same mouth come praise and cursing. My brothers and sisters, this should not be. (James 3:9–10)

And so, my friend, always present your case in gentle, non-blood-pressure-raising tones. Your negotiating power escalates when sweetness touches the lips. But when all your Communication 101 skills fail and you end up in another Battle of the Petty Minds, remember my butterfat-baby's appeal: "Stop licking me! I am not ice cream!"

Then maybe ... just maybe ... you'll tuck your dripping tongue back in.

And, at last, keep quiet.

Chapter 17

Salute to Mothers

When my eldest daughter was still a toddler, I used to recount exaggerated observations and funny anecdotes while I cleaned her ears. The entertainment was a temporary diversion that kept her mind off the poking cotton buds so she lay stock-still on the bed. All these years, I didn't know that one particular absurd comment drummed into her consciousness—"Your ears are so dirty! I can plant yams inside."

Gullible Colleen took my hyperbole literally and believed that sweet potatoes actually grew inside little girls' ears!

I didn't realize she had this line of thought until one evening when I prepared vegetable tempura for dinner. Colleen took a bite of the orange-colored yams coated with crispy breadcrumbs. She was halfway done when she asked nonchalantly, "Are these carrots, Mama?"

"No, honey. Those are yams. Do you like it?"

I haven't even completed my statement yet when Colleen's eyes popped wide open. Her nose wrinkled and her eyebrows

MENU 3: HOLINESS IN RELATIONSHIPS

furrowed in a disbelieving grimace. Then she shrieked, "Eeewwww! I'm eating earwax!"

This amusing experience was one of hundreds that spiced up my journey as a mother. Inscribed in my memory, I prized them all, for I knew this parenting season would fly by swiftly.

The road from crib to empty nest can be incredibly short. Each adventure with our children is a privilege that will likely not regenerate.

That being so, I retired from gainful employment during my prime when my technical skills were most marketable and critical to business operations. It was a matter of choice which I didn't regret even when our family's budget stretched thin.

However, during the years I spent as a stay-at-home mom, a lot of people who knew my credentials shared their unsolicited penny's worth of insight. Many regretted the decision to swap my high-profile career, glitzy benefits, and VIP treatment for a life of cooking-oil-splattered aprons, soiled dish towels, and grimy kitchen sinks.

For years, I had to put up with dissenting, nagging voices. "Honestly, you're wasting your education," some friends said sorely.

"If you just wanted to be CEO of the kitchen, why did you even bother with post-graduate studies? Instead of business management, you would have been better off with home economics," others teased.

"Unemployed?! Really? I think you got kicked out because your boss didn't like you. You can't land another job? Maybe you're too picky! Get off your high horse!"

"You have so many talents you can use to earn money. Why waste them at home?"

I accepted all these tongue-in-cheek overtones with a smidgen of offense. What was so wrong about wasting my talents on my children? Didn't they deserve the best of me too?

I felt like a commodity under tough microscopic scrutiny. But despite these prickly, two-star customer reviews, I didn't ditch the laundry basket nor unplug the vacuum cleaner to salvage my waning career and recoup my lost financial rewards. I was adamant about staying home because I believed motherhood was also a venerable vocation no one had the right to disgrace.

Have you been in the same boat? Have you encountered people who raised eyebrows and dished out a not-too-palatable evaluation of your choices?

Language experts coined a new name for this. They call it "motherism", which runs along the same circuit as racism, except that the prejudicial pinch is directed towards stay-home moms. It is the same bigoted outfit that says, "Hey, we are better than you."

People who think stay-at-home moms are lazy, uneducated, or cannot be successful for dearth of mental acuity are "motherists". Perhaps, they haven't walked along both sides of the career-or-home fence to acquire a more balanced opinion.

If you, too, have to bear the false judgments of family and friends because you go against the flow and stand out differently from the crowd, hold your gaze up to the Lord who picked you for this journey. Do not always believe what people say about you. Sweep their cheap shots aside. Don't give them permission to injure your vulnerability to such a degree that your identity as child of God is lost.

You are not a good-for-nothing idler just because you opted out of the payroll. Just because your status reversed from revenue-generator to partial liability doesn't mean you guzzle the garbage people cram down your throat.

Do not allow the world to weigh your worth on their unscrupulous scales.

Remember, you are an heirloom in God's treasure-house!

MENU 3: HOLINESS IN RELATIONSHIPS

That is not a presumption so pocket it as truth. Indeed, you are a royal diadem of the Lord.

How can you not be, when you have an extraordinary Father who sacrificed His Son as an extraordinary gift? Logically speaking, as recipient of the Gift, doesn't that make you an extraordinary person too! At the cost of Jesus' blood, your humanity and spiritual substance truly aren't cheap.

If you are still not sufficiently convinced, check out what Scripture says. In Proverbs 31, the Lord details your description straight down from verse 10—

> A wife of noble character who can find?
>   She is worth far more than rubies.
> Her husband has full confidence in her
>   and lacks nothing of value.
> She brings him good, not harm,
>   all the days of her life. (Proverbs 31:10–12)

See ... right there in black and white! You are "worth far more than rubies." Therefore, by the measure of your rarity and brilliance alone, it goes without saying that those who receive you lack nothing.

For how can you not be counted as rare when you are singular? No one else has your frame, shape, mood, and humour. Therefore, celebrate your individuality. Weigh as joy the fact that even your temper, food preferences, neural connections, and mannerisms cannot be duplicated by another. Your psychological makeup is entirely your own. Isn't that amazing!

What it comes down to is this: You are special—fingerprint, mole, and all! The choices you make or any smear campaign thrown against you cannot diminish your worth. If God Himself never belittles you, then why do you allow people to cheat you of your true appraisal?

Do you know what else you can highlight in Scripture? Find encouragement as you read down to verse 28:

> Her children arise and call her blessed;
> >her husband also, and he praises her:
> "Many women do noble things,
> >but you surpass them all."
> (Proverbs 31:28–29)

You, woman of God and mother of precious children, hear this! You are blessed. Even without a fat bank account, you are blessed.

It is possible you may not stash an enviable financial booty by being domesticated, but your well-bred children become your matchless trophies that no sizeable sum of money can buy.

There is no way you can equally trade money or professional certificates for the priceless moments you spend with your children. Holding hands with your kids while you watch seagulls by the waterfront, cupping their teary cheeks after they blister their fingers, picking apples in the garden, building snowmen during wintry no-school days ... these are intangible souvenirs you can't easily accumulate with your head buried under stacks of office assignments.

Fortunately, it wasn't too late for me to realize this. After retirement, I still had plenty of opportunities to grab those rare "eureka moments" when my children's mild acts of notoriety were promptly switched into value-formation time.

One such opportunity happened years ago over breakfast. I caught my then seven-year-old daughter sitting with both legs folded on top of the chair, with her chest leaning forward on coarse knees. She stretched her sweater to cover her cold legs and ate awkwardly in that fetal position.

She put heaping spoonfuls of cereals in her mouth which bulged her cheeks comically. When eager to talk, those

MENU 3: HOLINESS IN RELATIONSHIPS

half-masticated crumbs and milk sporadically spewed out from her mouth like an eruption of volcanic ash.

As a mother, I had a fixation for good table manners. Those naive gestures never passed without a remark.

"Colleen, can you please sit like a lady and eat like a lady? Only put food that can fit in your mouth," I pleaded. I held out half a spoon of grains to display the exact small measure I suggested.

Obediently, she rested her feet on the floor, sat in a prim and proper style, and covered her spoon only midway. But instead of feeding once and gulping it down first before taking another bite, Colleen stuffed her mouth with successive half tablespoons of her favourite breakfast until her face looked like a plump cream puff again.

One ... two ... three ... four ...

The half-filled spoon just kept coming back in rapid sequence into that ravenous little crater.

Colleen stared at my interchanging expressions of amusement and frowns. Again, she spluttered more crumbs as she explained apologetically, "They can all fit in my mouth, Mama."

Oh, well! Not all teachable moments worked out as planned. But God knows I tried!

Children are the bellwether that indicate, at regular intervals, what an excellent job you've done in raising them. To the extent that they imbibe sound Christian values and become disciplined, then you know your presence at home has yielded fruit.

Your brain will not atrophy as other people may judge. Your education is not wasted even if you withhold the practice of a trade. In fact, practical, day-to-day issues at home can challenge your true mettle and hone it to perfection. You utilize your intelligence and skills repeatedly, sometimes creatively, as you sculpt young lives.

Therefore, look at your motherly vocation with a brighter perspective. Your sacrifice and investments may not multiply foreign dividends, negotiable instruments, and capital funds. Your family's economic cycle may rest on the downtick more than the upturn, with personal debts inflating faster than savings.

Regardless of the slump in your standard of living, believe you are blessed.

Your children call you blessed!

Because whatever you fail to keep in your hand, whatever worldly advantages you lose ... all these pale in comparison to what you harvest in spiritual gains.

During my daughter's preschool commencement rites, after assorted medals for academic excellence were pinned on a handful of students, the little graduates individually stood at the center of the stage to deliver a thirty-second parting tribute.

In front of all the parents, one child said, "When I grow up, I want to be a doctor." A couple of girls wanted to be teachers, while another wanted to be a dentist in the future.

When it was Colleen's turn at the microphone, she gave me a bashful smile then stated publicly, "When I grow up, I want to be a mommy!"

What a poignant acknowledgement!

Could there be a higher form of praise and credit than this—that a child would desire to imitate her mother?

What better recognition could we receive than the knowledge that motherhood is on an equal plane of intensity and value as all other professions in the field?

> For you created my inmost being; you knit me
> together in my mother's womb. I praise you because

MENU 4: CHRISTIAN LIVING

> I am fearfully and wonderfully made; your works are wonderful, I know that full well. (Psalm 139: 13–14)

Listen, dear sister. Read that verse again. Take comfort in it! You, who were chosen to participate in God's creative plan, wear your shawl of dignity with pride.

You, woman, whose womb touched the miracles of God's ingenuity, rejoice in your fruitfulness. By your acceptance of God's commission, your children were "fearfully and wonderfully made" within you.

On that ground, let no one brand you a Nobody. Let no one downgrade your person. No matter which mudhole you have sunk—with or without an ambitious career—you are still God's Somebody... worthy of the same privileges reserved to those He loves.

```
          With this in mind,
        we constantly pray for you,
 that our God may make you worthy of his calling,
        and that by his power
         he may bring to fruition
      your every desire for goodness
   and your every deed prompted by faith.
            2 Thessalonians 1:11
```

Chapter 18

Choices

One quick look at my three-month-old baby and I knew her daddy gave her a bath. The damp hair was not the telltale sign, but the outfit was a dead giveaway.

My husband slipped Chiara into a peach and mustard long-sleeved top with a Winnie the Pooh applique. Her pants were of a powder blue and white striped cotton print. She had a lime green and white buttoned sweater. Her socks were a solid yellow on the right foot and a plain blue on the left. Wrapped around the right hand was a pure white mitten while the other hand had a printed navy. To complete the ensemble, Alvin put on a crocheted toque on Chiara's head. Bright splashes of pink, cherry, and lavender covered her baby-fine hair.

Ugh! If I didn't know any better, I would have mistaken my baby for a rainbow. Or might this be a Halloween costume aptly worn on a cool February day? Nothing in her wardrobe matched! Not even the socks!

MENU 4: Christian Living

My left-brain-oriented husband had a style that was uniquely his. Practicality and effectiveness of the attire took priority over color coordination and harmony in design. It didn't matter to him if you matched burgundy with luminous jade and made the baby look like a Christmas wrapper. As long as the child was clothed warmly, chic trends were no big deal.

Fashion faux pas in the infant department were not his only trademark. After a flitting inspection of the bathroom, I also knew Alvin brought my son to the potty. The potty seat and soiled diaper, sprawled recklessly open on the floor, were booby traps ready to ambush any unwary foot. The roll of tissue teeter-tottered on the towel rack. Puddles of water dotted the bathroom counter. Light still flooded the empty room, the switch completely forgotten. Then tiny Pajo ran past me with a crooked boyish grin and a denim jumpsuit worn inside out.

This was my bone-weary and sleep-deprived husband's way of juggling things. This was how he coped while I washed burp rags and handled middle-of-the-night breastfeedings. No matter how often I pestered him about it, the result was pretty much the same. I could nag him until the sand dunes of the Sahara turn into plump vegetation, but he would never change his habits. He made his choices; there was no way I could charm and sway him with mine. Therefore, I decided to sail where the wind blew and simply let him have the freedom to approach his business—his way.

Freedom of choice.
Somehow, this experience reminds me of our own relationship with God. The Lord creates us with rational minds, with the power to decide and act on our reasoning. He gives us free will to see what we'll do with it.

God presents us with limitless options and possibilities to test our choices. Will we choose yellow socks or blue socks? Rainbow outfit or dull monochrome attire? Will we take up a career or answer the call to evangelistic missions? Serve in the corporate battlefield or chase the muddy splatters of tiny feet at home? Do we end a nerve-wracking day with grouchiness, a hair-raising scream, or a tranquil nod of acceptance?

On a deeper level, do we choose maturity and spiritual wholeness over tepidity in faith? Are we the catalyst that triggers a contagion of truth or lies? Do we abuse our free will by prying loose what is forbidden?

The Lord gives us freedom in order to determine how far we use our conscience to guide our choices. He goads us to thoughtful reflection so that our minds may incubate virtuous judgments. Overall, He wants our biases to land on the side of goodness rather than evil.

Sometimes, God switches the green light and permits us to wander beyond the fence to determine where our steps will lead. During these moments, when we push beyond the compass of moral restrictions, God exposes the true nature of our obedience to Christ.

Are we submissive to His will and strong in faith, undeterred by temptation?

Or is our obedience so skin deep that the desire to sin dominates our desire to choose Christ?

In point of fact, unless we curb our perverse appetites and anchor them under God's commandments, we'll end up with wrong choices that breed painful consequences.

It is written in the Book of Deuteronomy,

> See, I am setting before you today a blessing and a curse—the blessing if you obey the commands of the Lord your God that I am giving you today; the

MENU 4: CHRISTIAN LIVING

> curse if you disobey the commands of the Lord your God and turn from the way that I command you today by following other gods, which you have not known. (Deuteronomy 11:26–28)

Truly, God has implanted within us this beautiful gift of choice ...

The freedom to decide for Him or against Him.

The freedom to choose life or death.

A blessing or a curse.

He created us with the faculties for free expression and the drive for independence. But guess what? Deep down, He wishes that we let go of our sophomoric debates and dwell within the domain of His sacred will.

He wishes to elect for us what is most befitting—that we elevate His choices and voice above our own.

He grants us authority, but inwardly desires our submission.

Imagine the height of God's joy if we decide to relinquish this gift of freedom! Picture His nod of approval each time we nullify our impulses and say, "Not my wishes, Father, but your will be done."

Daily choosing virtue and mastering our weaknesses lead to true maturity in Christ. This may be plain-vanilla in theory, but not really as simple in practice. That's because the fallen nature of man, the constant pull of the world, and the influences of culture make it difficult for the Christian to conquer his desires and submit his will to God.

Even the apostle Paul admits,

> I do not understand what I do. For what I want to do I do not do, but what I hate I do. (Romans 7:15)

I love how another translation paints a vivid picture of man's inner conflict.

> What I don't understand about myself is that I decide one way, but then I act another, doing things I absolutely despise. So if I can't be trusted to figure out what is best for myself and then do it, it becomes obvious that God's command is necessary.
>
> But I need something more! For if I know the law but still can't keep it, and if the power of sin within me keeps sabotaging my best intentions, I obviously need help! I realize that I don't have what it takes. I can will it, but I can't do it. I decide to do good, but I don't really do it; I decide not to do bad, but then I do it anyway. My decisions, such as they are, don't result in actions. Something has gone wrong deep within me and gets the better of me every time.
> (Romans 7:15–20 The Message)

As Scripture indicates, we are fallible human beings. That being so, our choices are prone to err. Our minds pause because our desires blow hot and cold. Our determination to embrace good can be corrupted easily by the whim of a moment.

Therefore, by the strength of our intentions alone, we can never attain true perfection in this world.

We need the grace of God!

We need the Lord to crack down on our internal contradictions. We need Him to alienate us from our wicked predilections. We need God to teach us how to choose Him above all things.

Dear friend, I encourage you to use your free will as God originally intended—

MENU 4: CHRISTIAN LIVING

Use it to consciously reject evil.
Choose to be docile to His grace.
Decide to stay in communion with Christ.
Go at full-throttle, and let God's will be your will too.

Allow Him to mold your freedom to perfection as you direct your choices towards all that is morally upright and true.

Be prepared, as well. Once you choose to live for Christ, He will put you through the wringer to test the purity of your choice.

Did you pay mere lip-service when you declared your love for God? Rest assured that He will shake you down, stack you up, shape you all around, and plant you in the high and low ... He'll do everything to challenge your authenticity.

If you claim to choose Christ, He'll make sure your life legitimates and substantiates the choice.

I remember the day God did exactly that. I was driving alone on a busy highway with praise music humming through my ears. The bright autumn landscape and the uplifting lyrics drew the perfect tone for prayer. My *Parachute Band* CD was playing *To Live is Christ*, an all-time favourite that never failed to choke me up. With one hand raised in worship and tears that trickled without warning, I echoed the lyrics and owned it like a statement of faith:

> "For me to live is Christ
> And to die is gain
> No matter what price I pay
> I choose to give this life away."

Swelling with emotion, I refueled my love for God and vowed to release my whole life into His hands—regardless of cost.

With my own lips, I parroted the words, "No matter what price I pay, Lord, I choose to give my life away."

Within a full minute of my gutsy pledge, as I was about to turn left on a three-lane thoroughfare, the yellow light abruptly turned red, and a hidden camera flashed its blinding light to capture my traffic violation. I was caught on the act, right in the middle of an infamous intersection, illegally completing a turn when the light was a bloody red!

Oh blast my lack of concentration! Too much singing would be the death of me!

I actually had plenty of time to complete my left turn, but across from me was a humongous, oncoming sixteen-wheeler trailer which covered a wider arch to steer left. I paused and, out of courtesy, gave the other driver enough wiggle room to negotiate the sharply hyperbolic curve.

Oh blast my kindness!

Excessive generosity would be the death of my pocket too!

If I was slapped a red-light-violation ticket, $167 would slide down the drain in a heartbeat. My thirty-year driving record had been so squeaky clean; not even a parking or speeding infraction tainted my name. I prided myself for being too respectful of the law. Well, not until that morning when I had my karaoke moment!

No police siren tracked me down, but I was on pins and needles. The joyful tears I had just minutes ago became sobs of mental shock. I barked at myself for being the stubborn donkey that didn't understand reds, yellows, and greens.

When that wasn't enough, I thundered against God for letting it happen. He could have blown a fuse or caused a power outage so the traffic camera wouldn't work.

If pigeon poop was already partially blamed for the collapse of a Minnesota bridge in 2007, then it wouldn't be too ridiculous of an idea for bird dung to drop again and blur the camera lens— right?! And where in my donkey world could I find $167?!

MENU 4: CHRISTIAN LIVING

All sorts of absurd thoughts cluttered my head that day. The sense of failure and blighted hope became too strong that I forgot what I promised God earlier ... "No matter what price I pay, I choose to give this life away!"

Bam!

It suddenly hit me!

God's humour.

God's testing.

God's not too humorous testing.

"Did you just play a joke on me?" I asked the Lord. "I know it's bad to swear—but I swear, you're not funny!"

Then to myself, I gave the silent rebuke, "No matter what price I pay? Yeah, right! The ticket is only $167 and I'm already this much peeved."

God didn't have to be too literal. But literal was what caught my attention and delivered the message right through my thick skull!

For sure, the Lord exposed my lack of credibility. My prayer had no genuine bite. I spoke the words too loosely that my faith overturned at the slightest pinprick.

The cost of following Christ was a measly one hundred dollars for me! Anything above that was obviously unnerving. Anything beyond that and I became insanely cantankerous. Boy, I never realized I was a cheapskate!

My friend, don't be a cop-out like me. Put your money where your mouth is. Once you use your free will to choose Christ above all else, steel yourself.

Don't back out when the Lord tests your integrity.

Never let your convictions be too anemic and weak that they sway at the slightest upset.

Remember, God can see through you.

See, I set before you today
life and prosperity,
death and destruction.
For I command you today to love the Lord your God,
to walk in obedience to him,
and to keep his commands, decrees and laws;
then you will live and increase,
and the Lord your God will bless you
in the land you are entering to possess.
But if your heart turns away
and you are not obedient,
and if you are drawn away
to bow down to other gods and worship them,
I declare to you this day
that you will certainly be destroyed.
Deuteronomy 30:15-18

RECIPE

you are beautiful because GOD created you xxx and there is no imperfection in anything GOD touches

Chapter 19

Where Beauty Lies

A few weeks on to my fourth pregnancy, my husband and I had this discussion over breakfast.

"When the baby's born, I hope he looks like you." Although my mouth spoke the words, my heart was so pumped up and my mind psyched to find a "mini me" in the next baby. After multiple miscarriages, Alvin and I were overzealous to see this pregnancy through. "How about you? Who do you want the baby to look like?"

With a smile as wide as my hips, Alvin proudly said, "Of course, I like the baby to look like me!"

It was an innocent remark, but surprisingly, I was offended. I guess, like any expectant parent, my husband simply wanted everybody to recognize him as the father who's totally smitten by this new child. He had no idea his statement hit a touchy nerve and opened up a floodgate of emotions. Unintentional, yes. Nonetheless, his response spotlighted painful grudges that transported me back to my childhood.

MENU 4: CHRISTIAN LIVING

For more than two decades, I held this secret. I was so tight-lipped about it—not even my family knew. Sitting obscurely behind my bubbly front was a lot of self-loathing. I hated myself for being too ugly and envied others who were endowed with the right kind of genes.

Such perception sprang from hurts I harbored against relatives who taunted me about my physical appearance when I was a kid. Though they didn't bluntly say I was the ugliest in the family, being the butt of their ill humour sealed that impression.

Some teased that while my cousins and aunts were fair-skinned, I fell on the darker shade of the color wheel because I tripped on cow dung. They said that on the day God rained down blemishes from the sky, I had no umbrella and so received a generous ration of pimples. The blow of their mockery often stung; it made my eyes fluid and my nose runny. For this, I was branded a cry-baby.

While my cousins had well-shaped legs and perfect curves in the right places, I was dissed for lacking symmetry, for having "logs" instead of "legs", and for flaunting the vital statistics of a pyramid. When I was about eight years old, my brother and cousins fell in line and mimicked a duck's walk to mock my protruding bum and fat tummy. As gullible as I was, my brother convinced me that I was adopted.

When I was twelve, I casually asked my mom when I would start wearing a bra like my peers. I didn't intend to crack them up, but my aunts nearly bust their guts laughing.

"What's there for you to cover? Just use a band-aid. It's cheaper."

I guess they didn't mean to make fun of me, but I never forgot how awful I felt and how embarrassed I was for asking.

From that point onwards, my self-esteem became so depleted that I actually believed I was nature's freak accident. No wonder

I felt indignant about my husband's legitimate reply. My twisted perspective fueled the fire and pushed the wrong conclusions into my subconscious. I thought Alvin didn't like the baby to take after me because I lacked glamour. I thought he would be humiliated if his son inherited my drab features.

Of course, none of these thoughts ever crossed my husband's mind. Still, God used our good-humoured banter to expose my inner conflict and cruel judgments. He wanted to bring back dignity into my life.

This event became a preamble to an even deeper pruning by God. Shortly after the spat with Alvin, both of us attended a weekend conference which spoke about celebrating our humanity. I had no initial expectations about the forum. As the hours ticked, though, I realized God had something meaningful and life-changing in the agenda. He transfixed me in that place for a reason.

The words of Pastor Ambrose were razor-sharp and stabbed where they should. Though I couldn't play back his words verbatim, the nub of his message hummed in my memory and became the guidepost for future decisions. If I wrap the whole conference down to a short and sweet capsule, he said,

> "God judges you by what you are inside, not by how you appear outwardly. Reflect on this—do you treasure yourself? If you are not satisfied with what God has given you, God can't give you more. God was not playing a joke when He made your nose small. He didn't run out of clay so that He can't put more shape where it matters. God made you as you are, and you need to be happy about it.
>
> "Let us grow a sense of wonder and view each person as a miracle. Look beyond the surface; embrace your self because you are beautiful. You

are irreplaceable. The greatest tragedy is to wish to be somebody else. Appreciate your own body, and stop envying others. Because if you can't accept your nature and love your uniqueness, do you think you have the capacity to hold others in high regard? If we do not value this life and what we are now, we will put everything to waste, for God will not give us another life.

"Don't be deceived by what you see. All of us are, in fact, created equal because all of us have dignity. Nothing and nobody can snatch away the beauty and worth of each of us. People's negative judgments will not incapacitate our lovability in God's eyes, for God doesn't appraise our value according to physical appearances. He doesn't rank us according to our personal success stories. He values us based on our inner growth—according to our potential."

The minute these words whirred in my ears, I knew God was trying to stitch old, gaping wounds. He peeled off my fake disguises to trigger healing on a grassroots level. In the process, He pushed out of the fog my nobility and true stature as daughter of a High King.

Though it never occurred to me until that day, much of what I assumed as concealed, became the actual driving force behind many past decisions. As a single woman, I was often noncommittal. Vagueness was my strength. I hemmed and hawed before accepting the marriage proposal because I knew I would be wed into a handsome family. I feared that I might not meet certain standards. It was a silly theory, of course, but one that made me jittery nonetheless.

I also remembered back in high school and university when I deliberately missed out on swimming parties. The mere mental image of my bulges in a bathing suit was already sickening. In fact, our honeymoon in world-acclaimed Boracay White Beach was the first time in fifteen years that I wore a swimsuit. I couldn't even claim credit for it. My mom had to plead with me for days before I gave a halfhearted "okay".

I had a bunch more of these experiences which bordered on my pathetic self-image. I supposed the Lord figured these were enough. It was time to turn the page and rewrite the story.

During the conference break, I decided to approach Father Ambrose for counseling. Inspired by his exhortation, I found myself sharing about my history and the cowardly product that I had become.

"Did somebody actually tell you that you're ugly?" he wondered out loud, his deep-set eyes growing wide. "I ask this because I think you're very beautiful."

That was perhaps the first time I heard someone compliment me with sincerity. The sympathy in his voice choked me up. Tears flowed unashamedly because what I thought to be a very humiliating disclosure turned into a sweet pat-on-the-back indulgence.

"There's no need for you to bring this excess baggage into your marriage. Leave the past behind, and work towards your future. Don't let people's false judgments of you destroy your relationships. I'm sure your husband is not so shallow as to marry you only for your looks. If others insulted you before, forgive them. They're probably speaking from their own wounded past."

Father Ambrose couldn't underscore enough the beauty of God's design and the need to hold such creative power in highest reverence.

"This is what I suggest you do," he said. "Each day, face the mirror, look at your body, and say aloud with conviction, 'I am beautiful!'"

MENU 4: CHRISTIAN LIVING

It was humanly impossible to produce a throaty croak and piggy snort as idiotically as I did after hearing his proposition. I laughed and cringed at the same time, imagining how ridiculous I would look in front of the mirror.

At the end of the day, I left the retreat house feeling more positive about myself. Wacky or not, I was stoked to give a resounding "yes" to my own question—"Mirror, mirror on the wall, am I fair or not at all?"

I never realized what cumbersome weight I carried for years and how liberating it was to trash them away. I was finally freed from this stifling imprisonment. And was I glad the Lord orchestrated the bail out!

The Bible has a lot to say about the standard by which we should calibrate beauty. In 1 Peter 3, it says,

> Your beauty should not come from outward adornment, such as elaborate hairstyles and the wearing of gold jewelry and fine clothes. Rather, it should be that of your inner self, the unfading beauty of a gentle and quiet spirit, which is of great worth in God's sight. (1 Peter 3:3–4)

Do you believe you are beautiful?

Don't answer nonchalantly, "yeah, sure" then leave the matter to the dogs. Dwell on it a bit more. Stare at your reflection and call out, "You are God's beautiful creation!"

Do you take every word of it as gospel without flinching?

Or is there anything uncomfortable in your past that you also keep under wraps? Do you entertain corrupted images of yourself and count yourself inadequate against the world's benchmarks? Do you knock your value down a peg lower than your neighbour's because you tip the weighing scale at over two hundred pounds?

Today, God wants to probe into your oppressive thoughts so that you stop belittling yourself. Do not write yourself off because God never does. Now is the time to get out of your escape hole where you hid and indulged in your pity parties.

Do you remember that private mental cavern where you retreated with your tears and where you wasted time bad-mouthing yourself? God sequestered it. It is now closed and out of business!

Do yourself a favor. Be still for a minute. The Lord wants you to be quiet and stop thrashing around. Let Him scoop out your repressed memories and heal any bitterness. Allow God to scrape your wounds and expose what is depraved. He will shovel and hoe until He gets to the root of your pain. Acknowledge that it will hurt. You'll surely shrink with embarrassment, but all these are necessary for you to obtain true freedom.

God wants to release you from needless bondage because you were not created to be chained. God loves you so intensely that it tortures Him to see your bruises and scars. Allow the Lord to patch these up and mend you to wholeness.

You, the beloved of God, are beautiful because He created you. And there is no imperfection in anything God touches. Claim then the words of Scripture. Make it your own—

> Charm is deceptive, and beauty is fleeting; but
> a woman who fears the Lord is to be praised.
> (Proverbs 31:30)

Chapter 20

Our Father Who Art in Heaven

```
The Spirit you received does not make you slaves,
       so that you live in fear again;
        rather, the Spirit you received
    brought about your adoption to sonship.
      And by him we cry, "Abba, Father."
                Romans 8:15
```

The wailing was persistent. Too tiresomely loud, it started to annoy. Whoever's the source of the sound was in it for the long haul. Was it the neighbour's cat? It piped like an angry miaow, shrill ... but not quite feline!

The woman took a few steps closer to her doorstep, straining her ears, probing. The cries crescendoed with every stride. No, the irritant wasn't bouncing off from the neighbours'. It seemed to resonate from behind her own wall.

Slowly, the woman pulled the knob, fearful of what stalked on the opposite side. To her absolute disbelief, a newborn rested at her front doorstep, mercilessly dumped like a piece of broken, hand-me-down furniture.

MENU 4: Christian Living

A huge price tag dangled on the baby's scanty wrap. For a pathetic $160, a poverty-stricken mother sold her child, not because of a life-or-death urgency, but due to a corrupted need to support her husband's gambling addiction.

Though initially horror-struck by the idea of "purchasing" a destitute human life, and though thrust into an ineradicable responsibility against her free choice, the woman took pity on the baby. She worked on his adoption, had him baptized as David, and treated him so affectionately you'd think they shared the same genetic chain.

David had the best education in an expensive private school. He was spoiled like a prince, safeguarded like fine pearl. The surrogate mother invested her emotions on the adoptive child even though she faced the risk of intrusion from the real parents. She could only imagine. If a biological father was neurotic enough to gamble away his own son, what would he not do to milk strangers until their bank accounts dried like a dusty, drained well?

The woman raised a foster kid regardless of his sleazy history. No spotted background could impair the maternal love she was willing to give. Driven by the love of Christ in her heart, she wished to redeem David's trashed dignity and compensate for his rough start in life.

Do you realize that we were all Davids? You and I. We were a fractured people. All of us were sons of Adam, woven into the fabric of sin, sentenced to death from birth. We came with tattered wraps, fragmented by our guilt. We could easily be dumped as worthless baggage.

But God had a similar obsession in adopting us. Even though sin clung to our past like caked mud, He didn't put the adoption deal on the back burner. In the general scheme of things, our willful disobedience didn't matter. Our gobs of mistakes were not voted against us. Our character flaws didn't tip the balance. Why, you ask?

Because God's love is perfect. It isn't hinged on the seeds of displeasure we sowed. Notwithstanding the skunky stench of our sins, He welcomed us into His family and bestowed upon us the same privileges as His true family. As such, we are no longer cursed children.

Saved by grace, we are now co-heirs, with equal rights as the Son, to a rich eternal inheritance. We were formerly disenfranchised, but brought back to citizenship.

Yes, my friend. You and I ... we're heaven-bound, freed slaves because of adoption!

You must believe too, God is not a fair-weather Father. He is not an I'll-love-you-only-if-you-behave-yourself kind of daddy. God understands that somewhere along the road, we'll cross the threshold of rules and break them.

Even so, this big-hearted Dad wishes to bridge the frigid distance so that we'll unwind and breathe easy in His company. He wants us to team up with Him in an unburdened, casual way. There's no need to be aloof, stiff, and official with a Father who aches to be personal. God forged an adoption agreement so that He ceases to be a blurry hypothesis that floats with the clouds.

Really, what a great privilege, that by praying "our Father who art in heaven", we are basically accepting our designated status as adopted children of God!

Just as a proud parent is restless to see his newborn baby, God was teeming with excitement when He saw the adoption contract with His name stamped alongside yours. His joy burst like a thousand gushing dams. In fact, He was soaked in too much pride and euphoria that He ignored everything else, even your birthmarks—those deplorable blotches left by Adam's fall.

MENU 4: CHRISTIAN LIVING

Realizing now that God initiated and sealed this relationship into permanence because it is His pleasure to save the unworthy, what should be your proper response?

There's no higher honour you can offer God than imitation. The simple truth is: God wants you to bear His resemblance. Not only should you mirror His identity, you too must lock His heart inside yours.

Every proud parent knows this. Even before the first light of the sun kisses a newborn's face, mom and dad already start arguing over whose dominant gene made the baby's nose sharp. Mom states a fact, "Her hair is as wavy as mine." Dad counters, "Those gorgeous brown eyes are definitely mine."

As the child grows, the comparison flows. "Wow, Henry, you play the violin so well. You're just like your mom."

"You made it to the soccer try-outs? I'm not surprised. In his younger days, your dad was an athlete too."

Just like our earthly parents, the Heavenly Father's heart softens upon finding His living portrait sketched on us. The divine thumbmark rubbed on humanity—this gives Him joy!

God forges us into the shape of His character and nods His approval as we strive to imitate His holiness. Imagine the Lord's validation, "Hmmm, my son's self-control has finally improved."

Other times, God observes how we rebound from the fury of a storm and warmly acknowledges, "Well done! Your faith has gained strength."

Even before poetic wordsmiths coined the famous expression "like father, like son", God already inscribed this in Scripture. His version, an all-time favourite, reads, "Be perfect, therefore, as your heavenly Father is perfect" (Matthew 5:48).

God elects Himself as the ideal model for His children. It pleases Him to find in us a flawless reflection of Christ. But do we really make every effort to be His imitators?

This question calls to mind an experience we had when my daughter was only eight. If there was one thing that could make her beet red in embarrassment, it was this observation spoken by any adult—"You look like your Papa."

Each time, she would stomp her feet in protest, crumple her nose, and snap with a resounding "Noooooo! I don't have a mustache!"

One weekend evening, the family arrived home very tired, a couple of hours past Colleen's usual bedtime. Naturally, she was grumpy and her whining topped the decibel charts. Alvin reminded her to brush her teeth before sleeping, but Colleen only made a fuss.

You see, since she was four, this child created a solid hierarchy of "hateful routines". She painstakingly debated her way out of anything hygienic. Showers, washing of hands and face, combing of hair—this little girl recoiled from them all. With a posture of defiance and cries that could awaken a hibernating grizzly, my daughter disliked toothbrushes the most.

That night, primed for battle while moaning sleepily, Colleen pleaded, "Papa, can you please brush my teeth for me?"

Without hesitation, Alvin took Colleen's toothbrush. With eyes shut but mouth stretched wide, Colleen lazily waited for her Dad to start the chore. But when Alvin didn't swing an inch, she sneaked a curious look.

"Why, Papa?"

"Before I do this, I have one condition." The Dad's prankish smile was teasing.

Colleen wasn't a bit flustered. Viewed from all angles, ANYTHING was better than dental hygiene.

"Okay, what?"

"Tomorrow, when you see Aunt Bambi and Uncle Billy," Alvin said "I want you to tell them 'I look like my Papa!'"

MENU 4: CHRISTIAN LIVING

A fairly effortless demand, you might think. Hilarious even. But Colleen squirmed like no human body could possibly squirm. Her internal sparks and sirens sounded off. As if kicked on the shin, her droopy eyes immediately flickered in panic.

"Aaaaawwww ... Papa!"

By her tone of defeat, you'd think her dream of orange-plaque smiles was crushed by a giant toothbrush. Indecision crumpled her eyebrows. Serious study narrowed her eyes. One look at her face and you'd presume the world's future hung in a tightrope.

Drumroll broke the silence.

Bargaining chips lay flat on the table.

What would the deal be?

Would Colleen admit her striking resemblance to her Dad? Or would she surrender to the power of the toothbrush?

"Alright, Papa," Colleen finally made a choice. Taking back the gadget from Alvin's hand, she conceded. "I'll just brush my teeth by myself!"

Sounds ridiculous?

Maybe.

But many of us Christians make similar absurd choices.

Instead of choosing to be an ideal image of our Father, we fancy other alternatives. The burning question is ... why? For what reason do we withdraw from God? Why do we dissociate ourselves from a Father who is overrreaching and straining to hold our hands?

Because it is tough to imitate Christ!

To be like Christ means to suffer like Christ.

To be like the Father means to give up the world and all its deranged affections.

Humans, however, love to pick roads with the least humps and craters. The lesser the resistance, the higher the entertainment value. Comfort, as the world defines comfort, seems to be man's default setting.

Yet, God challenges us . . .

Be perfect as your heavenly Father is perfect.

Be holy—set apart in purity—as your Father is holy.

Be patient and forgiving as your Father forgives.

Love genuinely as He loves. Always in triple measure, without exclusions. Push kindness to the extreme even when love is not reciprocated.

In all things, show the world that you are His family—a living portrayal of Himself.

Bear Christ's face. Towards your neighbour, be His tangible image.

For truly, besides this, there's no greater gift you can offer your adoptive Father.

```
See what great love the Father has lavished on us,
   that we should be called children of God!
         And that is what we are!
   The reason the world does not know us
         is that it did not know him.
                1 John 3:1
```

Chapter 21

Lead Us Not into Temptation

> For we do not have a high priest
> who is unable to empathize with our weaknesses,
> but we have one who has been tempted in every way,
> just as we are—yet he did not sin.
> Hebrews 4:15

Lead us not into temptation.

This is a modest request that every Christian with a sense of the bigger vision should pray. An awareness of the raging war among principalities should move us to seek God's protection so that we may not fall prey to temptation.

A wise Christian knows that to serve and obey God is to encroach into enemy territory. The deeper our love for God, the greater is Satan's compulsion to torment. Hence, it is with commendable prudence that we ask God, "Don't let us yield to the evil around us."

With or without our awareness, we enter into spiritual battle everyday. If we don't stay within God's turf and gird ourselves with His shield, we will be helpless before the onrush of evil. Temptation

MENU 4: CHRISTIAN LIVING

presses on every side, and like a bastion, we stand secure for as long as we invite God to reinforce the walls.

Back in kindergarten school, I took a front-row seat and observed how influential peer pressure had been to my five-year-old kid. Whether in the playground or in the classroom, Colleen was always a compassionate and well-behaved child. She never had the barefaced brass to pick a fight.

When pushed to mediate in a squabble, she automatically sided with the aggrieved party who shed the most tears. That was how she gained intimacy with her friends. In fact, most of the children dearest to her were once underdogs who found relief in Colleen's protective side.

Therefore, it came as a shocking revelation to me one day, when a teacher summoned me because of Colleen's "misdemeanor". Colleen was charged with bullying in school!

My daughter?

A bully?

Did they really mean this sweet girl whose heart bled for pitiful little down-and-outers? Somehow, things didn't add up.

Diving into the bottom of the story revealed peer pressure as the hideous culprit. A small gang of pretty, cherub-looking, young toughies in pigtails rallied behind Colleen and forced her to push a small kid during recess. Those little tyrants threatened to banish Colleen from their circle of friends if she didn't comply.

Colleen momentarily struggled between misguided obedience and group acceptance. But in the absence of adult supervision, she didn't stop to consider the moral issues involved and just shoved the target as instructed.

Whoosh!

Just a little elbow work and the task was completed at rocket speed. No sweat at all!

However, in the same split second that it took to complete the job, the teacher turned her head. Uh-oh! Colleen was caught with the proverbial hand inside the cookie jar!

You see, temptation has a way of bearing down on people as peer pressure does. When evil inclinations border us on all sides, and our righteousness sticks out like a sore thumb, we can be overcome unless we rest on a solid foundation.

Young people who are tempted into premarital one-nighters usually reason out, "Everybody's doing it anyway." An undergraduate decides to smuggle answers in an exam and he rationalizes, "Who has time to study?"

Jesus teaches us to pray "lead us not into temptation" because He recognizes our susceptibility to sin. Our Father, however, will not completely spare us from temptation. These will still come occasionally to test the fire of our faith and weed out the downsides in our character.

This fact shouldn't inspire fear, for as Paul says,

> No temptation has overtaken you except what is common to mankind. And God is faithful; he will not let you be tempted beyond what you can bear. But when you are tempted, he will also provide a way out so that you can endure it. (1 Corinthians 10:13)

Though it may sound unbelievable, temptations can be constructive to our growth. Through them, we become more dependent and focused on God while less presumptuous of our own spiritual muscle.

MENU 4: CHRISTIAN LIVING

Years back, while working in the strategic planning division of a huge conglomerate, I met a young, attractive man who crossed the boundaries of professionalism and showed me more attention than was mandated by his job.

Part of my responsibility was to brief local and foreign investors on the operational highlights of our company since our shares were actively traded in the stock exchanges. For this reason, it was not uncharacteristic for me to accept business lunch invitations over which I discussed economic trends.

I had occasional meetings with this client. Initially, our discussions bordered on rudimentary facts. Later, however, he turned his charm full blast and, with enthralling blue eyes, alluded to his personal tastes in women. His business tone turned too dangerously casual for my comfort.

Even as I channelled the conversation back into mainstream industry, he sidetracked again towards the topic of girlfriends. Being on gracious terms with him, I paired him off with some single women I knew. He brushed every suggestion aside in a wink. Finally, with boldness, he flirtatiously spilled out his feelings for me. Blindsided by the confession, I was speechless. His words packed such a strong wallop that my emotions ran riot.

This man knew I was married. It was no big secret. I even brandished my wedding band each time I went out with clients to voluntarily ward off any impression of intimacy in the meeting. My ring served to maintain the distance and keep the business relationship in focus. And I had been quite successful at it, until that moment.

I was aware of the savage temptation that whacked its full fury upon my heart. Nonetheless, adultery was never an option for me. I wouldn't deny that I found the floral bouquets, gifts, and starry-eyed interest flattering. But yielding to temptation and purposely offending God was not part of the Lord's agenda for my future.

To this day, I am still grateful that He yanked me away at the exact moment my own wall of avoidance crumbled. My spiritual discipline skidded downhill, but God's safeguards prevailed.

God didn't give the devil a chance!

The prayer says, "Lead us not into temptation." What weight of influence those words bear!

The phrase, tiny though it may seem in appearance, is a forceful blow against the enemy. It is a plea God can't refuse. For at the crux of this prayer, we ask the Lord to extinguish our carnal impulses which push the old self into disobedience. This plea slides the carpet from under the devil's feet so that he is powerless to exploit our fragility.

By God's grace, no longer can the adversary thrust us toward temptation's suicidal consequences.

Friends, let us peel the blindfold that sabotages our discernment and limits our ability to see the devouring mouth of the lion.

While keeping in mind the weaknesses of our human nature, let us acknowledge the power of God, behind whose back we hide when temptation raids.

```
     Submit yourselves, then, to God.
Resist the devil, and he will flee from you.
                James 4:7
```

RESENTMENT is a venom that embitters the Hearts & ruins GRACE

CHAPTER 22

If I Could Change Things

If for one day, God gives me power to change things in the world, I will:

   a) List maple walnut ice cream, tiramisu, and Bavarian cream profiteroles under the same health food group as broccoli and spinach,
   b) Distribute pucks to each hockey player so they won't have to wrestle and suffer concussions over one,
   c) Store sleep and time in bottles, and sell them cheap in convenience stores,
   d) Enlarge all holes in golf courses to the size of manholes,
   e) Redefine cellulites, voluptuous thighs, stretch marks, and receding hairlines as the archetype of beauty—the kind of stuff commercial models crave for and photographers feature in magazines,
   f) Let the hormonal fluctuations of adolescence turn teenagers into the sweetest of angels,

MENU 4: Christian Living

  g) Create a remote control "pause" button that can silence tantrum-throwing toddlers.

If I have power to change things, clutter is a home decorator's dream. Household chores are fun recreational sports. And spouses never wake up with bad breath.

If I have power to change things, Monday is a holiday. The government remits monthly tax refunds. And dust is a precious resource that can be deposited in your bank account.

If I have power to change things, hazelnut and almond chocolates are maintenance medicines. One hundred and seventy pounds is a five-foot woman's ideal weight. Arthritis is a status symbol. Teeth won't need brushing. Tooth Fairies are for real, and they pay the month's rent.

I will do all these and more ... if power rests in my hands.

But look at my list.

It is vain and self-indulgent—a clear picture of wasted power. It's not at all the frivolous list God will draft.

The whole Bible gives testimony to the power of God—

From the creation story of Genesis to the final judgment in Revelation.

From the parting of the Red Sea and the flooding of the earth, to the healing of the sick and the raising of the dead.

All these reflect the glory and majesty of a powerful Creator.

The power of His anger scatters the proud with all their evil devices.

The power of His love leads people to repentance.

The power of His hand designs life in the womb.

The power of His Word forces light out of darkness.

The power of His resurrection releases the chains that bind us to eternal death.

I am so glad that power rests in God's hands, not in mine.

> The heavens praise your wonders, Lord, your faithfulness too, in the assembly of the holy ones. For who in the skies above can compare with the Lord? Who is like the Lord among the heavenly beings? Who is like you, Lord God Almighty? You, Lord, are mighty, and your faithfulness surrounds you. (Psalm 89:5–6, 8)

We don't call God, "Almighty", just to give in to an arbitrary whim. We do so because we acknowledge His authority.

Nothing in this world has enough capacity to bottle up His greatness. God's influence is too preponderant; no one can transcend Him. No one can predominate and rip off the splendor of His crown.

As the Psalmist professes in verse 6, who can compare with the Lord? Definitely, there is no one more powerful.

We welcome this fact in our heads. But the question is—do our hearts discern it too?

One afternoon, my daughter, Chiara, asked, "Mama, can God do everything?"

In a snap, I said, "Of course!"

"Really? Anything?" She rolled that last word out of her tongue in a strange drawl.

"Yes," I wasn't sure what was so unbelievable that Chiara had to verify my response. "God can do everything. With people, there are so much stuff we can't do. But with God, nothing is impossible."

MENU 4: CHRISTIAN LIVING

"Really?" Chiara's expression was reflective. "You mean, God can also shoot lizards out of His eyes?"

"Whaaa—?" I had to look up from slicing vegetables to double-check where that came from. "Uhm ... well ... I guess so?"

My belief system melted right there! I was pretty sure those leaping lizards ran off with my faith!

Hesitation betrayed my lack of conviction. I wavered for what seemed like the longest millisecond of my life.

Oh, an epic fail!

I just declared with my own mouth that God could do all things ... except shoot lizards out of His eyes! Locusts? Maybe. But not lizards.

God performed surgery on me that day. He sliced me open, down to the living marrow. He sifted and probed—only to discover that my belief in His omnipotence was very shallow.

Do you ever find yourself in a similar spot? You don't exactly doubt that God is mightier than the rattling thunder and swollen seas. You don't argue that He can flick untamed cyclones out of the map and calm the winds with just a word.

But when it sinks down to a personal level—when it is your crisis that is on the chopping block—you begin to fluctuate. You are convinced God's power is not ginormous enough. The mountain is too steep. The squall is too fierce.

This malignant cancer is incurable.

The debts are too stratospheric; it makes you dizzy.

The job description is too ambitious for your paltry qualifications.

The justice system is too unbalanced, and your voice is too small.

Your enemy is too eloquent, but you can't stand in defense because you are not English savvy.

When problems smack your face hard, isn't it that your faith swings and waltzes in many directions? Major trust issues sprout out of nowhere—

Why are you so quiet, Lord?
Where are you when I need you?
When will you answer my prayers?
Am I so unlovable that you abandoned me?
How long do I have to wait?
Oh, God, can't you see how much I'm struggling?
Did you forget your promise, Lord?

Do not allow these questions to plague your mind and mess up your sleep. Instead, feed your thoughts with memories of God's boon, blessings, and bail-outs.

Recapture His faithfulness.

Your life is inundated with God's gifts, but your distractions smeared it into a blur. Go then and jog your memory to revive your appreciation of God's power. Feel the pounding of your heart and the warmth of your breath. You are alive. That alone is a miracle!

Let us reflect and reason as the Psalmist did:

> "Will the Lord reject forever?
> > Will he never show his favor again?
> Has his unfailing love vanished forever?
> > Has his promise failed for all time?
> Has God forgotten to be merciful?
> > Has he in anger withheld his compassion?"
> Then I thought, "To this I will appeal:
> > the years when the Most High stretched
> > out his right hand.
> I will remember the deeds of the Lord;
> > yes, I will remember your miracles of long ago.

MENU 4: CHRISTIAN LIVING

> I will consider all your works
> and meditate on all your mighty deeds."
> (Psalm 77:7–12)

Hammer this down in your consciousness. Remember this throughout your waking hours. Dream about it too, if you must.

We have an influential God who is clothed in power. He can forge ahead and change things in your favor ...

And He exhibits this power, not only for a day.

—⚬⚬⚬—

Chapter 23

The Lord Is My Shepherd

It was the summer of 1977. I was only nine. My dad planned a ten-hour road trip to his hometown and we packed our luggage with enough clothes to last a week's adventure.

On the morning of our departure, just when we were all dressed and ready to board the car, I picked up from hushed adult conversation that my mom back-pedaled. She no longer wished to travel with us. Feeling torn and confused, I also shifted ground. I orchestrated last-minute flip-flops in plans for which I was severely criticized.

As the other half of the family paraded out of the house with plump suitcases, I stuck around to keep my mom company.

Obviously miffed, my father grunted, "You're so fickle-minded!"

The heavy-hearted departure and criticism were chiselled in my memory as if the sour exchange happened only yesterday. Why? Because those were the final words I received from my dad.

MENU 4: CHRISTIAN LIVING

On their return trip, while cruising along the freeway at an unreasonably high speed, a truck changed lanes and sideswiped our car. My dad lost control of the wheel, and the vehicle careened on one side. Somersaulting several times down an embankment, the viciously crumpled car landed on its roof with tires still fiercely rotating.

My father was pinned against the steering wheel. Without the protection of a seat belt, twisted metal brutally lacerated his liver.

My poor brother, only thirteen years old then, was tossed out of the car like a spineless rag doll. His budding adolescent frame suffered major abrasions and a broken collarbone.

The other passengers were no less severe. In spite of their fractures and traumas, they were still fortunate to have survived the ordeal. My dad was not as lucky.

Whenever I circle back to the night of the tragedy and recapture the pain of our loss, I am floored by how I cheated death. I was within a hair of becoming a victim myself! If the Lord didn't cast a shade of indecision in my head, if He didn't dampen my enthusiasm and pull me out of the family vacation, then I might have been picked up from the debris as one unrecognizable corpse. At nine years old, I had no personal knowledge of God, but He sure was quick to save my life.

Haunted by this grim memory, Psalm 23 quickly evolved into a warm blanket of repose for me. The words invited silence and drew me back to my center of tranquility.

> The Lord is my shepherd, I lack nothing. (Psalm 23:1)

I grew up in the city and had never grazed a living, honking, bleating, squawking, or neighing farm animal in my whole life. I have friends who are bankers, architects, bakers, and accountants.

The last time I checked, none in my circle were nomadic shepherds. The only thing I know about sheep are the hundreds I count before my mind vegetates to dreamland. The only full-bodied sheep I have ever stroked is my daughter's Pillow Pet plush toy. The only authentic sheep I came close to touching was my Irish Aran wool sweater!

Having said that, I can't attempt to comment on Psalm 23 with all its pastoral images and metaphors. I am not qualified to post a theological debate about the complexities of flock administration or the scientific basis for the anointing of oil on sheep.

But as a teacher, I got a handle on grammar. So let me demystify one word ... is.

Which "IS", you ask?

The Lord IS my shepherd.

That "IS"!

The immediacy of the present tense is so beautiful. It feels current. Very near. Prompt. And deeply involved.

David's psalm reminds us that the Lord is near. He is our shepherd in the now. Nowhere in the Bible does it read, "the Lord WAS my shepherd" as if God already resigned after accomplishing a colossally exhausting Red Sea stunt. He didn't run out of steam after jacking up the loaves and fish supply for a motley crowd of five thousand. Neither was the Lord so physically drained of energy after redeeming the dead Lazarus that He scaled back his stewardship functions for us present-day "sheep".

The Good Shepherd is not shepherd emeritus who was discharged from professional duty. God still takes care of us today with the same momentum and meticulous precision as in the past.

We are never cut off from God's safekeeping.

What a soothing thought!

MENU 4: CHRISTIAN LIVING

The same Good Shepherd whom David loved is still within reach of our generation. The centuries that passed between us didn't rupture the bond. The weight of God's devotion didn't shift. We need only to attune ourselves to the Shepherd's voice to realize that He is still in the active trade of leading men to "fields of green pastures" where restoration is complete.

> Even though I walk through the darkest valley, I
> will fear no evil, for you are with me; your rod and
> your staff, they comfort me. (Psalm 23:4)

If you think that God's accountability over you is tentative or that He is frugal with His aid, you have another think coming. Like the sheep herder whose preservation of the flock doesn't taper off after sunset, God's mindful eye stretches beyond our waking hours.

Our Keeper never nods his head off to sleep. Even if we walk through the darkest valleys, terror will not defeat our spirits. God puts a hedge of protection around our faith. Hidden threats cannot pounce on our hope. And though our expressions of gratitude for these undeserved benefits are few and far between, God doesn't quit doing His job.

Years ago, we lived in a single-detached home that backed onto an untamed greenbelt of invasive cogongrass. These four- to five-foot-high weeds encircled several acres of open fields which farmers cultivated during growing seasons.

One afternoon, an unusual commotion beyond our rear fence stirred my curiosity. A huge throng of people stampeded across the grassland towards our home. They rushed headlong into the tangled thicket of wild cogon which outlined our wall. The reason for the pandemonium was unclear as quivering, panicky voices overlapped with each other to form an incoherent cacophony.

The disturbance dragged on for hours until police officers arrived with a hysterical mother.

Apparently, an elderly farmer was clearing the grass with his sickle when he unearthed a cadaver within the bushes. Leaning against our concrete fence was the remains of an innocent nineteen-year-old boy whom unidentified men rubbed out by mistake. Led off track by a confused impression, they committed the atrocity towards a false target and wasted a human life in the most barbaric way.

Upon hearing the police officer's account, beads of sweat lined my forehead. The revolting crime brought goosebumps all over my body as fear of another episode of killings hounded my imagination.

And then I remembered the previous night when our dog barked wildly ... something which she didn't do unless there was a stranger within hearing distance.

Whenever Poochie made noise after sundown, it was my habit to open the outdoor lights, survey the yard from the second floor windows, then go back to bed. That particular evening, however, I heard the mutt's howl. But for some strange reason, I couldn't peel myself off from the pillows.

I guess it was God's way of preserving our family. If I stuck to the routine, I could have been an unwilling witness to the assault and a sitting duck for a backlash.

You see, we once settled in a town where eyewitnesses didn't live to tell the tale. If the perpetrators of the crime saw even just a flicker of light, they'd figure someone in the house was an intrusive bystander. Make no mistake about it. These people would stop at nothing to sweep up the loose ends.

In a separate incident, God spared us from a potentially fatal smash-up even though we forgot to pray for His protection

MENU 4: CHRISTIAN LIVING

that day. A young couple in their early thirties took driving lessons around our neighbourhood one late afternoon. The woman maneuvered the manual-transmission car while the husband, an unlicensed instructor, dished out the directions.

Without warning, a rowdy pair of stray dogs crossed their path and threw the amateur driver into a state of panic. She floored both the clutch and gas pedal—mistaking them for the brake—thus causing a continuous loud rev of the engine.

Vroom! Vroom!

Like a sports car that sizzled on its tracks as it burned rubber, the deafening roar added to the driver's panic.

Startled by the sound, her left foot slipped from the clutch which made the car lurch at breakneck speed. Losing control of the steering wheel, the driver missed the sharp curve of the one-lane road. Instead, she crossed over an empty, furrowed tract of land and slammed the vehicle onto our next door neighbour's gate.

The entire front of the car crumpled up like a loose wad of paper. The windshield smashed to smithereens. The passengers, who made the reckless blunder of not wearing seat belts, were bloodied and too traumatized to remember the impact.

The ill-fated driving practice took place at 6:30 p.m. At roughly the same time, children in our neighbourhood routinely played basketball at the exact spot of the collision.

God's perfect game plan for the day didn't include casualties. As fate would have it, parents broke convention and called in their kids prematurely since dinner was served early.

What's more, the car rammed onto the patio's cement post and metal grillwork. If the driver swerved from its course even by a whisker, they would have bashed our neighbour's parked van.

In retrospect, there was a string of other blessings which brought us down to our knees in gratitude. For starters, the homeowner was a physician who just came off hospital duty. She was at hand to promptly administer first aid when everyone else was too overwhelmed and spaced-out to move a muscle.

The trail which the wayward car crossed was the same cul-de-sac my husband and I normally passed to enter the garage. That evening, the distracted couple would have directly hit us if we weren't stalled at the gas station a few meters away.

Coincidentally, we stopped for gas and pumped air on the tires. If not for the brief interruption, we would have knocked them head-on. I understood then that God synchronized both events and prompted the delay so that we would reach home without a scratch.

These experiences throw the spotlight on God as a devoted Shepherd. If you take a closer look at your own life, you, too, will find myriads of adventures in which the Lord whisked you from harm's way.

Recall the time you narrowly escaped from a fire or a calamitous flood. Perhaps you had a close encounter with a thief or a gun-wielding lunatic in a shopping mall.

Remember how you had a safe landing despite the pilot's in-flight announcement of severe turbulence ahead.

How about the time your car skidded on black ice and you came to a full stop only inches away from a crossing pedestrian?

Just think about it!

You, too, had many close calls! Many times, you didn't even realize what rotten luck you could have had.

Bad news.

Bad breaks.

Bankrupcies.

And headaches.

God saved you from many of these worries. You were surrounded by many enemies, but He made mincemeat out of them all.

MENU 4: CHRISTIAN LIVING

You wonder why? There's only one reason. As the Shepherd's "sheep", you—and you alone—are the focus of His interest!

You may not even know what kinks and knots to unravel because the Lord already intervenes before you spot the whole problem. Sometimes, God deciphers our cryptograms even before they become larger brain twisters we can't unriddle. Such is the faithfulness of our Good Shepherd!

To top it off, His care doesn't ebb and flow.

He is constant. Consistent. Always present in times of distress.

Therefore, my friend, hush your pounding heart. Put your faith in this—our security rests in the Shepherd's mighty hand.

And with Him, we lack nothing.

```
        Surely your goodness and love
      will follow me all the days of my life,
  and I will dwell in the house of the Lord forever.
                    Psalm 23:6
```

Chapter 24

Through Heaven's Gates

Ten years of experience in the financing sector taught me a lot about maximizing investment yields. Through regular exposure to market fluctuations, I learned how to play with interest rates, manage capital, and increase savings.

However, it doesn't require an Einstein to figure out the basic economic principle—the more you spend, the lesser your reserves. The more income you invest and save, the better your financial posture. Any amount you consume is counted as a permanent deduction.

God challenges this logical equation in dozens of ways. As far as He is concerned, giving and sacrificing adds up to blessing.

Money unselfishly shared is money received in double proportion. A ten percent contribution from one's paycheck, voluntarily offered for the work of the church, will store up an inheritance of a more sizeable dimension.

This is one postulate that is lacking in scientific basis. I think even the most meticulous accountant will have trouble justifying the inconsistency. But such is the law behind obedient tithing, and God Himself proves it.

> "Bring the whole tithe into the storehouse, that there may be food in my house. Test me in this," says the Lord Almighty, "and see if I will not throw open the floodgates of heaven and pour out so much blessing that there will not be room enough to store it." (Malachi 3:10)

Another translation reads,

> "... Bring your full tithe to the Temple treasury so there will be ample provisions in my Temple. Test me in this and see if I don't open up heaven itself to you and pour out blessings beyond your wildest dreams..." (Malachi 3:10 The Message)

Focus on the compelling phrases used to highlight God's promise. *Throw open the floodgates of heaven. Pour out blessings beyond your wildest dreams.* What mind-blowing words on which to rest our security!

God didn't say these just for the sake of conversation. He wasn't speaking metaphorically nor was He attempting to wax poetic. God had no hidden meanings. He really meant every word as stated.

If we honour Him with the first fruits of our benefits, His generosity will drench us beyond our expectations—and that is not a tall tale!

God has inexhaustible riches. At the right time, He sends them down to us from His heavenly depository.

We can test the credibility of His word. Watch if He will not reload our storage bins. See if He will forget to stock up our pantry shelves. We can prove if the Lord will, in fact, replenish up to the last drop of blessing.

God is by no means frugal in raining down benefits upon those who sow cheerfully. He loves those who surrender their wealth with unclenched fists—people who don't tithe out of mere obligation.

God's returns do not cascade in trickles, like light dewfall. Instead of a drizzle, expect a dramatic torrent of His goodness.

It offends God when people give with long faces and gritted teeth. What pleases Him are men and women who tithe with an eager detachment, for in them is a godly spirit. They view the glamors of this world as short-lived. Everything else is of lesser worth compared to the treasures of the Kingdom.

> Each of you should give what you have decided in your heart to give, not reluctantly or under compulsion, for God loves a cheerful giver. And God is able to bless you abundantly, so that in all things at all times, having all that you need, you will abound in every good work. (2 Corinthians 9:7–8)

God appreciates enthusiastic giving. He can't help but smile at people who jump for joy when they see church ministries expand because of their charity. To these people, God is never stingy with His privileges. He is equally delighted to requite at more than double their sacrifice—for there is no living being who can claim to be more bighearted than God.

God's generosity recognizes no boundaries. No coupon discounts. No cutoff periods. No rainchecks. And no fine-print restrictions. He lavishes on His children like there's no tomorrow.

I took God at His word and had proven it to be true. I challenged Him and found myself teetering from all the miracles we

MENU 4: CHRISTIAN LIVING

witnessed. So much physical evidence surfaced. Limitless rewards, stowed in bundles, popped out of nowhere.

Even when times were exceptionally tough, my family never lacked anything after we gave freely to the Lord. Always, resources landed on the table just when we downed the last swig of milk.

I remember when we started operating on a single income, tithing became a harsh discipline. The outflows of funds didn't slow down but the inflows did. The temptation to cut back on the gifts was so fierce. I made justifications for the irregular tithing. However, lame excuses like "we're facing abnormal circumstances" or "we'll try again next month" never got past my husband. Alvin had always been adamant about returning to God what appropriately belongs to Him. This, for him, is part of prudent stewardship.

Consequently, we tightened our belts several notches. We trimmed off the "gimme that or I'll throw a tantrum" and prioritized the "buy this now or we'll die!"

The deprivation didn't escape God's eyes. Though at times, the inconveniences we put up with were minor, He never belittled our sacrifice. With gladness, He opened the gates of heaven and through it passed the stockpile of His house.

In one of many similar instances, our pantry was totally cleaned out. We finished the left-over food in the fridge, and I had no idea how we could get by for the next meal.

No sooner had I popped the question than our next-door neighbour, whom we never met before, knocked on our door with a bucket of live fish. They went on a fishing trip and were fortunate to haul a big catch. They gathered too much fish that even after giving away a bucket-load, it would take them weeks to consume the extras.

Fresh fish!

Fatted, glistening fish with eyes pleading, "Eat me! I'm all yours!" What a superb treat indeed!

But that wasn't all. In the same afternoon, my mom phoned me for help. Apparently, my brother who departed for Malaysia, had excess baggage in the airport. Airline personnel forced him to leave behind loads of ready-to-cook goodies.

My mom had no freezer space to stash away the groceries, so she wished to distribute the surplus to us. Bulky piles of frozen meat lined our fridge for days. Imagine! These supplies even exceeded the average quantity of food we normally bought each month!

> Give, and it will be given to you. A good measure, pressed down, shaken together and running over, will be poured into your lap. For with the measure you use, it will be measured to you. (Luke 6:38)

Tithing didn't come naturally with me. I had to tussle with it for years. The meticulous, penny-pinching side of me crossed out tithes in the budget. Somehow, rescheduling the gift to a later date became a bad pattern ... until God criticized me for cheating Him.

> "Ever since the time of your ancestors you have turned away from my decrees and have not kept them. Return to me, and I will return to you," says the Lord Almighty.
> "But you ask, 'How are we to return?'
> "Will a mere mortal rob God? Yet you rob me.
> "But you ask, 'How are we robbing you?'
> "In tithes and offerings." (Malachi 3:7–8)

Such strong words spun me around.
Me?
A thief?

MENU 4: CHRISTIAN LIVING

I felt like someone doused cold water on my face to bring me back to my senses and swing me to the proper point of view.

God makes it plain in Scripture that all the relationships and possessions we enjoy in this life are on loan to us.

On loan!

We cannot claim any stake on it. As matters stand, we are not being fair and noble by sharing from our excess.

Sometimes, our logic can be muddled. Our moral compunction can be knotted into a confused mess because of our desires to control money. When this happens, God wants us to start afresh and view the situation from His perspective. Faithful tithing doesn't put God in a position of indebtedness to us. We are—and always will be—indebted to God.

All the harvest of our service comes from Him. It is His money which we borrow. We have no right to be selfish and stingy with what isn't ours from the beginning.

To identify with how God feels, let me use this analogy to underscore the point. Imagine ...

You asked a friend to keep your money in her purse. Then without regard for your opinion, she rushed out on a shopping binge and came home with the coolest fashion accessories and top-of-the-line electronics. She indulged herself but never reimbursed a single dime of your money. Realizing her thoughtless haste, she said, "I'll pay you back some other day, okay?" Then she left without remorse—not even a slightly pricked conscience. Emotionally high, she walked out, carrying everything with an avaricious grip.

If this actually happens to us, how do we feel?

Definitely rotten.

And yet, God has to patiently choke back the same feeling until we come to terms with our own lack of prudence and decide to slip the money into His "purse".

God wants to make it clear that we are not accumulating "good works" by tithing. Our contribution doesn't make us an exceptional model of philanthropy.

As God's people, it is our duty to help build the Church. To the extent that we provide food for our own family, we too should look after the needs of the Church with the same degree of diligence and responsibility. Consequently, we shouldn't expect a pat on the back when we give ten percent of our wages. We don't deserve the commendation.

For tithing is a commitment.

It is a decision—something that is expected of a faithful steward.

It is not the amount as it is the positive disposition of our hearts as we give that merits God's applause.

God has set in place a clear foundation for tithing that it is now difficult for me to ignore the discipline. When selfishness raises its hideous head and tempts my fingers to clench over my wallet, I whisper a prayer to regain my equilibrium.

"Lord, please protect the money. Don't let me spend it recklessly."

One memorable Sunday afternoon, our family finished errands at close to two o'clock. Famished, we decided to grab a quick lunch in a Japanese restaurant. Though our apartment was nearby, we voted against dining at home. Food preparations could take another hour, and we were too hungry to wait.

"Do we have enough cash?" Alvin asked.

We really didn't have extra funds even for a casual McDonald's drive-thru. But tucked in my wallet was the tithe I planned to drop in the collection basket in a day or two.

I considered it harmless to single out a twenty-dollar bill from the envelope. I promised to return the equivalent amount the minute we earn it. To my mind, it was an innocent decision cooked up by a gurgling tummy.

MENU 4: CHRISTIAN LIVING

Off we went to the mall. Unfortunately, the parking lot was packed with last-minute Christmas shoppers. It took a while for us to find a spot some distance away from the restaurant.

When we finally did, it was 2:05 p.m. on my watch. As we stood at the foyer, as I was about to push open the glass door, a restaurant employee suddenly flipped the door sign from "open" to "closed". I was speechless at the precise timing!

There were still a few patrons inside—probably licking their chopsticks of the tiniest sushi leftover—but the crew refused to welcome additional customers. Only then did I see the notice plastered on the wall. Restaurant hours were strictly from 11:30 a.m. to 2:00 p.m. Business would resume at 5:00 p.m. for dinner service.

After overcoming my initial surprise, I had to stifle a laugh. I knew instinctively that God's hand padlocked that swinging door. He never forgot my prayer to protect our tithe. And He found the perfect opportunity that afternoon to do the exact favor I asked.

Years later, shortly after we moved to our new neighbourhood, a thief broke into our van. It was a rainy night, and the stealthy burglar left muddy scuff marks all over the floor mat. He emptied the glove compartment and every little stowage on the dashboard. The trail of clutter proved how far he violated our private space, and it seemed like the air bag was the only thing he didn't touch. All the coins we hid were gone. No penny, nickel, or dime survived the carnage.

The bizarre thing, though, was that the thief didn't bother with our praise CDs or church envelopes. If he only pulled one or two envelopes from the box, the man would have kidnapped a few twenty-dollar bills! A day before the break-in, I replenished the tithe in time for Sunday's collection. This was something I didn't do as

[194]

a habit. But that single instant when I did keep a huge amount of money in the car, no filthy hands with evil impulsion came close to touching it.

In both these stories, the money reached the rightful recipient. Thank God! But more than the aftermath, these experiences taught me how to worship the Lord with my finances.

Truly, God's cup never dries out. His blessings come fresh every minute and lift your spirits like the whiff of brewed coffee. Its constant overflow touches our lives with pathbreaking abundance.

We can trust Him with our poverty, and watch Him return all that the locusts of difficulty have eaten.

We can test the reliability of God's words and find it unerring.

Because God's promise is a bedrock in firmness.

And He is faithful to prove Himself trustworthy.

CHAPTER 25

Loved Beyond Boundaries

God loves you!

What does this statement really mean? This expression is so timeworn with habitual use; for many, it already sounds like a cliché. The freshness of the message is gone. The impact is diffused, and the comfort it gives somewhat feels weak, dull, and stale.

Have you ever wondered how God can love so unconditionally? What's the catch? How can sinners like us who never seem to pick up from past downfalls be accepted, let alone loved? Is there someone foolish enough to embrace our true nature—stink, venom, and all? Who is willing to reinstate us to full glory when we're worse than damaged articles packed away for spring cleaning?

These pitiful reflections flooded my brain even as I was supposedly a mature Christian. It was really unfortunate that my early childhood pains became breeding ground for theological skepticism.

God, however, doesn't want any of His children to live blinded by defeatist thoughts. He cleared the fluster in my head, challenged my concept of a "father" point-by-point, and probed into every single assumption I had about His love. In time, He straightened all the crooked paternal philosophies I coddled through the years.

But before I recount how this happened, let me explain why, in the first place, I became a miserable bundle of mixed-up theories.

HISTORY OF CONFUSION

You see, my childhood wasn't exactly pink, rosy, and dripping with marshmallow goodness. Throughout my young life, I didn't witness a respectable father image. I never really experienced a stable and nurturing relationship with my own dad. Apart from my late grandfather, none of the adult men in our family became pillars of outstanding virtue. It was against this backdrop that my maladjusted ideas about God were forged.

I grew up in a dysfunctional home. My parents played out an obligatory farce, pretending that we were one small, happy family. For a limited season, my parents managed to coexist under the same roof despite the impenetrable tension, constant absence, and lack of communication between them which my immature mind already perceived.

My dad's adulterous affairs took its toll, and the wall of secrecy behind which my parents hid finally crumbled to the ground. With divorce not yet a legal option at that time, they decided to separate.

My brother and I were periodically shuttled back and forth from house to house so that we may tolerate some time with our estranged father. Since my grandparents constantly lambasted my dad for breaking his nuptial vows, I learned to harbor suspicions and withheld from him my respect.

I still had fragments of pleasant memories about my father, but these didn't stretch far enough to overshadow the countless frustrations he caused our family. I couldn't blot out the bitter imprints which his infidelity left behind. Even as I entered adulthood, I still smarted from the blow of his betrayal and consequently developed distrust towards people—men in particular.

My father was a publicly-acclaimed leader, a genius in business, and an achiever on all fronts. He pushed these credentials upon me, dreaming that someday I would also blaze a trail and be a titan in my own field. But he had a very meticulous streak, and he often lashed out verbal abuses each time I didn't perform up to par.

Whether in terms of academics or household chores, my dad demanded perfection. He stingily mouthed praises but leapfrogged at every opportunity to criticize. Thus, I grew up believing I had to be exceptional before I could win his approval—that until I carve my own niche, substandard sacrifices didn't deserve love.

Sadly, my relationship with God took a similar turn. I considered His love and blessings too fluid and slippery for my grasp. I just couldn't grab and own it!

Each time the Lord promised blessings, I instinctively tempered my hopes to protect myself against disappointments in case He changed His mind. In as much as "Doubt" became my internal default setting, I could very well be crowned the "new Thomas"!

On account of my dad's unorthodox methods of discipline and the frightful rod which he whipped not too sparingly on any protruding body part, I learned to view the "Other Big Dad" with

MENU 5: LOVE

a great deal of dread. I pictured the heavenly Father as a judge who likewise maintained an infallible point system. He kept a ledger of faults which legitimized the use of sanctions if I so much as tipped the scales of justice the wrong way. With all these musings, I managed to convince myself that the "God is love" banner was pure gimmickry.

PREAMBLE TO CHANGE

After many years of wrestling with my twisted impressions, God triggered change. The Lord no longer wanted me to equate His perfect love with the finite, ambivalent love of my dad. To Him, no such connection exists.

God is of a nobler league, and His love shall never find a human parallel. He is always constant, never fluctuating in purpose. He is neither flighty nor random in His affections. My dad's love was impaired and speckled with narcissism; it was a pity I found in him a poor earthly example.

With the past buried in the past, the Lord reversed my beliefs and drew me closer to the true meaning of "Abba" as Jesus himself portrayed it.

I once attended a conference where the theologian interpreted the parable of the prodigal son. He painted a dramatic picture of the contemptible behaviour of the young man in contrast to the father's testimony of grace and charity.

According to the speaker, when the father saw his prodigal son returning from his aimless walk, he couldn't extinguish his excitement. Too eager to see him, he ran swiftly towards the lad, in direct defiance of Jewish tradition which prohibited patriarchs from taking the first move. The father's sympathy was so far-reaching; he didn't bother to re-examine his son's mistakes. Instead, he wrapped the boy in a tight squeeze, rained down kisses upon his crestfallen head, and ordered a pageantry of culinary masterpieces fit for a king.

Such drama silently spoke volumes about the father's humility. Not for a single second did he allow Jewish practices, or his dignified position, to inhibit him from initiating the welcome. He didn't evaluate the consequences of breaking tradition. He didn't put weight on the backlash by naysayers or how they might wag their gossipy tongues for weeks on end. Extending his boundless forgiveness was forefront in his mind. And if there was a faint chance the boy would return—if there was even a hollow hope that he'd drift along the fringes of the neighbourhood or the farthermost outskirts of town—the father would already leap for joy.

The theological description helped me to further create a mental picture of the scene. The father spotted the child from a great distance. Doesn't this reveal how he anticipated the prodigal son's homecoming? Perhaps, day and night, he kept vigil by the window, enduring the dark circles under his eyes or the wooziness and muscle pain which sleep deficiency could trigger. No sacrifice was too great for the possibility of eyeing even a shadow of his son's robe.

To direct the son's steps, imagine how the father must have flooded the path with beacons of light brighter than the midday sun. And when he caught sight of that familiar silhouette, the burst of energy that pushed his heels to a fiery sprint debunked any claim that he was a sleep-deprived man.

The boy didn't deserve a scrap of hospitality, but the father, dumbstruck with wonder, treated him like a dignitary. It didn't matter that scoffing onlookers counted it a waste to slaughter the fatted calf in honour of a child who already depleted the family

MENU 5: LOVE

fortune. It didn't matter that the pigheaded kid wasn't amply apologetic to be in sackcloth and ashes. As far as the dad was concerned, the lanterns could now be snuffed out because the boy was finally home. The knotted mess was now untangled. The edge-of-your-seat wait was over. It didn't matter that his son's primary motive was to sever patrilineal ties and seek employment in exchange for food. Repentant or not, the prodigal son's presence alone was enough!

For he who was given up for dead has returned to life.
Amazing?
Definitely!

It's the same tear-jerking stuff that makes soap operas a hit. But somehow, I couldn't identify with this kind of love. In my life, I never encountered such brand of affection from my dad. All that I bore as a child, I accepted as justifiable, whether it was a spanking, a cursing, or silent treatment.

God, however, found it in His heart to reveal a fresh dimension in my relationship with Him. He nursed old wounds and showed me that I am treasured even when I am hateful.

In the fifth chapter of Romans, it says,

> But God demonstrates his own love for us in this:
> While we were still sinners, Christ died for us.
> (Romans 5:8)

Our value is beyond calculation. There is nothing God will hold back to achieve our redemption—not even His Son's blood, moans of agony, or abandonment in the Garden of Gethsemane.

It was not just the fatted calf that God put on the butcher block. He traded His sinless Son as payoff for our deliverance and weighed upon His shoulders all the punishment we deserved. Without a word of complaint, Jesus embraced the pillar of whipping and the cross of sacrifice at the exact point in time when we were most abhorable. The lashes that should have cut the skin of the prodigal, fell upon the slaughtered Lamb!

Such exchange spells only one word ... LOVE!

LOVE IN THE CONCRETE

> For you make me glad by your deeds, Lord; I sing
> for joy at what your hands have done. (Psalm 92:4)

Once the scales of bias slide off from our eyes, it is easier to spot the miracles each day brings. Just like the congenitally blind man Jesus healed with a mixture of dirt and spittle, we gain pure insight after washing away the mud from our eyes.

Our blindness, built through years of brokenness and pain, gives way to intuitive perception. And what joy it is to latch onto a wider field of view, to recognize the gazillion occasions God tirelessly pursues us!

I recall with emotion the time I almost got stranded while driving alone in a multiple-lane highway. I was stuck for hours in twisted traffic when the engine belched grey smoke through the hood. To my dismay, the needle on the temperature gauge vacillated towards "hot" faster than my jaw could drop open. The thought of conking out in a fenced freeway, several kilometers away from the nearest gas station, threw me into a bout of mixed tears and prayers.

Ironically, there was nothing "express" about this expressway. The road looked like an oversized parking lot during the morning rush hour. Every few inch of movement caused selfish drivers to squeeze mercilessly into other people's lanes. I knew that if my old, stick-shift car stalled, I'd worsen the congestion,

MENU 5: LOVE

and no irate driver would spare an extra minute to tinker with my overheated engine.

With feverish haste and passion I repeatedly sobbed, "Lord, please help me! Please help me!"

Synchronous with my full volume outcry, the trail of cars before me started to budge. From first gear, I shifted to second ... then to third ...

Before I realized what was happening, I broke free from the tangled vehicles while the rest of the lanes stood perfectly immobile. Just when I thought I was hopelessly trapped, my personal Red Sea parted in such a dramatic way!

No other driver dared to change lanes and cut in front of me. Since my hood dangerously spewed thick smoke and hot water, people must have figured I was a ticking timebomb. I myself was scared spitless. I was pretty sure my face was paler than blanched cauliflower. The car also pitched forward in such an erratic fashion that if my lane slowed down to a halt, the engine would no doubt expire.

I knew it was not a quirk of fate but the hand of God that worked that morning. Not only was I able to exit from the freeway in a wink, every intersection light switched to green as I approached! In no time, I wheeled through the ramp of the nearest gas station where, as if on cue, the engine died. My haggard face dissolved into relief when the in-house mechanic took over the scene and skillfully patched up the drained radiator.

There is no other way to describe this experience. Plainly, this is the love of God in tangible terms.

Here's another story—

Years ago, as part of my weekday routine, I tagged along with my husband on his drive to work, got off at church, spent a few hours there in prayer, then rode the bus for the return commute.

Jacob, a jolly-faced, salt-and-pepper haired man who also dedicated his mornings in prayer, habitually occupied the front seat in the church. After he was done, he would slip by my favourite back pew for pleasant chitchat before crossing the exit.

One particular morning, as he softly shuffled his way through the middle aisle, he extended his free hand toward me. At the tip of his fingers lay a shiny two dollar coin which he insisted I keep.

I must have shot him a quizzical look because he explained without delay, "Go ahead and give this to your daughter. I was cleaning the house and saw a lot of coins lying around which I'm giving away to children."

I thanked this sweet Grandpa for the unexpected token. After we parted, I walked straight to the bus stop to head back home. A minute before boarding the bus though, I realized to my absolute horror, that my purse was empty!

I had my Bible and every non-essential whatchamacallit women normally shove inside their handbags, but money was nowhere in sight! No yen, no rupiah, no demonetized shillings, and definitely no Canadian currency whatsoever! I couldn't pay the fare with lipstick. Face powder would probably give the bus driver an asthmatic wheeze. I wondered what kind of beating I would get if I asked for an IOU and if I could fend off the ambush with my ballpen. Rummaging through my purse, those were all I had to swap for a ride.

Completely discombobulated, I chided myself for being so scatterbrained. Right before I sprung into my fifteen-kilometer endurance marathon, a thought bubble suddenly popped.

Wait!

MENU 5: LOVE

  I didn't need to hike home. I remembered Jacob's two dollars gently tucked inside my shirt pocket. What a stroke of divine fortune! A toonie was all I needed to purchase a one-zone bus ticket!

  I must have looked like a freak that morning—upset and flustered one second, then giddy with happiness in the next. Imagine! I wasn't even aware I'd get into trouble somewhere down the alley, yet my loving Father already had a solution waiting in the wings.

  I could almost hear Him chuckle, "Honey, you left your wallet, but don't worry. Sit tight. I got you covered. It won't hurt to exercise, but I know your legs can't walk the distance. Barter no longer happens in this day and age, my dear, so perish the thought, and keep your lipstick. Accept my gift instead, and all is well!"

> I will praise you, Lord, among the nations;
> I will sing of you among the peoples.
> For great is your love, reaching to the heavens;
> your faithfulness reaches to the skies.
> (Psalm 57:9–10)

  I remember another autumn day when I picked up my daughter from school. The air was very nippy; I silently wished some kind-hearted parent could hitch us a ride home.

  We lived along the main artery which most members of the school community regularly passed. For a stretch of five blocks, a leisurely fifteen-minute walk on a warm summer could bring you to our humble apartment. However, the temperature then was too Siberian for comfort, so walking was out of the question. With no funds to restock my dwindling supply of bus concession tickets, I begged the Lord for ways to save our day's bus pass.

  That afternoon, many familiar faces in flashy cars whizzed by with a friendly wave, but none gave us a lift. Friends left us high and dry to just hoof it. As my daughter and I briskly ran along the pedestrian lane, a few acquaintances paused in their tracks for a courteous "hello". However, none were too generous to squeeze us into their half-empty vans.

Tut-tut! This wasn't one of those lucky days when philanthropy overflowed. I didn't take offense, though. I could understand. People had to go places, and there wasn't much room for altruism when dinner needed to be thawed and roasted pronto.

As things panned out, Colleen and I waited again for our favourite bus driver in the same old corner shed. When we boarded the bus, just as I was a teeny fingerbreadth away from the ticket validating machine, the darling driver gestured me to stop.

"No, no!" he said with a broad smile and an earnest wave of the hand. "My machine isn't working today. Forget the ticket. Just go in."

A free ride?

Goodness gracious! I was too overwhelmed for words!

I only breathed a mindless wish, yet the Lord honoured it. Not wanting to leave us with shattered hopes, God sprinkled the moment with a fancy surprise and allowed us to keep two unused bus passes for another school day!

Do you see now what a loving God we have? He is a real, down-to-earth Father who is submerged in our details. He is never too engaged to be bothered—never too wound up in other people's agenda to keep tabs on you. Though self-absorbed folks may lack sensitivity and turn a blind eye when you flag down for help, God never plays the avoidance game. He comes to your rescue and offsets the deficiency with a miracle more grandiose.

God loves to do the unthinkable. I call them "Hallelujah" moments—times when your tongue is tied and words fail you.

MENU 5: LOVE

Those are points in your journey when God suddenly prepares a "prodigal son's feast".

The spectacle is too large scale, it makes your head swim.

The plethora of heavenly help is too mind-blowing that you can only conclude—God's love is at work!

His love causes a torrent of emotions that leaves you speechless.

In the end, your eyes can only blink tears and your lips declare, "Amen! Hallelujah!"

True, there are so many episodes when the Lord displays His enthusiasm at being a Father. You just need to open your eyes to see them. Fatherhood is a serious business with Him—a role He hasn't yet failed to perform.

Even if your issues seem too puny, God considers them just as important as creating the universe. Even if there are billions of people vying for His exclusive attention, He still defends you as single-mindedly as a mother does an only child.

It may be that your biological dad flunked his own parenting test. Believe that God is more than willing to compensate. His doting presence heals. Therefore, throw away that mental picture you have of God as an irritable ogre or a frowning, unscrupulous, ledger-toting accountant.

Because God doesn't use a caliper to size up the thickness of your flaws.

He doesn't write an index of your crimes and ungodly behaviour, sequentially arranged by date of transaction.

He doesn't take blame-and-shame strolls down your sinful life's memory lane.

Instead, He measures the grace and favor you need to become a saint and rejoices at the prospect of your return from purposeless pursuits. With the torch of His forgiveness ablaze through the night, He waits for you to crawl out of darkness to live sanctified in the light.

> Because of the Lord's great love
> we are not consumed,
> for his compassions never fail.
> They are new every morning;
> great is your faithfulness.
> Lamentations 3:22-23

God flanks you on every slouching side. It does not matter which way you twist, slump, or roll. His love is there.

Chapter 26

When a Bandage Is Not Enough

One dollar broken down into dimes, nickels, and pennies. That's all I had. One pathetic dollar. I had no credit card. No income. No purchasing power.

I usually didn't mind being cornered in tight spots. Our well ran dry far too often; I've learned to live humbly to deal with many shortages.

But that particular spring morning, I couldn't come to terms with the pinch. The bold red ink on many bills was always under my nose. Misery was knocking at my door, and I was tempted to invite him in. Not even the robins twittering by my window nor the vibrant display of tulips sprinkled happiness.

Relatives from the wealthy side of the family were in town for a vacation. That should have been a source of excitement and relief.

MENU 5: LOVE

However, my relatives were already nearing the end of their two-week stay, and I had yet to catch a trace of their shadow. I rationalized that they were way too busy with their whistle-stop tours to be slowed down by a visit to our apartment. Again, I didn't mind.

It was already the last weekend of their visit when my aunt dropped a courtesy call.

"We couldn't pass by," she said apologetically.

At first I refused to understand the big idea behind what she said. We didn't live in the outer fringes of the city. Our building was just two whoops and a holler from where they stayed.

"We're stuck in the house," she complained. "I couldn't take the weather and came down with a bad cold. I'm sorry we won't be seeing you this time. I really feel bad 'coz we can't even take a tour of Vancouver."

"That's alright." It was the only polite thing left to say. How else could I bury my disappointment? If only I had one more dollar, I could buy myself a bus ticket and be the one to pay them a visit instead.

My attempt at courtesy succeeded in hiding my bitterness. For little did my aunt know that I caught her trying to cover her tracks with a lie. Prior to this farewell call, my telephone echoed in the room. I picked it up only to hear the rustling of a purse interrupted by some muffled conversation in the background. Apparently, somebody's mobile phone keypad was accidentally pressed, and it speed-dialed my number.

"Hello? Hello?" I repeated. "Who's calling?" No one picked up because nobody had the intention to call.

I was about to return the handset to its cradle when I overheard a recognizable accent.

"Look over there! Wow, the mountains are covered with snow." It was my aunt's voice. "Quick! Get the camcorder and take a video!"

Judging from the car passengers' "oohs and aahs", I figured they were driving north, feasting on Vancouver's picturesque terrain. I dropped the phone a bit too forcefully as if my hand was weighed down by steel. The heaviness of my arm, though, was no match to the deadweight of my heart.

I felt betrayed.

Left behind.

Alone.

This double-dealing violation of trust twisted my entrails in knots. The pain punctured at the very gut, too deep to console, because it was a gash inflicted by family—people you never expected to deliberately dump you.

No bandage was big enough to wrap around my wound. But it was precisely when the bandage wasn't enough that God's love filled the gap.

A week after my relatives' return flight, the phone rang.

"Hi Ginger," came the strangely familiar female voice. "Guess who?"

It was the most pleasant surprise I've had in years! The whole Espinosa family, long-time friends from California, crossed the border for a week's vacation in Vancouver. The children were on spring break, so they decided to tour a widely popular tourist destination in British Columbia.

"We're going to Victoria Island tomorrow," she announced. "Can you come and join us?"

Though terribly excited at the prospect of exploring the provincial capital for the first time, I forced a damper on my wildly racing heartbeat. Reality check! I still had one dollar! We had no money to cover extraneous expenses like travel. It was an excess frill we couldn't afford.

[213]

MENU 5: LOVE

"That's great," I said, a bit half-heartedly. "But …"

"Don't worry about anything," Marycar cut in, apparently perceiving my reluctance. "Just get ready tomorrow at eight. Manny will pick you up. Just give us your address. We'll try to catch an early ferry so we can spend the whole day in Victoria."

Marycar's eager interest was infectious. And so I found myself pitching in on the plans for the trip, momentarily forgetting about our empty pockets.

The following day, I emptied the pantry and packed anything handy so that Colleen and I wouldn't be forced to shell out money for food elsewhere. Alvin opted to stay home so we could scrimp the twenty dollars we borrowed. Yes. We were twenty dollars richer, though I doubted this was adequate for the ferry. Entrance fees for the day-tripper attractions in the isle would surely hurt my wallet too.

I tucked in the bill with a candid prayer, "Lord, please let this money stretch far enough."

Before leaving, I gave my eight-year-old daughter a thorough lecture on what I judged as proper behaviour.

"Honey, no matter what happens, please don't ask me to buy you anything. And I mean ANYTHING," I said emphatically. "We don't have money for souvenirs, okay."

"Yes, Mama," Colleen said, her face already painted a guilty look.

"So don't go around pointing your fingers at anything you want," I repeated. "Are we clear?"

"Yes, Mama." Fully satisfied with her promise to rein in her cravings, we geared up for a rare escape. And what an insane adventure it was!

To put it mildly, we rode in style aboard a luxury SUV which the Espinosas drove all the way from San Francisco. Like a child with a new toy, I stared open-mouth at that sophisticated clump of well-polished metal rigged with soft leather seats and a whole lot of fancy. If not for the view of the open road instead of wispy clouds, I would have mistaken the drive for a business-class flight!

When we reached the ferry's point of entry in Tsawwassen, my hands started to sweat with anxiety. The fare turned out to be a steep sum, and my twenty dollars became a pathetic contribution.

"Here's our fare, Manny," I said. I bent forward to give his wife the lone bill in my wallet.

"Just keep it," he said. "I'll take care of this."

"No, please take it." I insisted, but the couple just smiled at me and refused to budge. And so it was that Colleen and I entered the ferry terminal with the twenty dollars still intact.

Cars were already maneuvering up the ramp into the ferry when we reached the tail-end of the queue. We didn't know how many vehicles were already packed inside the boat, but we silently hoped the parking levels were not yet crammed. The next ferry trip was a good two hours away, and we didn't want to waste time waiting in the adjoining building.

Luck and good speed weren't on our side. We missed our ride and were forced to idle away the hours in the shoreside lounge. The kids were hardly disappointed. The delay gave them a chance to eat breakfast in the self-service restaurant.

When faced with a spread of nibbles and goodies, my daughter's eyes popped off their sockets. There was a neat selection of subs and sandwiches, chowders, gourmet casseroles, pepperoni and Hawaiian pizzas, and other lip-smacking desserts. Even the whiff of freshly-brewed Columbian coffee made my stomach gurgle.

To my dismay, Colleen started ordering a slice of pizza from the server behind the counter. She had breakfast at home; I was pretty sure hunger was not an issue. With my daughter somewhat

MENU 5: LOVE

hemmed in by our party, I couldn't express my disapproval without them noticing. I had half a mind to pull her aside.

For a brief second, though, I caught Colleen's attention. I squinted my eyes to signal her to stop. But instead of being discreet, Colleen shouted above the cafeteria noise, "What, Mama?!"

She failed to get the hint.

Beet red with embarrassment, I tried to inch closer so I could whisper, "Please don't order. We have food in the car."

By then, Manny already finished consolidating all the menu requests, and the attendant was gingerly serving the pizza slices on small white plates. It was too late to back out!

Manny turned to me and asked, "How about you, Ginger? What do you like to eat?"

Unlike Colleen, I didn't have time to grab a bite before leaving the house. I was packing hastily that morning when our ride came. Hence, I was bitterly tempted to satisfy my hunger, not just with a cup of coffee, but with a medley of breakfast treats.

Instead of surrendering to the lure of my taste buds, I managed a feeble smile. "I'm okay. I don't need anything."

"Go ahead, Ginger. This one's on me," he prodded.

I could stake my last dollar; Manny was a mind-reader! Never prone to abuse anyone's generosity, though, I simply admitted, "I wrapped something in the car. I'll eat later."

The brunch was relished and decimated into indistinguishable crumbs. Still, I haven't spent a dime. I wasn't being stingy. It's just that nobody wanted to accept my payment for Colleen's meal.

Soon after, a brood of stuffed travelers marched out of the lounge and finally boarded the ferry. Throughout the trip, the couple put on their thinking caps and weighed which attraction to explore first. Since we were behind schedule, we'd be lucky if we saw more than one.

Their animated discussion went on as I basked in the unspoiled beauty of the islands we passed. Cool, fresh breeze whipped my hair in all directions as Colleen and I stood on the deck, hoping to steal a glimpse of a whale or any life form in the open waters. It was a moment to take pleasure in God's creation. It was a moment to thank God for the very miracle of this unexpected trip.

The picture-perfect view around me provided an ideal ambience for a prayerful retreat with the Lord. As I relaxed on the sun deck and gazed at the striking formation of feathery clouds against the turquoise sky, the Lord impressed His words clearly in my heart.

> "Can a mother forget the baby at her breast and
> have no compassion on the child she has borne?
> Though she may forget, I will not forget you! See,
> I have engraved you on the palms of my hands …"
> (Isaiah 49:15–16)

"See how deeply I love you?" the Lord said further. "Men may ignore and forget, but I never do. I pay attention to your desires—no matter how small these are, no matter how secret. My love extends past the juncture where human love fails. My love saturates. Man's love fluctuates. Come to Me then for I am sufficient. Allow my love to drench you till all gaps are filled, until what smarts is healed."

There was no question about it. God was trying to bandage my wounded spirit with a vacation more fantastic than the one I missed.

The day ended and left sweet footmarks of God's faithfulness. Colleen and I had heaping treats of burgers and fries as well as peanut-sprinkled chocolate ice cream on huge sugar

MENU 5: Love

cones. We walked along the harbor and reveled in the extensive display of totem poles, native sculpture, and other First Nations handicrafts along the sidewalk. We marveled at the ornate designs of the Parliament building, the historical Empress Hotel, and other heritage architecture. We took pictures of horse-drawn carriages steered by men and women in Victorian period costumes, and of street actors in clown garb doing mime or musical performances.

The best part was that we had all these for free! Not even the packed lunch nor the lone dollar in my coin purse was touched.

Indeed, when God splurges his love on you, He does so in a unique fashion. When He blesses, He withholds nothing.

Therefore, my friend, rejoice in this love.

Be delirious with happiness.

Shout hosanna all day!

For God flanks you on every slouching side. It doesn't matter where you droop or drift. It doesn't matter which side you twist, slump, or roll. God's love is always there.

You are completely surrounded!

On such grounds then, put the weight of your troubles on His hand. Because when you are ailed by a gash too big for a bandage, His love is more than enough to cure all.

How priceless is your unfailing love, O God!
People take refuge in the shadow of your wings.
They feast on the abundance of your house;
you give them drink from your river of delights.
Psalm 36:7-8

Chapter 27

Love in Broken Cups

Stephen was a sprightly four-year-old boy with dimples highlighting his puffy cheeks. It was Father's Day, and he wanted to create something special for his Dad. Stephen knew his Daddy loved to drink coffee while scanning the morning news. So that particular Sunday morning, he tiptoed out of bed early to rustle up a surprise.

Quite noisily, he dragged a stool to the nearby hutch so that he could isolate the Royal Albert teacup which his mom pulled out only on special occasions. He didn't want to pick the old cracked mug stacked inside the dishwasher. His Dad used it every single day; the grungy baseball print was hardly visible.

With pudgy fingers, Stephen reached for the set, careful not to touch any of the crystal champagne goblets on display. But the tea cup was barely an inch from his short outstretched arms. If only he could extend an itty-bitty more ... up ... up ... gotcha ... ooops!

Oh no!

The cup handle slid smoothly through Stephen's index finger, but the saucer nose-dived to the floor. Luckily, it landed

MENU 5: LOVE

on the area rug, but not without grazing the side of the stool. Crouching to inspect the damage, Stephen was relieved to see that only a quarter of the gold rim chipped off. At least, the old-rose pattern was still intact, and the dainty saucer was not broken into more fragments than he could count.

Now that he hooked the perfect cup, Stephen tottered to the kitchen, careful not to knife his feet with the shards of porcelain scattered on the floor. His mom repeatedly warned to never play with the coffee maker, so he didn't attempt to brew. Instead, he grabbed his Daddy's favourite instant decaf. He had the foggiest idea how much teaspoons to put, so he threw in the granules until the cup's bottom disappeared. He poured water from the tap, sprinkled sugar, and emptied his milk carton until his Daddy's drink turned off-white. Stephen was mighty proud of himself, glad to have accomplished all these without adult help. It felt awesome to behave like a real grown-up.

The whole time Stephen was tinkering in the kitchen, his father jerked awake. Dad wanted to find out what caused all the thumping, so he quietly slid out of the room to check. Marching down the hallway, he shot a curious look at Stephen's tousled and empty bed. He deftly tracked the trail that the noise made, careful not to wake up the rest of the household.

In the formal dining room, Dad was puzzled to see that the buffet hutch door was wide open. Bits and pieces of fine porcelain were strewn on the ground. Stealthily, he took a peek at the kitchen and was aghast at the cluttered sight!

On the hardwood floor were puddles of milk that dripped from the granite countertop like tiny waterfalls. The faucet was left open, and water leaked continuously. Stephen was busy stirring what appeared to be a thick, syrupy cup of milk. His baby blue pajamas were damp and had dotted light brown stains all over. Everywhere within a square meter of Stephen was a tropical paradise for ant colonies—sugar and coffee powder lavishly coated every visible surface.

Sensing his presence, Stephen looked up from the kitchen island where he made an exhibition of his unique coffee blend. With a bright dimpled smile, he cried out, "Daddy, happy Father's Day! I love you! Do you want to see my surprise?"

At this, the father's heart melted. He couldn't anymore bring himself to discipline his son for the eyesore he made of the spick-and-span house. How could he possibly scold a boy who worked his fingers to the bone in order to dote on him?

Gently, Stephen balanced the cup and saucer flat on his palm. The mixture was recklessly dispensed to the brim. So as Stephen inched towards his Daddy, his unsteady hands tipped off most of the liquid. He dumped a few spoonfuls on the fractured saucer, some on the floor, and on his already grubby night clothes.

By the time his father reached for the beverage, it was in a totally messy, half-empty state. Stephen's wide, irresistible smile radiated so much passion that it tugged at the deepest seat of his emotions. It encouraged him to hug his son and unbuckle his genuine paternal affection. Stephen displayed to him all the obsessive attachment that made this Father's Day an extraordinary memory. No measure of junk or Reign of Terror in the kitchen could dampen that deep father-and-son connection.

Did you notice?

Did you spot the strong parallel between this story and our own relationship with God?

Like Stephen, we wish to love our Father and give Him the best of what we've got. However, our crooked and decayed human condition smudges our love into a substandard gift. Try as we might,

MENU 5: LOVE

we mishandle and reduce our "coffee cups" to a mucky, disfigured, and almost depleted shape.

Shrugging off our defects, God heartily accepts our sloppy "surprises" as if these were never inferior to begin with. His vision sears through the souls of men and beholds instead the pure motives that rest inside.

God never underestimates the devotion that we give Him, and He prompts us to look at ourselves in the same way. Just like Stephen who was so thrilled to serve his Daddy despite the limitations of his age, God wants us to hold nothing back. He wants us to splurge in our giving. Never mind if the love that we share seems to make no dent at all. We are invited to love extravagantly nonetheless.

It doesn't matter if our little acts of charity appear too incidental and pointless considering the wider need. Deliberately bathe others with goodwill and mercy, knowing that God doesn't pucker His eyebrows and say, "Well, child, that just isn't good enough."

Touch humanity with a profuseness of compassion. Believe that the Lord never eyes our sacrifice as worthless hogwash that delivers little joy. Therefore, even if folks think our deed of kindness is too small that it dangles on the lowest margin of acceptability, we should still lend a hand and be as bighearted as we can.

God urges us to take the risks necessary to make a difference in people's lives. Like Stephen, He wants us to give liberally from a love-plump heart even if the final outcome still leaves a lot to be desired.

In one of the old apartments where I previously lived, I met an elderly, crippled lady who took that risk. Years ago, Andrea was a victim of a hit-and-run drunk driver. Today, she is extremely grateful to God for having survived that nightmare.

With a sturdy walker, she moves around the building at a snail's pace. The chronic pain on her legs makes it excruciatingly difficult to accomplish much in a day. Grateful for the second lease on her life, this woman transcends her disability and lavishes love even to strangers.

Once, I coincidentally met her in a public coin laundry room. Andrea finished unloading her warm, freshly-scented bedspread and was on her way back to her suite. Meanwhile, I was preparing to swing our wet, clean clothes to the next vacant dryer. Behind my back, Andrea sneaked a dollar into the slot to keep her machine going. Then before waving goodbye, she turned to me and said, "Ginger, go ahead and use this dryer. I'm through with it.

Obediently, I crammed my stuff in. I assumed that the dryer Andrea left running would just operate the few residual seconds in the timer. I waited for the dryer to automatically shut down so that I could insert my coin and reactivate the machine. Two minutes … five minutes … ten minutes passed. The motor was still humming.

Twenty minutes … thirty-five …

Before I figured out what was happening, the appliance had already completed the full hour, and my clothes were all dry. It was only on hindsight that I finally inferred the meaning behind Andrea's telltale smile shortly before she left.

That was Andrea's voluntary act of kindness. To this elderly woman, the one-dollar token might not have been worth an ounce of attention. However, that modest spray of love meant a great deal to me who relished the advantage. No doubt, her generosity, which she premeditatedly struck off the record, didn't escape God's eyes too.

The Lord, who accepts with untold pleasure even the little "broken cups" that men give, treasured Andrea's love like it was the most spectacular gift ever to unfold.

MENU 5: LOVE

The love we have for God may be tarnished by our addiction to blind self-worship. It may be watered down by earthly distractions and changeable feelings. Our passion and worship may be as sloppy and imperfect as Stephen's broken cup.

But God takes them.

He applauds each gift with fresh delight—not for what they're worth, but for a stature more noteworthy than our gift's true merit.

Because all acts of love and kindness, though fairly small, mean a whole heap to Him who receives the advantage.

Do nothing out of selfish ambition or vain conceit.
Rather, in humility value others above yourselves,
not looking to your own interests
but each of you to the interests of the others.
Philippians 2:3-4

Chapter 28

Beyond Rhyme or Reason

For I am convinced that neither death nor life,
neither angels nor demons,
neither the present nor the future,
nor any powers, neither height nor depth,
nor anything else in all creation,
will be able to separate us from the love of God
that is in Christ Jesus our Lord.
Romans 8:38-39

Clack ... clack ... clack ... clack ...

From behind, I heard the escalating rumble of an approaching motorcycle. I looked through the rolled-down car window to see a red-head biker swerving from side to side, trying to overtake every vehicle that was sticking to the sixty-kilometer-per-hour speed limit.

My husband, always the cautious driver, left a comfortable distance between our car and the Pontiac ahead. However, oblivious to the risk, the cyclist cut our car sharply and claimed the fifteen-meter gap Alvin intended as his braking distance. Instinctively,

MENU 5: LOVE

Alvin pounded on the brake and successfully evaded the motorbike's tail. Keeping his cool, he didn't grunt or blare the horn to lecture the negligent biker.

A few seconds later, the skittish red-head again tried to swing over to the other lane. This time, he wanted to glide by a narrow margin, hoping to race past the Pontiac in front of him and the huge semi-truck on his right. He attempted once but backed out. He tried a second time, but just couldn't squeeze through the tight pass.

I watched the over-speeding battle between cyclist and truck driver with sweaty apprehension. For a moment, it was nip and tuck as to which wheels would cross the intersection first.

The truck driver was too elevated; he most likely didn't notice the side-to-side, in-and-out tango of this wannabe Evel Knievel. When the middleweight daredevil took the final attempt to overtake, he miscalculated his swerve.

Trying to steer clear of the Pontiac's back, his motorcycle slanted at a sharp, acute angle from the ground. This threw the biker off balance. As a result, he whacked the truck's off-road tires. He somersaulted into the air, landed with a thud on the street, and rolled over mercilessly.

The cyclist's momentum seemed unstoppable. His bike dragged on for meters, making a painful impact with his body. The grating sound of metal scraping the asphalt pierced our ears as Alvin and I shrieked out of shock. Everything happened in double-quick time.

Unaware of what hit him, the flabbergasted trucker came to a screeching halt and left long, black tire marks on the road. He managed to stop just short of the bike and its rider who lay bloodied near the pavement.

Alvin immediately pulled over in front of the accident scene. Jumping out of the car, I almost dropped the cellphone as I stood on jello legs. I looked over at the moustached trucker and his wide-eyed passenger. Paralyzed in their seats, both men's faces looked haggard and anemic.

The truck driver seemed too traumatized to help, so I ran towards the cyclist to check if he was knocked unconscious. To my relief, the lad slowly straightened to his feet. As he removed his helmet, I saw that his freckled face was also drained of color. Obviously disoriented, and with wind taken out of his sails, he fumbled for his bike handles. As he did so, blood trickled out of his knuckles and arms. He awkwardly moved the two-wheeler away from oncoming traffic—too unhinged to note the serious injuries he sustained.

"Don't move," I sternly instructed him. "Stay there. I'm calling for an ambulance."

I couldn't gauge which of my extremities quavered more—my legs or my arms. With jerky fingers that resembled an epileptic fit, I dialled 9-1-1.

"Ma'am, where are you located? Can you please give me your street?" The operator's calm voice was in stark contrast to my teary, out-of-control staccato.

"I-I-I'm at 88th Avenue," I stammered while scanning the street markers and the horrible gridlock that we caused. Many passersby reduced their speed to snoop, but none stopped to help.

"Ma'am, it's a long stretch. Would you know the last cross-street you passed?"

Running back to our car, I frantically asked Alvin for directions. When I stuck my head through the window, I realized my husband's face was pasty white, too. Apparently, his mind kept replaying in slow motion the boy's bone-crashing cartwheel. His heart leapt out of his chest as it dawned on him—this was no theatrical stunt. There was no hidden harness, no inflatable mattress

MENU 5: LOVE

to cushion the fall. This was real-life drama, and we were reluctant actors playing an unscripted role.

"I think we're between 144th and 148th," I said.

"Don't worry, ma'am. We're sending an ambulance right away."

While I was listening to the operator and fretfully pacing back and forth on the road, the truck driver and his passenger finally found their bearings and approached the injured teenager. Strange, but instead of lending a hand, they both blew off steam by talking dirty.

The men cussed the biker as if this very act would drum the guilt and make him more apologetic. They verbally skinned him raw until the boy perhaps wished he could crawl back inside his mother's womb.

Embarrassed, the boy rode his bike and tried in vain to resuscitate its motor. Judging him to be past the crisis stage, the men belittled the kid's injuries. They threw fiery daggers with their stares. Without a second thought, they clambered back inside the truck cab and sped off, leaving the rest of us speechless with outrage.

"Wait! Wait!" I told the boy who was also decked to run. The 9-1-1 operator on the other end of the line listened to the commotion. "Where are you going? I called for help. Just wait for the paramedics. You need to go to the hospital right away!"

Freak accident or not, premeditated or unintentional, the biker somehow knew he was at fault. His crumpled eyebrows, tremulous lips, and beads of sweat were all the signs of one who was too scared to face police officers. He looked barely eighteen. I wonder if he even owned a driver's license.

He must have feared a reckless endangerment charge or eye-witness accounts of him wildly weaving through traffic from start to finish. Whatever his motivation, this child went against his better judgment and dismissed all my vicarious mothering.

"No, no!" the red-head protested. "Please don't call 9-1-1. I have to go now. I don't need help." He brushed the dust off his pants, wiped some of the fresh blood on his arms, and covered his head with the battered helmet.

"Ma'am?" I totally forgot about the operator still waiting for an update.

"T-t-the driver who hit the b-boy just ran off!" It wasn't cold but I couldn't control my tremors. "And the victim here wants to leave too. What should I do? I'm just a witness here."

"Did you manage to write down the truck's plate number?"

"No. Sorry. I panicked. I didn't think."

"That's alright, ma'am. It's okay. Things like these happen." The lady's voice was gentle. "You can just give your name and phone number to the boy. Let him know that you are available as witness should he decide later on to press charges."

I don't know exactly why, but right at that moment, a wave of compassion washed over me. I wanted to reach out to the child and reassure him that all would be well. For how couldn't it be? He wrestled against the odds and looked blanched as death itself. But he survived!

His jerky movements betrayed his anxiety. I myself was spooked when I wasn't even the one who skyrocketed into space like a gutless rag doll. It wasn't my place to do so, but I wanted to bandage the boy's wounds, to sew his torn sleeves, to sling his arm around my shoulder, and help him with his limp.

I knew that somewhere out there was his real mother, waiting for his peaceful return. I could imagine her pacing the floor, impatient, all nerves worked up, grimly staring at the clock, and counting every second of this peculiar delay.

MENU 5: LOVE

I didn't want this mother to see him blood-smudged and dirty. I didn't want her to open the door and be greeted by an emotionally-crushed and purple-faced child who, only moments ago, left the house without the slightest crease on his shirt. I didn't want this mother to beat her chest in grief and say, "Why didn't anyone help my son? Is this what the world has come to?"

With the truck gone, the circuitous traffic began to clear. I turned my attention toward the boy and gave him a firm warning to drive responsibly, straight to a doctor.

Like a reflection on a pond, most of us may discover a mirror image of ourselves in that foolhardy boy. Through the rough and tumble of life, we miscalculate moves. We plunge ahead without analyzing consequences, give in to earthbound passions without thinking beyond the heat of the moment.

We idiotically push our way through narrow passes that we know are dangerous, believing that we can wing it. With a devil-may-care attitude, we draw decisions that end in an emotional upset. We create a labyrinth of secret sins, but we can't fix the awkward mess once the public gets wind of our shame.

However, though knocked down by our failures, though hammered by the penalty of our stupidity, God doesn't drench us with curses.

He doesn't pin us to the ground with crippling negativity.

He doesn't cuss.

He doesn't dirty our name. Truth to tell, we already do that to ourselves, without anybody's help.

Friend, today may find you in the middle of a crisis. Your life may seem like a war zone with the wreckage of your sins tossed everywhere. You don't know how to conceal the embarrassment and pain. Your conscience suffers the pinch, but you don't know how to start over.

To you, the Lord says, "Come away with me."

Stop the fruitless journey. Hide in God's presence. You've fumbled blindly through the duststorms long enough. Now, the Father is calling His weary traveller to rest from the effort. He is wooing you back with the gentlest of words.

Even for a moment, stop probing the world. Stop flirting with its iniquities. Withdraw from the noise. You, weary soul, disengage from your willful fight, and be alone with God. Enough of the drunkenness. It is time to rush back to your Father.

Do not be afraid. No matter what defiance, perversion, or indiscipline caused your fall, the Lord won't deal with a brusque hand. He will not jerk and kick when you're already down with repentance. He will not wag His finger at your face.

He will not add salt to your wounds or disregard your pain with a sarcastic, "I told you so!"

He won't scratch his head in skepticism and nag, "You messed up again! When will you ever learn?"

No. God is not like that at all!

Because God is pure love.

Surely, we make a fool of ourselves on more counts than statistically possible. But each time we do, we know we can expect mercy and gentleness from the Lord.

Misfortune is not ours to bear alone. We have a Father whose love smoothes over the brutal consequences of our mistakes. With this love, He heals. With this love, He reclaims the dignity we dumped with reckless abandon.

We're awfully lacking in noble qualities, but God loves us still. His compassion is free—never predicated on proof of human eligibility. We may not be able to wrap our tiny brains around this, but it is true. God's love has no rhyme or reason.

MENU 5: LOVE

It is irrational.

No mental faculty can dissect its logic.

God's love has no strings attached. No legal limitations. No ifs, ands, or buts. His love has no abridged versions, with omissions here and there.

Therefore, weary traveller, rest your troubled heart in God's loyalty. You can't be cut off from His love, no matter how hard you try.

Remember, you are in the limelight of His foolish love. He'll take all avenues necessary to woo you ... even when you're at your meanest, most repulsive, and contemptible worst.

```
        All of us also lived among them at one time,
              gratifying the cravings of our flesh
            and following its desires and thoughts.
                       Like the rest,
           we were by nature deserving of wrath.
          But because of his great love for us,
                 God, who is rich in mercy,
                 made us alive with Christ
        even when we were dead in transgressions—
          it is by grace you have been saved.
                     Ephesians 2:3-5
```

Chapter 29

The Power of "Small"

The ninth month was perhaps the worst stage in all of my pregnancies. Fluid retention was so pronounced, you could press any part of my body and it would waggle like a waterbed.

My tummy ballooned to such scandalous proportions that people often assumed I was carrying triplets. I was very clumsy too. Any attempt to peek at my toes would tip me off-balance and send me rolling like a barrel of beer. There wasn't even a way for me to check if I slipped into identical shoes.

If these weren't enough, my nose also stood like a pink, disfigured blob on the center of my face. The skin tone around my neck turned terra-cotta brown and much too scaly that you'd think I was half unbathed human and half iguana.

Imagine then the pits to which my fragile self-image sunk. Any delusions I had of being crowned beauty queen were chased by nightmares of my husband selling pounds of post-partum flab in the butcher shop.

MENU 5: LOVE

One afternoon, while cooling down in the mall, I met the gaze of an elderly couple walking leisurely hand in hand. Guessing by the wrinkled skin, the cane, and the luminous silver hair, they must be in their early seventies. Without any hesitation, the woman smiled at me, warmth and angelic glow bursting from her face. She reached for my arm with unsteady hands and said in a bashful tone, "You look beautiful!" Her husband nodded in agreement then beamed and waved as they walked in the opposite direction.

You look beautiful.

The words chimed a harmonic song in my ears.

What on earth did I do to deserve a compliment? That was too random! I bet my sweet pajamas they weren't runaway psychiatric patients who found humour in flattering strangers.

I didn't exactly cut a fine figure. My oversized jumpsuit wasn't fetching. Not by a stretch! Every pore in me was screaming "pregnant", and my gait was just a pinch better than that of a web-footed penguin. There were no hidden cameras, so this couldn't be a reality TV show. It wasn't April Fool's and nobody's laughing, so this couldn't be a practical joke.

You look beautiful.

I didn't dream it up. That was precisely what she said.

Whatever prompted the old lady to speak, it seemed like she knew I needed encouragement that day. It was a small deed done on impulse. It might have been an observation casually dropped. No matter. The words still had a rich, perky effect on this hormone-overloaded mom.

Why? Because love broke the surface. The melodic tune of acceptance whistled through her lips. The couple created a ripple of rosy thoughts which erased any touchiness I had about my image.

Theirs was a small deed with a humongous impact.

We may underestimate small deeds, form quick opinions that they're too negligible to matter. It is so easy to raise the excuse that their advantages are so marginal, it's not worth the disturbance. However, God knows that everything we do leaves an impression that can either profit or trouble others.

Acts of charity—though small in the onset—are true heavyweights because they snowball into wider extensions of mercy and grace. Love influences and grows exponentially. Give love today, and that love multiplies to impact a larger community.

Whereas those who experience generosity reciprocate, those who receive bitterness retaliate. In the same way that kindness spawns kindness, an intimidating deed annihilates and propagates until what you see is a wider circle of angry people.

The Lord honours even the littlest favors. Jesus restated this when He sent out His disciples with instructions.

> "And if anyone gives even a cup of cold water to one of these little ones who is my disciple, truly I tell you, that person will certainly not lose their reward" (Matthew 10:42)

A tiny cup of water? What's the deal with that? Did Jesus have to attach a colossal value on something as trivial as a cup to drink?

Jesus understood the kindness principle.

The point is not so much the value of what you gave but the condition of your heart when you extended your hand. It doesn't matter if you gave water, lemonade, or a cup of piping hot cappuccino. What motivated you to fill in a need? Was it respect for the weak? Compassion? A desire to serve with Christ-like love? Or perhaps, an urge to brag? Was the deed fodder that fed your ambition for publicity?

MENU 5: Love

Once, I had the misfortune of meeting one man who didn't think small acts mattered much. The burly man with a walrus moustache was rushing out of a Costco parking lot onto the main road, poised to break the speed limit. With one hand on the wheel, he reached behind the passenger seat to grope for something in the back of his van. He decided that pulling over was too much of a drag and that a quick turn of his head couldn't possibly hurt. He shifted his attention off the road for just a few seconds. And what an almost fatal mistake that was! In a bat of an eyelid, he zigzagged smack-dab in the middle of the opposite lane and headed straight for our car.

Instinctively, I angled my sedan away from the disoriented man. I was only an arm's-length away from a fleet of cars parked at the curb. Everything happened in a snap. All I could do was stop, blast my horn, wait for the collision, and pray that my airbag would disengage as the car dealer's sales pitch once promised.

The red car behind me lunged to a halt as well. The lady with ash-blonde hair stared, her mouth agape, alarm clearly etched on her face. The approaching driver was only a foot from my fender when he tilted his head in response to the hooting. He instantaneously wheeled the vehicle back on track and zipped past us without a gesture of apology. Such ruthless man didn't even care what heart attack he almost gave me and my passenger.

Initially, I was so upset because I didn't have it in me to roll down the windows and scream my two-cents worth of incriminating speech to agitate the man's sense of good citizenship. I turned to look at my cousin who gripped her chest with trembling hands, tears cascading down her cheeks. For a split moment, she thought she would never see her three young children again.

Here was a fool who didn't realize how his casualness could harm another. Here was a man who thought that parking his car was a time-consuming interruption not worth the bother. And yet, he triggered a wave of stressful consequences towards the strangers he disregarded.

These two episodes teach us never to belittle the power one can wield with the stroke of a small deed. It may just be a goofy laugh, a firm handshake, a handwritten note of cheer, a shared box of Krispy Kreme doughnuts over a cup of hazelnut latte, or a tall glass of orange juice given to your local garbage collector.

Everything matters.

Little courtesies and random extensions of blessings do not only leave you with a warm, I-feel-like-hugging-a-fluffy-bear brand of sentimentality. More importantly, they set in motion another upsurge of kind deeds from those touched by your humanity.

It all then becomes a cycle of self-sacrifice and altruism.

Or a cycle of errors and bungled steps.

The choice is yours.

You have the power to influence the outcome—and it depends on the decisions you make and the opportunities you seize. So choose your steps well, and never misjudge the power of "small".

Chapter 30

Shortcuts

> Enter through the narrow gate.
> For wide is the gate and broad is the road
> that leads to destruction,
> and many enter through it.
> But small is the gate
> and narrow the road that leads to life,
> and only a few find it.
> Matthew 7:13-14

As a homeschooling parent, I needed to come up with creative ways to teach the basics of English without drawing psychedelic stares from my young kids. While going through my grammar lesson plans one day, I myself had to scratch my head because I couldn't decipher some illogical word patterns.

Now please resolve this for me—

The plural of "goose" is "geese", but the plural of "moose" can't be "meese", nor "choose" ever be related to "cheese". How could I explain that "fought" is the past tense of "fight", but "brought" can't be "bright"?

MENU 6: STRENGTH IN SUFFERING

Like the ambiguous riddles of the Mad Hatter, a lot of things in life are this confusing. One evening, instead of grammar, it was spelling that had my then grade-nine daughter glassy-eyed.

"Papa," Colleen called out from the computer desk. She was working on a Social Studies essay and wanted it done in a dash. "Can you give me an example of a terrorist?"

"Osama bin Laden," Alvin suggested.

"How do you spell that?"

"O-sa-ma bin La-den." My husband syllabicated the name so that my daughter could figure out the spelling on her own.

"I don't know how," Colleen was in no mood to think.

"Okay, write Brutus instead."

"Who's Brutus?" Colleen turned a questioning face towards her Daddy.

"You don't know Brutus?" he smiled. "Brutus ... the enemy of Popeye!"

What a convenient shortcut! Can't make heads or tails of a word? Then think of something simpler to write even when the replacement doesn't make sense. That's the goofy ideology my husband subscribes to when on-the-spot answers escape him.

However, this homeschool educator is a spelling and grammar police. As long as you can match antecedents with pronouns and know where to insert your apostrophes, we can cross pinkie fingers and be friends for life.

Having said that, I will never let a bearded cartoon scoundrel pass for a terrorist, nor spinach-gobbling Popeye pass for a Canadian Prime Minister just because my daughter can't spell Joseph Philippe Pierre Yves Elliott Trudeau.

Almost daily, I prod my students, "Show a little more effort. Burn the extra brain cell, and dig a little deeper. No shortcuts, please. And that means, use an eraser. Don't just rub the mistake off with your licked fingers!"

Incidents like these jog my memory and push into the forefront a well-used line in the Bible. It reads, "Enter through the narrow gate" (Matthew 7:13 NIV).

A more contemporary translation reads, "Don't look for shortcuts to God" (Matthew 7:13 The Message).

This verse encourages us to take the less-traveled road though it requires a little more trekking, a little more stretching, and a share of discomfort.

God gave the command to enter. God wasn't asking, "Would you like to enter?"—like He was half expecting a "yes" or "no" reply.

Neither was He groveling, "Can you please enter?"—as if we're irate customers walking away from a sales pitch gone bad.

God made it imperative for us to walk through the narrow by giving the instruction, "Enter."

Mind you, the gate isn't too impressive; there's no window dressing to encourage a second glance. The doorway is too plain; it doesn't use flattery to cajole. The passage is too tight; you'll have to let go of nonessential baggage to get through.

However, though the entrance may be off the beaten track and the inner network is too circuitous and uphill, the view in the end is like no other!

"... Small is the gate and narrow the road that leads to life ..." (Matthew 7:14 NIV). Jesus himself spoke the promise during His Sermon on the Mount.

Yes, this ugly road points to life.

At the perfection of the journey, in the eleventh hour, all our struggles will wrap up into a crown ... the crown of eternal life!

Today's Scripture verse rings true in many areas of our lives. We can't assume our walk with the Lord to always be smooth-sailing. That said, we are encouraged to press on in faith even when life throws us a curve ball.

MENU 6: STRENGTH IN SUFFERING

The gate is tight.

The road is rugged.

And yet, it is to our benefit that we enter.

We should walk the extra step though the path is unfamiliar and only half-defined.

We need to understand that gardens do not flourish without the scraping of the rake and pounding of the hoe.

The best masterpieces are crafted with a lot of hard work, testing, and persistence.

Therefore, we should not quit in the middle of the pilgrimage. Though we do not have the agility to proceed or the wisdom to grasp God's full road map, victory is on the horizon as long as we stay the course.

My friend's grade-two daughter brought home a science questionnaire one day. The teacher left instruction for the class to pick a planet in the solar system, and fill in the blanks with information gathered from research. Kaley chose Neptune and scribbled her thoughts without reading any resource materials. Just to scratch the assignment off her to-do list, she didn't fuss over Google searches and wrote logically from the top of her head.

To her horror, Kaley's mother read these gut-busting answers:

> Q: What is the temperature in that planet?
> A: Very cold.
> Q: What is the distance of that planet from the sun?
> A: You cannot say because it is very far.

Caught between a frown and a giggle, her mom said, "Kaley, there has to be a number. The temperature in Neptune should be about negative 220 degrees. It can't just be 'very cold'."

While easy cop-outs like these are charming because they involve innocent children, adults who make it a habit to choose fifty-fifty bargains in life are no longer making cute, funny decisions.

Scripture reminds us to never take shortcuts on the road to God. The path through life is tricky; there are no easygoing formulas to achieve what God requires. The road to heaven has numerous high-pressure points, and you can't simply drive through a bypass to avoid the obstruction.

Sickness. Natural disasters. Cash outflows. Marital conflicts. Business collapse. Fractured self-esteem. Raising teenagers. Aging and taxes. There are no alternate routes to avoid the inevitability of these speed bumps.

Though you can't retreat from life's frustrations, you can choose to face them with the end of the footpath in view. Yes, the way is narrow, but you know it leads to an endless fellowship with God.

The smog of your struggles will soon shift and lift. Grope through the gloom with the Lord's grit, and you'll eventually reap the crown of salvation as reward for your perseverance.

Withdraw from the struggle now, choose the easier road, and you know the picture at the end of your life will not be very pretty.

Those who take the wide road, those who skip through life footloose and fancy-free—giving in to every whim, and skirting around hard places to avoid the uphill climb—these people make themselves candidates for destruction.

Many enter the broad gate where the turnpike is paved with compromise and convenience. Diligence and stamina are not mandatory skill sets because traveling the long haul isn't on the job

MENU 6: STRENGTH IN SUFFERING

description. Instead, those who choose the broad gate think it is cool to loaf in self-gratification.

That highway is teasingly wide.

And many take it.

The problem with most people is that they fall in love with the expressway. Life is too lovely. The itinerary is so much fun. There's a whole wardrobe of pleasure to try on for size.

They just love the road!

But the road is not where we're supposed to pitch a tent. We can't be stuck in the freeway. God created us for so much more than the romantic tour. It's the destination that's relevant, and we're headed for Heaven.

My friend, do not stop dreaming of a forever with God. Do not be overly invested in the feasts of the present moment that your vision of eternity gets too fogged up.

Don't fall for the broad-gate lifestyle even when you are outnumbered. Don't deviate from your True North even when the trail is saw-toothed and harsh on your feet.

God warns that only a few find the road to life. What a sobering thought! The fence that opens up to God's warm welcome is disguised with thistles of tears and weeds of suffering. Therefore, be vigilant.

Keep moving.

Without concentration, you might miss the gate.

CHAPTER 31

Even Death Cannot Part

His deeply furrowed brows betrayed the pain he suffered. Oxygen tubes inserted through his nose did little to ease the labored breathing. Besides the raspy sound of his breathing, the hum of the blood pressure monitor disrupted the silence in the intensive care unit.

I crouched at his bedside and held his leathery hand that fell limp with fatigue. With tears of worry, I kissed his wrinkled cheek and let my other hand stroke his thin gray hair.

Though he was asleep, I knew he could hear me, so I whispered "I love you" more times than I could count. It was my lame attempt to atone for all the opportunities I wasted—those forgone seasons to express my gratitude to this honourable man.

It was only a few weeks ago when I shared a light moment with my grandfather inside his austere one-bedroom home. He seemed to be in tip-top shape then, tending his small vegetable patch or taking short leisurely walks in the village. It was thus a shock for

MENU 6: STRENGTH IN SUFFERING

the family to hear about the abrupt reversal of his health. It never seemed like he could be a candidate for a massive heart attack.

On the hospital bed, he no longer looked like the brawny, strong-willed man he used to be. He lay like fragile bone china. Age irrevocably ravaged his body. His voice was reduced to a faint, coarse sigh; his eyes lost the sparkle of courage and purpose. His careworn body was giving up on him though his spirit was desperately trying to hang on.

The angiogram showed that my grandfather's main arteries calcified. Only a heart by-pass could save his life. The cardiac specialist maintained it was nothing short of a miracle that he was still alive. But could his body survive major surgery? It was a fifty-fifty gamble that didn't give us the guarantees we sought.

The family had to make quick decisions and, in a country where healthcare was not within the scope of government benefits, private funds also had to be raised. Money was no object. But though we were willing to take extreme measures to prolong his life, my grandfather's beleaguered body seemed to have plans of its own. He didn't have the tenacity to fight the inevitable.

Many times, I stayed by my grandfather's side to read him the book of Psalms. I repeatedly prayed with him as he closed his eyes in quiet acknowledgment. Such moments brought him relief and hope.

The little speck of optimism we held was snatched away in no time. His condition took a sharp nosedive. By then, we knew that God's answer to prayer was no longer physical restoration but eternal peace.

During his last moments, when the very act of speaking weighed him down like a millstone tied around his neck, he still managed to say what was topmost in his mind. Calling out for his beloved wife, his lips quivered his endearment, "Mommy."

Although the medical intervention in his body brought serious torture, my grandfather's mind was far from himself. He stood dangerously near the threshold of death, but all he cared about was the woman he dearly loved for more than fifty years. My grandfather spoke only one word, but we understood the deep emotion and dread that choked him up—"What will happen to my wife? Who will look after her?"

"Papa, it's time to let go," my aunt said. "Don't worry about Mommy. We'll take good care of her."

We couldn't bear to watch his agony any longer. We knew he was only holding on to life for our sake. Like a burning stake driven through our hearts, the pain stabbed—our hope torched to ashes. But though it crushed our spirits, we had to release my grandpa and reassure him that it was alright to go. God was waiting with a warm welcome. It was time for his heavenly homecoming. It was time for him to witness the rapturous worship of the saints before God's throne. And we, who would be left behind in grief, had to face the change in faith and obedience.

That evening, we drove back to the same austere one-bedroom home, not really sure of how to break the sad news to my grandmother. The day we left for the hospital, she was full of expectation that doctors would do their best to patch her husband back to peak form. We didn't explain the grim scenarios to her. My grandma also had a weak heart, and an emotional breakdown could do serious damage.

But the moment we stepped into the house, we realized that she already knew the fight was over. Without being brought up to speed, somehow she knew. Somehow, she felt the intensity of his presence during the dark hours of her loneliness. She felt his spirit lingering, warming her up inside. No words were spoken, but my grandma knew. With misty eyes and trembling lips, she looked up at her daughter's defeated face and allowed the tears to slide.

MENU 6: Strength in Suffering

"Papa," she silently lamented.

The love my grandparents had for each other was built on fifty-seven strong years of marriage. Their relationship ran deep and survived the many kinks and curls of life. Separation was cruelty to a relationship buoyed by this much loyalty.

Friend, perhaps you too are grieving the loss of a dearly loved. The angel of death arrived without warning, and suddenly you are immobilized. You can't make sense of your life, but you need to pull yourself together to arrange a funeral. No matter how hard you focus, your days pass like a motion blur. Your sadness doesn't lift—like a blanket of gray fog that wraps around you and confuses the outline of your future.

Everywhere you look is a reminder of how the dead used to live. The favourite chair, the dinner plate, the fresh-smelling clothes, the toothbrush by the sink, the empty bed, the cold shoes no one else will wear again ... everything rings up a memory, pinches the heart, and forces out a tear.

Do not stonewall and resist the sorrow. It is alright to mourn. Allow yourself the freedom to linger in the past and to hold on to your richest memories. Let your heart bleed for as long as you need, until you are ready to move forward again.

Cry.

Heave.

Hyperventilate.

Collapse, if you must, until you are ready to let the past go.

All these, God understands.

As Psalm 116:15 reads, "Precious in the sight of the Lord is the death of his faithful servants."

The spouse, the friend, the parent you lost ... they are not only precious to you. As a Father to fondly treasured children, God is crazy in love with them too. Therefore, God understands your heartbreak. You are not alone in your paralyzing depression.

Take pause and reflect on this for a little while.

As Jesus hung on the cross—His body exhausted from the flogging and nails, His divinity debased by humanity's sin, and His imminent separation from Mary signalled by His ebbing breaths—He thought of His mother. Forgetting His own pain and the humiliation of the crucifixion, He only thought of the heartbroken widow weeping at the foot of the cross. Jesus could turn a blind eye on His calvary but couldn't turn a deaf ear to the sobs of the woman He would leave behind.

The story of the crucifixion unfolds in the book of John.

> When Jesus saw his mother there, and the disciple whom he loved standing nearby, he said to her, "Woman, here is your son," and to the disciple, "Here is your mother." From that time on, this disciple took her into his home. (John 19:26–27)

Near the hour of His death, ignoring His throes, Jesus handed over the guardianship of His mother to John, the saint He trusted and loved. Jesus knew that the night would be long and dark for His grieving mother. Having recently bled through His personal Gethsemane, Jesus understood only too well the pain of abandonment.

And He knew Mary would be inconsolable.

He knew she would need warmth and comfort.

He knew that until His Resurrection, Mary would suffer the insults of people who would mock her as the mother of a crucified criminal.

MENU 6: STRENGTH IN SUFFERING

Friend, through your darkest hours, when the rawness of your loss writhes and sickens you, God comes. Just as Jesus knew His mother shouldn't be alone, He knows not to leave you stranded at the black pit of sorrow.

By your side He clings, mending and consoling until you retrace your steps to calmness and stability. He doesn't sneak off, not even for an eyeblink.

Because just as the child who entered eternal rest is dearly beloved to Him, so too is the heartsick child who was left behind.

And this affection God has for you is too deep.

It is a love not even death can part.

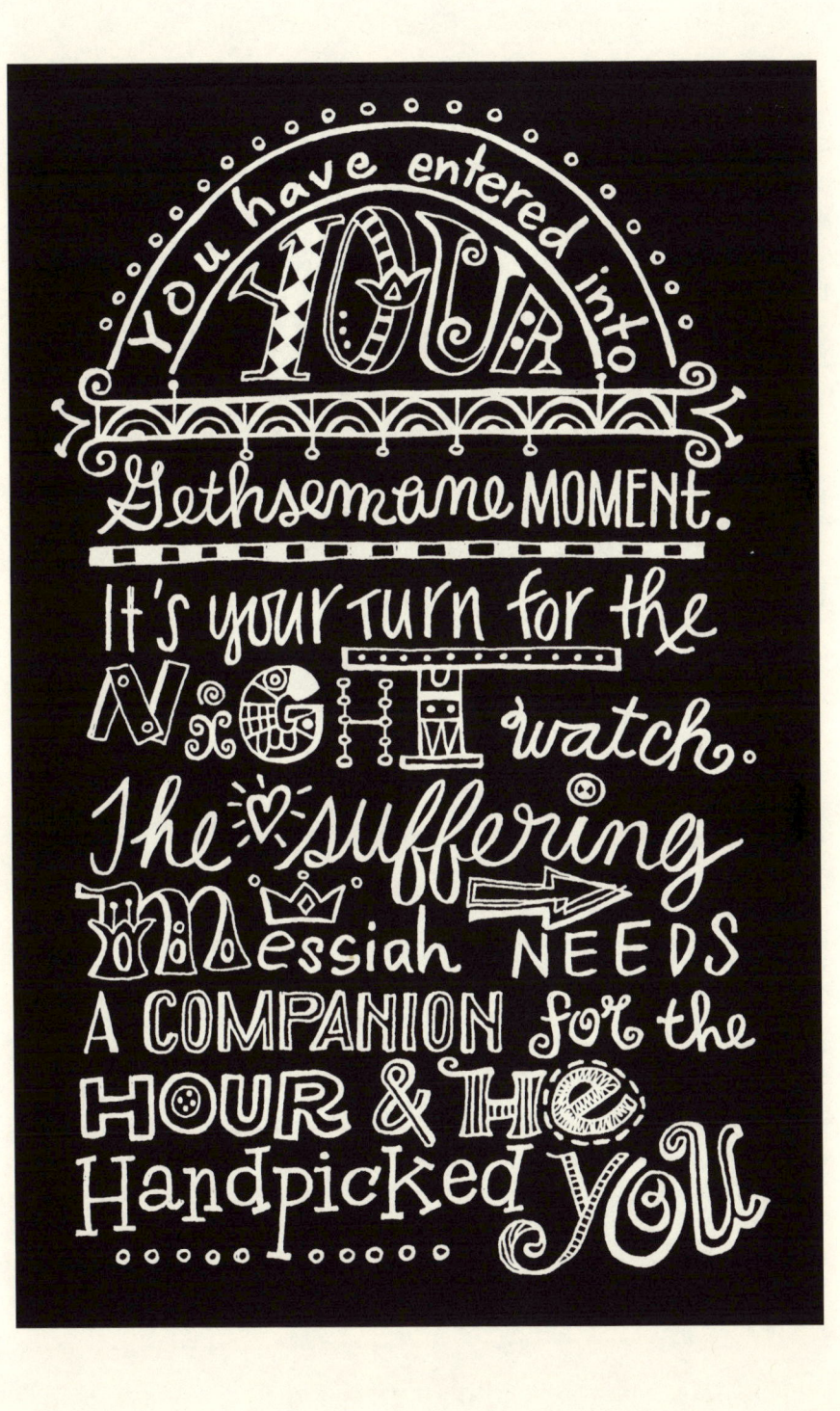

You have entered into YOUR Gethsemane MOMENT. It's your turn for the NIGHT watch. The suffering Messiah NEEDS A COMPANION for the HOUR & HE Handpicked YOU

Chapter 32

When God Says "No"

> "I have told you these things,
> so that in me you may have peace.
> In this world you will have trouble. But take heart!
> I have overcome the world."
> John 16:33

Colleen was eight when she surprised me with a vibrant, hand-painted poster for my birthday. Using multi-colored felt markers, my daughter scribbled a list of things I did for her which she appreciated the most. She wrote:

Top 10 Things I'll Remember

1. Watching movies together
2. Teaching me math
3. Doing chores without complaint
4. Teaching me how to draw
5. Checking my grammar and writing
6. Playing Scattergories with me
7. Giving me advice

MENU 6: STRENGTH IN SUFFERING

> 8. Working so hard for the family
> 9. Helping around the house even when you are sleepy
> 10. Loving me

Colleen punctuated the last entry with a huge red heart and bursts of color that popped each letter out of the page. It was a touching compliment that elevated the prosaic into the sublime. Through the tribute, dull routine dignified into honourable treasures—demonstrations of love which my daughter hugged reverently in her heart.

From time to time, it is a good practice to knock our memories and applaud others for favors we received. It is an even better exercise to recapture the years God Himself has clothed us with bounty.

Many of us will probably draw up lists of answered prayers. We have no trouble remembering occasions of healing. We are grateful for the job promotion and the economic perks attached to the title. We bathe in the majestic view of glaciers during an Alaskan cruise or reminisce the seaside stroll in Hawaii. We sigh with contentment after we seal a mortgage contract and transition to a brand new home. Our smiles stretch a kilometer wide when projects run hassle-free or when relationships in the homefront flow placidly.

We gloat about our feasts as if famine will never strike.

We look at our top ten lists and say, "God is good! He has done great things for me."

But what if He doesn't?

What if God keeps silent and refuses to lift a finger?

What if He deliberately waits until we tire of praying the same requests over and over again?

What if He ruffles our feathers and life goes berserk? If in place of benedictions and advantages, we receive criticisms and injury. Instead of empowerment, we are dispossessed. Instead of the liberating warmth of summer, endless, dark winters sicken our souls. Instead of a landslide victory, we pick up our losses and drown in debt.

Will we still declare with the same good-natured cocksureness that God is good?

If there is one thing my daughter is passionate about, it is reading. Bring her to a library, and her eyes twinkle with excitement. Her attachment to books is almost obsessive.

One afternoon, my husband decided to drive my daughter to the public library. An hour later, Colleen skipped out of the place with a stuffed bag of paperback novels. With a smile that outshone a blazing Mediterranean sun, you might guess she cinched the winning lottery ticket.

Looking up at Alvin, she said, "You're the greatest Daddy in the whole world!"

Colleen's affirmation gave my husband the warm fuzzies. "Why do you say that?" he asked.

"Because you bring me to the library." She was really tickled pink.

Alvin's eyebrows furrowed. "What if I don't bring you to the library?"

Colleen kept silent.

As an only child for eleven years, my daughter used to equate love with getting what she wanted. Like most kids her age, she had no problem believing in the love of her father for as long as we indulged her hankerings and appeals. Once her requests met contradiction, her young mind failed to appreciate the discipline and misjudged the deprivation as a deficiency in love. In a surly mood, her eyes would roll like a whirlpool and her frown would look no less rumpled than the face of a flat-nosed pug.

As I skimmed through my daughter's list, I realized that I treated God in the same way. I only remembered seasons of joy when God granted my heart's wishes.

MENU 6: STRENGTH IN SUFFERING

But when God seems distant, when His answer to prayer is as unpalatable to me as the charred bottoms of dry, over-baked cookies, must I question His goodness?

Does He cease to be the greatest Daddy in the world when He says "no"?

Do I simply forget interludes of heartaches and grief through which God triggers greater good?

Whether or not we accept it as true, God is good, and He accomplishes great things. You can bet your old boots on it! It doesn't mean, though, that God will always deliver what we want. What the Lord has in mind for us, though not to our taste, bears monumental significance for our salvation. It is reasonable to expect that what He delivers may not always be delightfully sweet.

Years later, during a break from our homeschool lessons, my little boy engaged me in a silly wordplay which he picked up from reading cartoon clips.

"Mama, if an ice cube can talk, what will you tell him?" Pajo asked.

"I don't know. What?"

"You're cool!"

"How about a pebble? What can you say to a pebble?" Pajo asked again.

I still had no clue, so my son continued, "You rock!"

That made me chuckle until he dished out more. "Mama, try this one. What will you tell an oven?"

By then, I understood the pattern so the answer was pretty obvious, but my other children jumped into the bandwagon and volunteered, "You're hot!"

Amidst the giggles, a tiny voice chimed in, "Ooh, I know one more, Mama. What will a tree say?"

I couldn't venture a guess until one kid piped up, "Mama, I think you're a tree! You're stumped!" By this time, my family was one noisy crowd, snorting and sounding like a laughing kookaburra.

When the racket settled down, I asked, "Pajo, out of all these statements, which one describes me? Am I cool or hot? Do I rock?"

My son gave his signature prankish look then with tongue-in-cheek jazz said, "You stink!"

That naughty rascal didn't get away from me without a battery of tickles. But after the wide grin faded, the thought throbbed in my head with a rapid-fire insistence that was difficult to ignore.

Life is sometimes like that. It stinks! Problems and puzzles leave you stumped. With agitations raging left and right, you can't be cool. The absurdities of your situation are no longer laughable and cute, and they leave you jalapeno hot ... hot-tempered, that is.

Your cobwebs are sticky.

Your knots are tight.

The briers are prickly.

And the lamp bummed out; there is no light.

Your foot is stuck in the rabbit hole.

Life, as you know it, simply stinks!

On such occasions, can we still profess the goodness of God and keep our allegiance to Christ firm?

When life is a valley of trouble and imbroglios greet you at every turn, hold tight to your faith. You have entered your Garden of Gethsemane. It is all a test to see what solidity your spirit consists.

Will you be a quitter or a conqueror? Will you be subdued or will you overcome? Will you be the warrior who rises to the occasion? Or will you be the cynic who slinks away in abject fear long before the rough-and-tumble begins? Will you cut your victory speech mid-sentence and retract when it seems like you can no longer hold the fort?

MENU 6: STRENGTH IN SUFFERING

My friend, do not be the loser who backs out of the boxing ring without an offensive punch. Fight your battles, and do not give up. The burden you carry is a test of faith to turn the worrier and naysayer into a victor.

When God says "no" or when the answer to prayer is too foggy to understand, do not feed your mind with despair. Let hope be the fodder for your soul. Do not degenerate into a skeptic who scoffs at the goodness of God because your life is not a picture of perfection.

Imitate David who was staunch in piety despite the sneers and pillages of his enemies. It is alright to sulk like the psalmist who wondered, "How long, Lord, will you look on?" (Psalm 35:17).

It is also fine to plead,

> Lord, you have seen this; do not be silent.
>> Do not be far from me, Lord.
> Awake, and rise to my defense!
>> Contend for me, my God and Lord.
> Vindicate me in your righteousness, Lord my God;
>> do not let them gloat over me.
> (Psalm 35:22–24)

Like David, you too may complain, if by so doing, you ventilate your anguish. But with the same breath, let your allegiance still remain in Christ. Even when your sighs are deep and your mouth is too bone-dry for words, announce with boldness,

> My tongue will proclaim your righteousness, your
> praises all day long. (Psalm 35:28)

Believe in the goodness of God even when you are engulfed by an avalanche of pain, and the world unleashes its wrath on you. You have entered into your Gethsemane moment, and it is an absolute privilege. It is your turn for the night watch. The suffering

Messiah needs a companion for the hour, and He handpicked you to learn from His cross.

Bleed with Him.

Groan with Him.

Be sanctified with Him.

For through your Gethsemane moment, as you collapse into the comforting arms of Jesus, you regain strength. Your calamity is a scourge that purges you of your weaknesses and teaches you to cling to the Rock of Ages. In this is your power!

Therefore, sit devotedly at God's side even when your heart is broken into pieces. Stay in the Garden, and keep vigil through the night. Today may seem like your crucifixion, but tomorrow, the glory of the Resurrection will come. God will mend you back into form with far greater strength than what you had in the beginning. With the Lord, you will never come away empty-handed.

Recognize that what ails you now is simply a test.

It will not last!

The countdown is on—soon this will be over.

Dear friend, by the grace of the Holy One who is in charge of this test, may you not flunk out!

> You will keep in perfect peace
> those whose minds are steadfast,
> because they trust in you.
> Trust in the Lord forever,
> for the Lord, the Lord himself,
> is the Rock eternal.
> Isaiah 26:3-4

Chapter 33

Of Boats and Bridges

I must have strained myself to the limit during the Easter celebration I had with friends. The straight rounds of board games coupled with a boisterous crowd of junk food stuffers stretched the fun up to the wee hours of the morning.

I knew I abused my throat quite severely with all the laughter and hubbub that accompanied the night's fellowship. The following day, I rolled out of bed with a funny, croaky voice. Irrepressible fits of coughing interrupted my every phrase. I thought it was an ordinary glitch that would fizzle out in no time—probably just a minor throat problem springing from excessive talking.

After a week however, my condition didn't peter out as I optimistically predicted. One morning, at the crack of dawn, an excruciating twinge in my left ear jarred me awake. The shooting pain felt roughly like sharp thorns being crudely drilled into my sensitive skin. The stabs were so piercing that I literally howled for help as I wriggled on my bed, unable to sleep.

MENU 6: STRENGTH IN SUFFERING

It was close to sunrise when exhaustion finally overtook me. With a limp body, I squeezed in a nap which was cut short by a strange heaviness on my left jaw. Hearing on the left side became awfully muffled. The surrounding noise abruptly dropped to a low-key volume just as you would expect with bad TV reception.

"Am I becoming deaf?" I was immobilized with fear.

Instantly, memories of my sickness in 1984 floated in my mind. Back in high school, my hearing was impaired for three to four months due to heavy congestion. The trips to the ear specialist were so traumatic that I balked at visiting the doctor again.

I could still recall how my hands turned clammy as I fretfully waited for my turn outside the doors of the medical clinic. As the doctor inserted foreign instruments into my ear canal and sucked out the stubborn blockade, my stomach somersaulted a hundred times. I remember how I almost squashed the blood circulation from my mom's fingers. I smothered her arm each time the pressure applied on my ear became too painful.

Even after several operations of this sort, the abnormality refused to fade. Consultations with brilliant doctors didn't shed light on how to alleviate the symptoms. Permanent healing came only through prayers. And what a long-drawn-out, grueling gamble with faith that proved to be!

Now this was no déjà vu. This was no illusion, nightmare, or prank. I, in fact, faced the haunting threat of reverting to deafness for no apparent reason. The speculation alone scared the living daylights out of me.

Judging from the frequency of my new visits, I almost became a permanent fixture in the doctor's clinic. Each consultation proved my hunch right. My hearing was going downhill.

The doctor's deepening frown lines and facial contortions hinted at how puzzling my case had become. Although the prescribed medication and restorative procedures reduced the swelling in my ears and the gruffness of my speech, I remained partially deaf.

The specialist had a gnawing suspicion that an undetected tumor could be the root of the problem. Normally, congestion affects both ears. However, since the malfunction was localized on one sphere, an ugly tumor was the most frequent culprit.

AT THE PRECIPICE

When the wonders of science failed to nurse me back to health, or even give a satisfactory diagnosis, I began to pray. How strange that God had to push me towards a gridlock before I caught His scent. How strange indeed that I initially snubbed God, dissociated myself from prayer, and considered Him a trump card reserved for do-or-die situations. Desperation hit when I touched rock bottom. It was only then that I voiced my heartfelt petitions.

Prayer should never be the last resort. The Lord should not be our stopgap measure. He isn't the remedy we grab on the eleventh hour. He is not the substitute we call when no other problem solver comes under the radar. I understand that now. But I didn't back then.

One of my most enlightening faith experiences emerged from periods of debility, when my hopes were dashed and life was one huge catastrophe. This season of deafness was one of those times. It was an age of grace when callouses thickened my knees, and prayer babbled from my mouth incoherently with the same rhythm as my tears.

During one of those intense moments of prayer, I received a mental picture of Jesus inviting me to walk with Him. In the vision, I

MENU 6: Strength in Suffering

watched myself drift towards the edge of a cliff. Its depth couldn't be calculated due to the abyss-like darkness at the base.

Connecting the crag to the other side was a narrow plank of wood, cut to precise length to fill the gap. The makeshift bridge had no overhang and appeared rickety. The slightest knock could slacken the edge, trigger an avalanche of stones, and cause the antiquated timber to collapse.

Despite this ugly view, God instructed, "Go ahead and cross."

If I obeyed my instincts and shaped my judgments from the irrefutable laws of physics, I would have raised an eyebrow and cynically said, "Are you kidding me?"

But the Lord, in my vision, was assertive. He repeated, "Walk over the bridge now. Keep your eyes on Me, not on the depth of the gorge. Raise your hope. I am waiting for you on the other side."

I understood right away that God was nudging me to take a step of faith. He didn't want me to form my opinion based on appearances. I had to believe God was reclaiming full function of my ear though it was inconsistent with my observation of facts.

IN THE STORM-TOSSED BOAT

> A furious squall came up, and the waves broke over the boat, so that it was nearly swamped. Jesus was in the stern, sleeping on a cushion. The disciples woke him and said to him, "Teacher, don't you care if we drown?" (Mark 4:37–38)

When I read this passage, I was positive it wasn't Jesus' disciple who chewed him out. That was me! All that tongue-lashing stampeded out of MY mouth.

It sounded so like me to blow a gasket and say, "Hey, don't you care? Please, wake up! I'm dying here! I'm the one who's deaf, not you. So why are you acting like you can't hear me?"

No doubt, I had an emotional connection with Jesus' disciples who were thrown into delirium when the gigantic waves of the Sea of Galilee whipped their boat.

The fishermen were veteran sailors. They were professionals. Yet, despite their knack for navigation, they couldn't bail themselves out of a sticky situation. They reached the end of themselves. Out of desperation, they barked at Jesus, "Teacher, is it nothing to you that we're going down?" (Mark 4:38 MSG).

When I became deaf for weeks, I could identify with the disciples' fright. It seemed like I also jostled on the same boat with Peter on that fateful night. I too felt the spray of cold sea water on my face and the violent winds knocking the breath out of my chest.

When the doctors announced that there was no cure for my specific case of Eustachian Tube dysfunction and that I could be hard of hearing indefinitely, I plagued God with my whys. Like the disciples, I nagged, "Don't you care that I am ill? Can't you pick a better time to sleep?"

I thought God chose the wrong time to be droopy. Disaster was already waiting around the corner, preparing for an ambush; but there he was, catching some zzz's.

> [Jesus] got up, rebuked the wind and said to the waves, "Quiet! Be still!" Then the wind died down and it was completely calm. (Mark 4:39)

Just like in the evening of the storm, when the agitation of the winds and waves quieted down at Jesus' explosive command, God only spoke the word and I was refreshed. My private conflict subsided even as I was still physically disabled.

MENU 6: STRENGTH IN SUFFERING

You wonder how this could be so? It's because throughout my personal ordeal, God disclosed an important contradiction.

While He can sleep unflustered during savage weather, He cannot sleep through our prayers!

Go ahead. Jump back. Read that line again.

God can't sleep through your prayers.

It is against God's code of love to remain oblivious to our suffering. He cannot keep His eyes shut, dream away, and snore through the night—not because His children are maddening pests, constantly interrupting His sleep, but because He cannot bear to see us in pain.

The Lord is a promise keeper.

When He said I could walk over a treacherous bridge, I should have accepted the statement as true. I wouldn't be flirting with danger if I passed the slim, wobbly lumber. God already vouched for my safety.

And God doesn't lie.

So there was no need to worry about dropping thousands of leagues into the precipice. If God promised He would wait for me on the other side, then there was no denying He'd be there as foretold.

In the same way, before Jesus relaxed his head at the stern of the boat, he told his disciples, "Let us go over to the other side" (Mark 4:35).

He didn't say, "Goodbye, compatriots. We shall drown together today. See you in Paradise ... if you're lucky!"

No!

He said, "Let us cross the lake."

Jesus had always been credible. So why didn't the disciples believe they would dock on the opposite coast with their body parts still attached? Whether or not the bumpy sail would leave them scruffy and emotionally shaken, they should have trusted God to bring them to shore as He already prefigured.

Brothers and sisters, God's words are never barren or pointless. His words precipitate blessings and fetch results. They are never bereft of meaning but return with hope, power, and vindication.

Each time the Lord discharges a promise, He is bound by honour to see through its perfection. He is the embodiment of truth. Fruitfulness is His trademark. Therefore, pay close attention. "Today, if you hear his voice, do not harden your hearts ..." (Hebrews 3:15).

TO RIDE THE WAVES

All of these reflections pushed guilt to the surface and painted my cheeks pink with shame. I reproached myself for doubting God's power.

God is our Deliverer; He can easily heave us from the jaws of death any second He chooses. We only need to wait through His own calendar, not ours. That's because God dances to a different rhythm. His cadence and punctuality is our presumed irregularity. His measure of promptness is often tardiness in the alarm clock of our impatient world. His silence is misread as indifference. We accuse God of being slow when He doesn't even take stretch breaks.

He is tirelessly testing our faith.

Fine tuning our patience.

Sharpening our obedience.

And redeeming our souls.

That is His job description—and that is what God did on the day my hearing was finally restored!

MENU 6: STRENGTH IN SUFFERING

One night, in a dream, I saw the same old timber used as makeshift bridge. I caught sight of the same bottomless rockface and Jesus standing on the opposite ridge with arms open in a gesture of welcome. The only difference was that I no longer stood frozen on my side of the summit. I was inching midway through the tight pass. I was still as tense as ever, with eyes cast on the foot of the black, yawning chasm. Nonetheless, I took a few steps forward.

It was then that I realized ... God's sermon on faith had already taken root.

Indeed, the best time to cultivate faith is right at the center of a field of testing—right in the middle of a stormy sea.

Storms do not hurl without end. Waves soon subside to a ripple. And the ocean, sooner or later, restrains its irritability. It is God's desire for us to calmly ride the moon-whitened waves.

For as long as God is in the boat, a bloody shipwreck will never be written into our personal narratives. Therefore, let us wait for the Lord to rebuke our whistling winds with the same forceful "Quiet! Be still!"

In the sidelines, watch as He subdues our inner tempests.

Then in His company, be the ones to sleep pacified.

He said to his disciples,
"Why are you so afraid?
Do you still have no faith?"
They were terrified and asked each other,
"Who is this?
Even the wind and the waves obey him!"
Mark 4:40-41

Chapter 34

He Knows Your Heart

"Oh, dear! Look at the time!"

I was seriously behind schedule. While on panic mode, I rushed through merging freeway traffic like a police officer on the tail of a runaway carjacker. I wanted to focus both on the road and on the speedometer with as little distraction as possible so that we'd reach our appointment with all our body parts still intact.

However, for my little passengers, road trips were as perfect a time for interrogation as any. My then three-year-old Pajo, with his gift of gab and prying mind, inundated me with random questions starting with, "What does a turtle eat?" This was followed by "what does an octopus eat?", "how about the crab, the giraffe, the bear?" and a long checklist of other species in the animal kingdom. After exhausting his vocabulary of living creatures, he looked at the steam coming out of factories and quizzed me about what things factories make.

MENU 6: STRENGTH IN SUFFERING

The volley of curiosity didn't abate until I finally said, "Honey, can you please keep quiet for a while. I'm having a hard time driving."

Obediently, Pajo kept silent after admitting in a whisper, "I am tired of talking."

My eldest teenager took this as a cue to grab my attention. Since Pajo carried on non-stop, Colleen couldn't even clear her throat or interrupt with a sigh. When she finally had the chance, all she managed to utter was, "By the way, Mama ..."

Immediately, Pajo shushed, "No! Don't talk to Mama."

"Why?" Colleen was amused at the sour, humourless crease on his brother's face.

Like a pompous peacock, Pajo raised his chin and looked down at his sister from the narrow barrel of his button nose. "Because Mama is CONCENTRATING!"

With puckered brows, I looked at him from the rear-view mirror. "Wow, Pajo! That's such a big word for a three-year-old! Concentrating?"

"Do you even know what the word means?" Colleen asked.

My peacock ruffled his feathers, and with much pride, declared with gavel-pounding firmness, "Yes! It means 'DRIVING'!"

Colleen and I doubled over, gripping our aching tummies as we roared. Pajo laughed along though he never figured out what the hilarity was about. As far as his innocent mind knew, he gave me what I needed—his silence. He was confident enough in his relationship with his mother to discern rightly that my "driving" or "concentrating" required his mute passivity.

Familiarity.

This is the key to understanding.

My son was so deeply familiar with me that he perceived what I meant. He understood even a shudder, a slightly upturned mouth, a wheezing breath, a hand signal, a raised eyebrow, or a wrinkled nose. Whether or not his preschool wordbook could accommodate fancy, high-sounding language like "concentrating", I had no doubt he got the picture.

Because, bottom line is … my son knew my heart.

As I reflected on my relationship with my children, the Lord reminded me of the same affectionate connection He has with His children. God understands us. How can He not, when he created our every fiber and filament, eyelash, toenail, and bellybutton?

You'll be surprised that the God who loves surprises is never Himself surprised. Our Father who knows everything about you—like the back of His hand—is never struck dumb. To figure you out, He doesn't have to dig around for answers. He doesn't need to probe and ferret out your personal trivia. Nothing jumps out and flabbergasts Him like we do with first encounters. You're so transparent; He doesn't need guesswork. God knows you through and through—

Whether you're upside down or inside out,
Rolling over or creaky on your feet,
Whether or not your humour is crazy,
Your bones are lazy,
Or your thoughts, hazy.
He isn't surprised.

There is nothing about you that grosses God out, even when you're at your ugliest. His knowledge of you is complete, updated to the last millisecond—accurate to the last count of hair on your head (or the last one that fell off the comb)!

The Lord catches the drift. He reads you like an overused, dog-eared book. Though shabby with torn pages, or printed with invisible ink, there is nothing you can hide in your life's storybook that He doesn't already know.

MENU 6: Strength in Suffering

Remember, He is the Author who assembled the twists and plot of your novel. He knows the valiant exploits you'll do in the future, the evil schemes and antagonists you'll battle, the tension, climax, and all the little victories you'll brag about throughout your saga.

Your Father's familiarity and intimacy with you is so unbelievable, it'll blow your mind away. Do you need proof? Let's see.

Here's one ...

> Before a word is on my tongue you, Lord, know it completely. (Psalm 139:4)

You can't win the Twenty Questions game against God. He knows all the answers!

Here's another ...

> You know when I sit and when I rise; you perceive my thoughts from afar. (Psalm 139:2)

You can't play Charades, either. God can read your mind before you act anything out!

God knows all your obscure details, the measure of your days, your moods, even your favourite sins. Such is the limitlessness and inexhaustibility of our Lord. Even with your best effort, you can't fool Him—

> Your eyes saw my unformed body; all the days ordained for me were written in your book before one of them came to be. (Psalm 139:16)

Further, the Lord says,

> "My eyes are on all their ways; they are not hidden from me, nor is their sin concealed from my eyes."
> (Jeremiah 16:17)

You might be thinking, "Okay, I get it. God is my stalker. So what?"

When you get down to it, you'll realize how comforting this truth really is—God understands.

When friends trample on your trust with clouded judgments, you can lean on the Lord who understands your heart. Are your scars too deep that they isolate you from friends who can't imagine the torture? Don't lose courage! God grieves with you, weathers the pain with you, and holds your hand through the night. Even the deepest sorrows and most suffocating shadows aren't too remote for His understanding.

Is your suffering too intense, you have no words to describe the torment? Are you too embittered, you don't know how to pray away the sting?

Are you at such a loss that you don't know whether to ask God to remove the calamity or to summon the grace of endurance?

Are you crumbling under the deadweight of sickness or abuse—pulled to the lowest, blackest valley in your life—that all you can do is groan in mourning?

My friend, though you're too choked up that groaning is all you can do, don't wrestle with your prayers anymore. You don't have to try so hard to explain what you mean. There is no need to scuffle and strain to be specific in prayer. The language of your groans is already clear to Him.

MENU 6: STRENGTH IN SUFFERING

    God's understanding is that extreme, even your tears are replete with meaning. The cruelty of your circumstance is so aligned with God that He gets the full picture.

    Be well then!

    Your Father knows His child's heart.

    And His understanding is your comfort.

GOD needs time to scrub your ChaRacter to a polished Elegance. He knows your FAITH can only grow by little {degRees} at a time and only the friction of PROLoNGed suffeRing can bring OUT your RaDiaNce

Chapter 35

Crucified

Shortly before my thirty-fourth birthday, then six-year-old Colleen asked, "Mama, how old was Jesus when he was crucified?"

"Thirty-three."

"Same as you?"

"Yes."

Upon hearing this, my forward-thinking girl raised a ruckus. "I don't like that, Mama," she moaned.

"What don't you like?" I was puzzled by her abrupt sniveling.

"I don't want my Mommy to be crucified!"

Many lips curled at this sweet anecdote. Maybe, you would too, if you share the same opinion. Let's be honest. Crucifixion—whether you take it literally or metaphorically—isn't something you'd want for yourself or for anyone you love.

People have an aversion to suffering that is as natural as a finger jerking at the prick of a rusty needle. The weight of the cross is as abhorrent as the idea of stretching in front of a speeding

MENU 6: STRENGTH IN SUFFERING

fourteen-wheeler truck. No one volunteers to be in the line of fire of a triggerman run amok. It is psychosis to intentionally choose pain and affliction!

The dusty, starless, gravel road of affliction is one that people dread to travel. Instead, we plan our journeys through life like we do a Monopoly game—optimistically expecting assets growth and indulgence at every roll of the dice.

Yet, the Christ whom we pursue and imitate is a suffering Messiah. Through His living example, we know that the bloodied wooden cross of Calvary preceded the lustrous throne of Heaven.

The crown of thorns foreshadowed the crown of gold.

There would be no prize of the Resurrection without the price of the brutal Roman scourge.

It totally cuts against the grain of the flesh to welcome suffering. That said, we are only able to accept the Gospel of the Cross if we have the Holy Spirit's empowerment. We need God's grace before we can cradle our misfortunes with a sunny posture.

We need the Holy Spirit to puncture, permeate, and invade the core of our souls. Only then can we see beyond life's nasty blows and grasp suffering's higher intent. Then like James, we can "consider it pure joy ... whenever [we] face trials of many kinds" (James 1:2).

Back in 1988, God tested my capacity to carry the cross with this brand of joy. From nowhere, strange boils erupted on both my feet. The numerous tiny bulges, initially itchy, became murderously painful. The skin ruptured and oozed a mixture of blood and gooey fluid.

Most of the boils covered the whole underside of my feet. A generous cluster grew in between my toes while a few swelled on top. Stunted mobility brought my life to a screeching halt. Walking became an annoying inconvenience. The spastic torture of every muscle shift pushed me through the doorway to madness.

The skin lesions persisted for almost ten years in spite of frequent stomach-turning steroid injections.

Ten hard-fought years!

Hands down, that was, by far, the worst blow I received in my life.

Throughout those years, leather shoes were death-row executioners that inspired fear in me. The tanned hides roasted my blisters and peeled dried wounds raw once again.

Sometimes, big flies swarmed on the exposed wounds, and I neither noticed nor felt the difference. I only realized it when people stared at my sandaled feet with obvious disgust. The mockery in their eyes silently criticized me for my sketchy hygiene.

People didn't know any better. They just assumed I was contagious. Suitably, many recoiled from me as if I had power to kick-start a new plague of leprosy.

Hundreds of times I asked God through gritted teeth, "Why me? Why this? What did I ever do to deserve such an ugly disease? The doctors may not know what to do, but you can easily figure this out, right? Why aren't you doing anything then?"

Instead of a straight answer, the Lord shed light through a poignant portrayal of the incarnation.

Jesus stepped down from His venerable image to become Emmanuel—God with us. He traded His eternal glory in heaven for a thankless ministry on earth. He swathed His omniscient power in a blanket of humility, embracing the stable's trough as the birthplace of His mission.

God the Son, who chose to become man, embraced all the restrictions, disqualifications, and inaptitudes of growing as man. He, who had legions of angels at His beck and call, and who was

MENU 6: STRENGTH IN SUFFERING

worshipped by saints in a palatial home, sank down to our level to be surrounded by sinners, traitors, adulterers, and murderers.

Such alienation from the Father must be excruciatingly painful. Yet despite the agony, Jesus relinquished His kingly reputation and took the form of a servant. He gave up all pomp and grandeur, not only out of submission to the divine will, but because of a love that's too deep for words.

What did we do with this privilege of Divinity touching humanity?

Word took flesh to bring salvation to fallen man. What did man do in return?

We defamed the Godhead.

We cast Jesus off like good-for-nothing trash.

Humbly, He succumbed to our ridicules and curses. Treachery and corruption. Whips and lashes. Anger and bloodshed.

If I may put it in crude, rhetorical terms, I guess what can help you imagine the atrociousness of Christ's condition is the analogy of a human being voluntarily taking the form of a squiggly maggot. A man ditches the luxuries of home, gives up an intellectually satisfying career, and enters the bug world in swaddling banana peels inside a stinky dumpster. He assumes a new identity, only to be eaten alive by scavenger birds. This rough sketch may not fully parallel the essence of the incarnation, but somehow, you get the picture.

Such was the sting of Jesus' incarnation. With this image in mind, how then could I still wince over my own wounds? Any sacrifice is too cheap in the light of what Christ endured on our behalf.

Really, all our troubles combined will still be too little a price to pay for the salvation that was won for our sake!

Suffering is no cool spine-tingling roller-coaster ride. There's no entertainment in it that makes one hanker after more. So how could anyone face trial with the same joy that James prescribes?

As years passed and the wounds outlived my stamina, I learned to aim my attention to God. He produced in me a healthy measure of forebearance.

God didn't permit a quick fix to my illness because He needed that much time to scrub my character to a polished elegance. He knew full well that my fragile faith could only grow by little degrees at a time.

Only the friction of prolonged suffering would bring out the radiance.

I guess, this is what triggers joy!

It is the knowledge that our trial and grief will result in the shaping of our character into the ideal profile of Christ. God designs suffering to elicit greater good in us. The burden then doesn't just give birth to wasted tears. It generates priceless intimacy with God!

Once, as I gazed intently at the crucifix and reflected on the Savior's nail-scarred feet, it dawned on me—Jesus had the same disfigured feet as I had for ten years.

Almost in jest, I thought to myself, "Jesus, why did you have freaky feet too?"

I was surprised when, in prayer, I felt Him speak.

"So that I'll know how to deal with your pain. I know what it's like and I know that soon, you'll need someone who understands."

Yes, God understands.

He understands not just my pain, but yours too.

You'll never encounter an ordeal that Jesus hasn't experienced Himself.

MENU 6: STRENGTH IN SUFFERING

And this brings relief—that before you are crucified, Christ has already numbed the agony by taking upon Himself the vicious blows of the Roman spikes.

> Not only so, but we also glory in our sufferings, because we know that suffering produces perseverance; perseverance, character; and character, hope. And hope does not put us to shame, because God's love has been poured out into our hearts through the Holy Spirit, who has been given to us. (Romans 5:3–5)

Storms are an inextricable part of life. It's been promised to us too. In the book of John, Jesus gave the warning to his disciples,

> "I have told you these things, so that in me you may have peace. In this world you will have trouble. But take heart! I have overcome the world." (John 16:33)

Therefore, my friend, do not be surprised by the pain you now bear. Stop asking, "Why me?" Think with submissive candor, "Yes, why not?"

Is it too surprising to take up a share of the cross' burden in the same way that Simon of Cyrene did when Jesus fell under its tiresome weight?

Is it irreproachably Christian to watch your neighbour suffer, commiserate from a distance, but not really understand how to extend compassion because your whole life has been problem-free?

Carry your burdens, and carry them well! It is your honour to be handpicked for the task.

If you think, like I do many times, that you don't deserve your suffering, you may want to reflect on the flipside to gain deeper wisdom. Let's take the opposite perspective.

We too don't deserve the blessings we receive, and yet we drink them all in without choking. If you want to file a complaint against your sufferings, why not complain about your blessings too?

Gain wisdom from the witness of Job's life who, despite the fatalities and forfeit of all his previous blessings, still honoured the Lord through his sorrow.

> "Naked I came from my mother's womb, and naked I will depart. The Lord gave and the Lord has taken away; may the name of the Lord be praised." In all this, Job did not sin by charging God with wrongdoing. (Job 1:21–22)

Friend, bear the thorn which the Lord drove through your side. There's a reason it is there. Receive the anointing of the Cross-Bearer because He is using your suffering to make you a deeper, wiser person.

For, in truth, scarred people are beautiful.

Those who passed through the crucible of fire with their faith intact, rise up in maturity, their beauty glittering like diamonds.

Yes, scarred people are beautiful.

They are more sympathetic and open-handed than those who've never been bruised deep enough to hurt.

It is broken men and women who know how to "carry each other's burdens ..." (Galatians 6:2) because they, too, had been roughened by life, patched up with God's grace, and healed back into usefulness with a renewed sense of purpose.

While in the middle of writing, I asked my then seven-year-old daughter to keep quiet so that I could concentrate. She zipped her mouth only for a minute, after which she threw monosyllabic grunts at intervals of a few seconds.

MENU 6: STRENGTH IN SUFFERING

Humph ... Humph ... Humph ...

Thinking that there was something painfully wrong with her throat, I asked, "Are you okay, honey? Does your throat itch?"

"Nothing's wrong, Mama," Colleen said. "I'm just exercising my voice 'cause I'm tired of keeping quiet."

With my creative juices pumped out and my train of thought already broken, she continued confiding about the silliest of things.

"You know Mama, when I cry, I collect the tears on my finger and lick it," Colleen proudly announced.

"And why would you do that?" I asked, bewildered.

Perhaps she wanted to experiment to find out if tears were really salty. Her answer was nowhere near my guess.

"'Coz I want to recycle my tears, Mama! My teacher said not to waste anything."

Now who would have thought!

Why did I tell you this story? Bear with me for a moment while I unfold the rest ...

You know, some of life's knots cannot be untangled. All we can do is hang tough till the end.

Cancer plagues. The untimely death of a child hounds your day with grief. Bodily paralysis limits your usefulness and quells your desire to serve. The epidemic swiped your family clean, and you are literally the last man standing. Your teenager drowns in substance abuse, and you can't seem to pull him out of his downward spiral. Blindsided by a concussion, your big-league dreams were dashed by a baseball pitcher's accidental stroke.

Problems without solutions—there are many such partnerships that pop out of nowhere.

True, you can't control the problems that pound on your door, but you can control your response to these hard-luck stories.

Brother, don't let storms drag you down. Sister, keep your hope up. Believe that "if we endure, we will also reign with him" (2 Timothy 2:12).

If, at the end of the day, tears flow without end, let it be. Just like my Colleen who recycled tears, God doesn't waste tears too. Every drop is counted for your future glory!

Weep as long as you want.

Soak up all the tissues.

Use a towel if need be.

But take comfort! God sees those tears.

And He who brought you to this dark, painful place, will vindicate and defend. Soon, you'll understand why He did what He did. What was unfathomable will be revealed.

The long-pending whys will find answers. The crooked will be ironed straight.

And with the same tears, you'll joyfully applaud God.

With genuine reverence, you'll thank Him for the transforming work He completed in you!

> I have been crucified with Christ
> and I no longer live,
> but Christ lives in me.
> The life I now live in the body,
> I live by faith in the Son of God,
> who loved me and gave himself for me.
> Galatians 2:20

Chapter 36

In the Quietness of the Night

One minute, he was giggling and tumbling around the living room carpet, with fingers exploring and ransacking the house. The next minute, my months-old cruiser was bearing a high-grade fever, screaming for attention and writhing in pain.

The sudden mood shift was alarming especially since Pajo had always been a show-your-dimpled-smile charmer since the day he was born. He was usually more fun than a barrel of monkeys.

A quick temperature check revealed a whopping 39.5°C. I immediately ran tap water on his mottled skin and scrubbed his body to release the heat. That didn't seem to pacify because Pajo pierced the quiet night with his shrill cries. His fingers dug at his tummy as if indicating the source of his pain.

In a blink, his whole body started to convulse out of control. It was more than a shudder that lasted longer than three minutes. My maternal instincts told me to wrap him in a towel. I hurriedly cuddled the baby and tried to control the spasmodic seizures while my husband grabbed the phone and dialed 9-1-1.

MENU 6: STRENGTH IN SUFFERING

Within minutes, paramedics rushed into our bedroom. I never felt more relieved in my life! When we were hanging by a hair, I wanted so badly to lean on people who had more than just a clue on what happened to my son.

The paramedics' presence lifted the pressure off my jerky nerves. They raced against the clock and moved with intent. A small oxygen tank and other equipment lay on the floor as they gently poked Pajo's half-naked body to check his vitals and oxygenation.

After they pacified and physically stabilized Pajo, they strapped me on a stretcher as I rested his limp form on my arms. It was 10:30 p.m., way past my son's bedtime. Though heavy-eyed at first, he became all alert the second he saw the strange contraptions and rows of first-aid medicines inside the ambulance.

The emergency room of the city hospital was so packed, even the hallway housed a long queue of stretchers. Elderly men and women, brought in by paramedics, awaited their turns.

In the adjacent lobby, more ambulatory patients counted the hours. Wrinkled brows mirrored both apprehension and impatience. The lingering clusters looked fixedly at the triage nurse as if mere stares could compel her to draw up patient charts and call out names.

The hospital was bursting at the seams, and every doctor on duty had a long line-up of distraught people. Though we were the last to pull in, paramedics wheeled us straight into the pediatric department.

I wasn't sure if I should feel privileged to receive special attention. Friends, who had been through this roller-coaster ride before, already warned me that prompt admission was a sign of grave health problems.

How right they were! I was shocked to hear from the pediatrician that my son displayed symptoms of bacterial meningitis!

What?! Life-threatening, ugly, meningitis that could snuff out the breath of my baby within hours?

At that point, I wished the doctor didn't tell me anything. At least, what I didn't know wouldn't cause my heart to grieve or my stomach to twist in knots. Ignorance could be bliss.

At the crack of dawn, I brought Pajo in for an x-ray—his first test out of a series. The merciless technician sat my poor baby up on a makeshift bench, buckled both his feet on a pole, and fastened both his hands above his head.

Naked except for diapers, my son was tied like a pig for the slaughter. He tried to wriggle himself free as his shrill outcry chilled me through the bones.

The ill-lighted room, the unfamiliar apparatus, and the menacing instruments pulled close to his face contributed in no small measure to his fright. Since I was four months pregnant and had to step inside a radiation-free enclosure, I wasn't within arm's length of my son, who at that time, craved the touch and reassurance of a mother.

Pajo wept mournfully as he stared at me through thick glass windows. His eyes pleaded for help. His voice turned husky from too much crying. His exhausted and feverish body shivered from the cold.

Tears flowed as he repeatedly called out, "Mama! Mama!"

When I tried to soothe my baby with soft words of endearment, the rude technician gave me a piece of his mind. Pajo inclined his head towards my voice, and this bit of movement made it difficult for the man to take an angled x-ray shot.

The sight of my restrained son was more than I could take. The operator treated him like a dog in a short leash. Out of compassion for Pajo's miserable state, I dissolved in bitter tears. I heaved and sobbed unashamedly. I let my son know that my love

MENU 6: STRENGTH IN SUFFERING

went out to him—that I suffered alongside him, and that his torment was mine too.

During this dark hour, God unmasked a different facet to His nature—His sensitivity to the human condition is so intense that He too weeps.

The Book of John gives us an account of the death of Lazarus and the emotion Jesus openly displayed among the Bethany crowd. Lazarus had already been entombed for four days. Many skeptics believed Jesus was too late to be the day's hero.

An extract from John chapter 11 reads:

> When Mary reached the place where Jesus was and saw him, she fell at his feet and said, "Lord, if you had been here, my brother would not have died."
>
> When Jesus saw her weeping, and the Jews who had come along with her also weeping, he was deeply moved in spirit and troubled. "Where have you laid him?" he asked.
>
> "Come and see, Lord," they replied.
>
> Jesus wept.
>
> Then the Jews said, "See how he loved him!" (John 11:32–36)

Let me emphasize this poignant fragment that is often skipped over—"...he was deeply moved ..."

The sentimental undercurrent was surprising. Jesus was not a stoic, distant God after all! He was not a cold and dispassionate onlooker who didn't understand grief. I could almost picture His quivering lips, reddening eyes, and flushed face as He asked to see Lazarus' remains.

And when His sorrow reached a crescendo that it burst the well of empathy inside His divinely tender heart, Jesus did the unprecedented.

He wept!

Jesus' vision clouded and oozed liquid without inhibitions. Releasing His bitterness over the loss of a beloved, He joined Martha and Mary in their open laments.

Imagine! The mighty, all-knowing Author of all things did what we thought only humans could do. It was counterintuitive. For why did God, who had power to re-create anything, drop a tear over something He could easily fix? How could a lofty, unreachable deity descend to our level and cry?

As I watched my inconsolable son duke out his life's first battle, the vision of Jesus sobbing over Lazarus lingered in my mind. This time, though, His heart didn't bleed over His best friend in Bethany. He fast-forwarded two thousand years later and wept once again—this time, in a cold hospital, over a distraught mother and her fragile baby.

It stands to reason that Jesus who was moved with pity over my trepidation also weeps over yours.

Have you fallen into hard times?

Are you, perhaps, reeling from some personal calamity, and your pierced heart is so poisoned that you can't bring yourself to pray?

Do not be discouraged! There's good news in the horizon. You just moved Heaven with your doleful tears, and God's hand is reaching out to set things right. What your lips couldn't form in words, your groans clearly spelled out for the Lord to read.

Therefore, wait patiently. God's glory will be revealed soon. You need only to honour Him with your hopeful silence.

MENU 6: STRENGTH IN SUFFERING

Your tear-jerking sorrows grieve the Lord with the same severity. Through the tenderness of His nature, He too shares the encumbrances of your misfortune. He cries with you when words are inadequate. He suffers when you are so numb and detached that you cannot kneel within reach of His touch.

God cries not because He is helpless to alter the outcome of your trial. He suffers not because He is powerless to extricate you from the entanglements of the train wreck you caused.

He cries only for one reason ... that you may realize you are not alone.

You are not on a solitary journey towards your condemnation. God is right beside you with a rope to pull you out of your black, bottomless pit. And nothing can break this affinity with your Lord.

In the quietness of the night, when the darkness of your circumstance leaves nothing else but tears of torment, know that God weeps with you.

He weeps—because He loves.

> I will exalt you, Lord,
> for you lifted me out of the depths
> and did not let my enemies gloat over me.
> Lord my God, I called to you for help,
> and you healed me
> ... weeping may stay for the night,
> but rejoicing comes in the morning.
> Psalm 30:1-2, 5

Chapter 37

Running on Empty

When my kids were still toddlers, our home operated like a three-ring circus. There was never a dull moment with my two babies—Chiara, "The Young" and Pajo, "The Restless". As a mother of three vivacious kids, all I could do was manage chaos, facilitate damage control, and check that scrapes and bruises were limited to five episodes a day.

Since my son learned to walk, I swapped bywords from "patience is a virtue" to "patience is a myth." It was impossible to establish a routine schedule, so I wised up and expected the unexpected.

One afternoon, I was busily sautéing when eight-month-old Chiara cried, begging for a burp. I picked her up, balanced her wriggling form on one hip, and continued cooking when I heard a loud crash from the living room.

My son's muffled "uh-oh" and ensuing silence pushed the alarm bells in my head. I knew he was up to something, but I didn't want to know what catastrophe it was.

MENU 6: STRENGTH IN SUFFERING

However, true to form, my eldest daughter squealed on him. "Mama, Pajo destroyed your plant!" Colleen testified. "He pulled the roots out. All the dirt's on the carpet."

Turning to his brother, she said, "Pajo! Look at that mess!"

I was afraid to look. My hands were already full; I didn't appreciate another chore in my to-do list. I wondered how badly a two-year-old could trash a pot of primrose. The flamingo pink blooms were a Valentines Day gift from my husband, barely two days ago.

Before I could plug the vacuum, Chiara vomited and covered her face and both our clothes with spit-up milk. The nauseating odor overpowered the smell of burnt food.

Dinner!

I totally forgot the onions and garlic I was cooking. Unattended on the pan, it had sizzled to a nasty charcoal black!

In the meantime, Colleen and her carpool buddy finished up their macaroni and cheese snack. They left behind a stack of pots, cups, and bowls for me to wash.

Chiara twisted again in my arms, now begging for a bath and a fresh change of diapers. Pajo, who discovered that potted plants were no fun, ran off to tinker with the water dispenser. He pressed down both knobs and flooded the kitchen floor with filtered water.

In the midst of all the hurry-scurry, the phone rang and a thickly-accented woman drove straight to the point.

"We're conducting a research on the feeding patterns of children less than two years old. I'll just take ten to fifteen minutes of your time. Are you the mother of …?"

"Three monsters," I wanted to butt in. But then I realized she said ten to fifteen minutes! Are you kidding me? I wanted to scream. I couldn't even take two seconds of my bathroom privilege to empty my bladder!

The relentless demands on at-home mothers like me could be overwhelming to the point of neurosis. And it didn't help that I had to spend the better half of a day scrounging around the house for our keys which Pajo playfully hid inside his daddy's shoe. It didn't make my load any lighter when I had to fish a baby bottle from inside the toilet bowl. It didn't help that Colleen couldn't figure the difference between the hamper and the floor, nor the difference between a coat-hanger and the doorknob.

Really! I would have been a proponent of the evolutionary theory if Charles Darwin said mothers could diversify into a four-armed species to survive the multitasking challenge.

I worked my fingers to the bone while raising three hyperactive kids. There were days when I was so exhausted, I could only cry. With Pajo's and Chiara's wailing, we formed a cacophonous choir.

I hungered for pause, wishing badly to zone out, shut off the noise, and be irresponsible for a change.

More than once, I ask God, "Who takes care of the caregiver? Who'll take care of me?"

One evening, God gave me the chance to refuel my empty tank and restore my emotional balance. After worship services, I stayed behind to have some quiet time in the church. All the parishioners had gone home, and the early darkness of the winter evening paved the way for deep contemplation.

As I knelt on the pews and looked up at the huge cross hanging on the altar, tears flooded my eyes.

The silence was soothing.

The gentle dimness was comforting.

For once, no child clung to my skin. No errand hung on my shoulders. I was alone with God—and I felt consoled.

I didn't have to utter a word. My sighs and tears were enough for God. He understood my needs. And He gave me the tranquility I sought.

MENU 6: STRENGTH IN SUFFERING

I was running on empty, but God, who knew what to do with every weary traveller, rekindled my lost fortitude.

Friend, are you perhaps running on empty too?
Have you lost steam?
Does it feel like a truckload sits upon your chest, and you can't breathe under the crushing weight? You didn't get a death sentence, but your anxiety feels just as heavy.
Are you immobilized by your burdens, stuck in an uncomfortable spot, and unable to cut yourself loose? Believe that the Lord put you there. He brings you into an entanglement that you can't unbraid on your own so that you'll nod a yes when He says, "Come."
Jesus says,

> "Come to me, all you who are weary and burdened, and I will give you rest. Take my yoke upon you and learn from me, for I am gentle and humble in heart, and you will find rest for your souls. For my yoke is easy and my burden is light." (Matthew 11:28–30)

An easy yoke.
A light burden.
And rest for the weary soul.
Jesus spoke these most soothing words in Scripture. You can almost experience the freedom and relief even as you read it. That being so, wrap your mind around these verses when encouragement is in short reserve.
The God of comfort invites you to come because He alone can reshape you back into form. No matter what kind of trouble depletes you to a vulnerable clump, He can restore. If it is a fractured relationship that unglues you, He can repair.

God rescues all you who call upon His mercy and grace. He resuscitates you, dear burned-out worker, and freshens you up with greater endurance.

He recoups what you counted as loss. He multiplies and enlarges what He returns to show you the extent of His generosity.

Those who have fallen into moral corruption, He regenerates into newness of life.

He reclaims the rights which arrogant powers ripped off from your person.

He melts your stony heart—stiffened by the consequences of sin—and recreates it with the warmth of His forgiveness to show you His magnanimity.

God can do all these ... and more.

Therefore, trust that whatever exhausted you, He can set right.

Weary soul, touch base with the Lord for your rest. Carry on a conversation with Him who wants to be inseparable from you. If you should gamble your life, gamble it on the Lord who will never waste the risk you took when you sought Him out.

When your world seems to cave in, give yourself permission to cry. Acknowledge that you don't have a grip on your life unless God grips you. There is nothing that troubles you which God can't mend.

Whatever it is that broke you spiritually, messed you up emotionally, or violated you physically, the Lord of restoration can heal.

Return to your rest, my soul,
for the Lord has been good to you.
Psalm 116:7

The FRUIT OF character is best nurtured under THE cultivating, SCRAPING PRESSURE OF the Great Gardener's RAKE

Chapter 38

Are We There Yet?

The weather was perfect for a trip to the mountains. The sky was clear and the air crisp. Though frost covered the roadside, no fog shrouded the spectacular view from the highway.

For the first few minutes, my little girl sat quietly in the passenger seat. As the car shifted to high gear, her eyes moved back and forth with unmasked enthusiasm.

As time dragged on, however, Colleen could no longer hush up her bubbling excitement. She looked out the window and waited for the evidence of urban living to yield to the rough foliage and steep elevation that defined our destination.

Dozens of times she asked, "What time is it?"

But more often than that, like a monotonous refrain, she kept saying over and over, "Are we there yet, Mama? Are we there yet?"

The freeway was clear, so travel time was cut back to just a little over an hour. It wasn't much of a wait, but the hundred-kilometer-per-hour speedometer reading wasn't fast enough for a kid who was anxious to try the massive Skyride. Colleen wanted to get

MENU 6: STRENGTH IN SUFFERING

a bird's eye view of Grouse Mountains' Douglas-fir-covered terrain and the picturesque Gulf Islands in the distance. In her opinion, minor spurts of impatience could be pardoned today because the thrill of backcountry hiking and outdoor ice skating with friends was just too hard to contain.

Are we there yet?

The words throbbed in my head as I thought of my own travels with the Lord. I am nowhere close to where I want to be. Truth be told, I feel like I'm not even moving. My life has been trapped in a school zone, with the cruise control programmed to drive no faster than thirty kilometers per hour.

Like my daughter, I have become an impatient passenger. I judge my driver to be a turtle who hampers my progress. I wish God is an ambulance paramedic who rushes to my desired destination in Guinness-world-record time.

I know it is arrogance, but sometimes, I assume He's crawling—purposely choosing jammed roads over speedways, and spacing me a mile behind my peers. I believe I have the muscle to do better navigation, if only I can fire the Driver from the job.

Through twenty shadowy years, life dealt me with many thumbs-down, slaps on the face, and forfeited opportunities. With the fusion of rejection and endless waiting, my dreams became too untouchable—it was delusional for me to even hope.

However, God helped me understand that no matter how long-winded the pilgrimage, I'm still a step ahead of where I was yesterday. I'm never stuck in the same pothole. With a little vision fine-tuning, it is possible to see the advantages behind God's dirt road detour plan.

"Are we there yet?"

This is a common question you too may have asked the Lord innumerable times. You wonder, when will life get any better?

When will healing happen? How long must you wait before you get off the shortlist and clinch the decent-paying job?

How much more patience do you need to wring out of your guts? How many more scrapes can your shoulders take before God lifts the weight of the cross?

When will your heartbreak give way to hope? When will the weeping, withered winter end?

When will the Lord of the Harvest enlarge your territory and replenish what the locusts of poverty have destroyed?

Will life change gears and shift to highways of blessing? You ask, "Oh God, am I even there yet?"

Questions. Questions.

I, too, had so many of these questions. Yet, instead of answers, God bounced back to me another question.

"Will you continue loving and serving me even if you don't receive what you want?"

That was a tough one!

In the beginning, when life was undisturbed, the journey was cushiony in its snugness, and we coasted on Easy Street, I said without qualms—

"Of course, Lord! What kind of a question is that? You know, I'll love and serve you forever. You don't even have to ask!"

I was such a knucklehead for saying so!

God forced this over-confidence through a stress test to show me the emptiness of my speech. My spiel had no meat. No backbone. No strength. It was all air!

In the years that followed, suffering came in a series. Feasts turned to famine. Plans misfired. Dreams thinned out to nothingness. "I quit!" became the banner cry. Discouragement and debts crowed their irksome, scraping tunes each sunrise. Hope was sucked into a cosmic vacuum—too far out in the heavens to even smell.

MENU 6: STRENGTH IN SUFFERING

Years dragged. The proverbial "light at the end of the tunnel" didn't show up.

Life became tiring.

Depression set in.

Relationships turned nasty.

Prayers felt dry.

This went on and on. Then God asked again, "Will you continue loving and serving Me even if you don't receive what you want?"

My "yes" didn't slide from my tongue as fast as the first one did. The voice was too feeble, even a whisper was blaring. Tears just fell, accompanied by many moans which I hoped God decoded as "yes".

This entire picture, the Bible has a label for it. In the beginning, I had no idea what the word meant, but I remember, it sounded really rotten. Pastors often used it to describe Job.

What was it called again?

Long-suffering.

See? Sounds nasty, doesn't it?

The name alone conjures bleak images of a nail that pierces without letup. It is anguish without relief. Prolonged cross without deliverance. A crown of glory delayed.

Long-suffering. By my crude definition, it is the polar opposite of happiness.

Friend, are you perhaps strained by a long-drawn-out battle? Is your patience already stretched to a thin, taut line?

Don't give up.

You are not the lost cause God threw into the throes of futility. There's a reason why the answer to prayer has not reached your door. God is not done yet, so hang around. Anticipate what He will soon do to deliver you.

Right about the twentieth year of my waiting on the Lord, when the gravity of the cross hunched my back and I wanted to quit, a profound thing happened. I witnessed a lunar eclipse! Right in front of my bedroom window, on a cloudless autumn night, the full glory of the moon shone on my face.

At three in the early morning, while the whole city was asleep, I stared up at the resplendent transformation, pensive in reflection. I cried to the Lord for help and asked Him why He seemed so far away. Uninhibited in prayer, I let go of the tears and snapped at God like a child with temper tantrums.

It was at this depth of misery that I suddenly felt God's calming presence. While the Earth slowly cast its shadow upon the moon, merging it into the blackness of space, the Lord impressed his word upon my heart. His voice was unmistakable, mellow against my inner turbulence.

"Look at the sky," the Lord said. "Though invisible to the eye at the moment, you know the moon is still there. Right at the spot where you watched it disappear—cloaked by the shadows—the moon rests. So it is with your Father. Child, I never abandoned you. Believe in Me. Though wrapped in ambiguity, I am near. Though you do not perceive Me, I never leave your side."

My long-suffering friend, be encouraged by these words. The Lord cast His shadow upon your life to teach you a lesson. He eclipsed on your soul so that there will be more of Him and less of the selfish ego within you.

While you seem lost in the shadows, He is in fact reshaping beauty in you. Your umbra is the platform out of which glory will soon burst.

MENU 6: STRENGTH IN SUFFERING

Just as the moon is most sublime at the totality of the eclipse, bloody in its splendor, a rare honour to behold, so too will you be most beautiful while in the darkness of your storms. While clinging to God in your pain, depending on Him for dear life, you become one with Him. Yours will thus be a soul awakened.

Through heartbreaks, you rise redeemed—transfigured in beauty!

Contrary to my original thought, there is immense joy in the pit of trial. It is possible to be happy in our defeat.

We can be content in scarcity.

And it is within our capacity to quash our jealousy in order not to begrudge those who surf the waves of material abundance.

When all's said and done, trial is still our best ally. For the fruit of character is best nurtured under the cultivating, scraping pressure of the Great Gardener's rake!

As God allows adversity to shake us up, He is in fact preparing us for His mission. He is laying in us a bedrock of discipline, humility, and detachment that will make us ready for greater work ahead.

God is in no hurry to finish what He has started. Preparations for His call may take years or a lifetime. It's possible we won't understand the direction He is taking until all are revealed in due season.

And so, are we there yet?

Perhaps, the answer may not be fully appreciated unless we accept the truth—God's timing and destination for us are different from what we plan for ourselves. His choices are far better than all the combined things for which we hunger!

Friend, unlike my daughter's field trip to Grouse Mountain, your life may not be headed towards captivating snowy peaks and mountain-top experiences. The Lord may not be cruising you through an ice-skating paradise of unlimited pleasure.

He may decide to take His sweet time, driving through zigzagged country roads, instead of transporting you in cozy, high-speed style.

It doesn't matter.

Because staying at the foot of the mountain produces equal joy. God's measured pace and deployment of pain bring to the surface the best virtues in every man.

There is empowerment in the wait.

And, ultimately, no matter how passive we judge God's stride to be, He is always prompt—accomplishing His anointed purpose in the appointed time.

```
       But as for me,
I watch in hope for the Lord,
I wait for God my Savior;
    my God will hear me.
         Micah 7:7
```

Chapter 39

The Litterbug, the Onlooker, & a Dose of Integrity

```
    Lord, who may dwell in your sacred tent?
     Who may live on your holy mountain?
        The one whose walk is blameless,
            who does what is righteous,
     who speaks the truth from their heart;
                 Psalm 15:1-2
```

While driving my daughter home from her bowling class, I rolled down my window and threw a wisp of hair into the blustery wind. The harmless act, though imperceptible to most, stirred a high-strung reaction from Colleen.

"Mama!" She almost yelled. "You littered!"

My jaw dropped. "Huh?" I feigned innocence. "That's just a tiny strand. What would that hurt?"

"You polluted the air!"

If not for the giggle she tried to muffle, I seriously thought a law enforcer was ready to slap me with handcuffs for dirtying the

MENU 7: GODLY CHARACTER

road with my hair. That afternoon, I realized curious eyes closely spied my every move. Really, a mother is never without stalkers!

My children were not the only sharp-eyed Sherlock snoops in town. I once played the part and became a surveillance camera with klutzy knees and toes. I was one very pregnant and very insecure mommy then. Every pound of flesh in my body bulged to such extent that a mere sneeze could bust a seam. My swollen nose was a cross between a Roma tomato in size and beetroot in color. Just to hide the dark lines on my neck, I favored turtleneck pullovers and scarves even in summer!

Insofar as I was overdue with the baby's delivery, we thought it best to stroll in the mall to induce labor. However, because of sporadic Braxton Hicks contractions, I rested on the benches at short intervals while my husband and daughter loitered nearby. It was on such occasion that I saw Alvin's eyes drift innocently towards an eye-catching, breathing, life-sized Barbie doll. The tall lady who stepped out of the elevator had all the good genes of a cheerleader and the vital statistics of a swimsuit model. Her skin looked creamy like vanilla pudding, and she walked with peacock poise. Her ash-blonde curls looked stunning compared to the chaotic haystack on my head that could be mistaken for a pigeon's nest!

Alvin did nothing to destroy his self-respect nor taint his love for God. As a man who upheld his integrity, it was farthest from his mind to cheat. For all I know, he might not even be admiring. But he looked. And for an insanely jealous wife heavy with child, that was the only ingredient needed to kindle self-doubt.

We never really know which one of our actions snatches another's attention. For me, it was my husband's harmless microsecond gawk. For my daughter, it was my littering. Some people may be peeved by simple mannerisms or a mindless comment. A neat freak may go ballistic over the carpet of weeds on the backyard which you refuse to mow. Another person may be annoyed by someone's narcissistic lifestyle.

Suffice it to say, we carry our testimonies with us wherever we go. Our lives are peeled and naked, open to public scrutiny at any random instant. Depending on the measure of honesty and moral purity our lives mirror, our influence can swing in either direction—good or bad.

There's a magnetism in each one of us that draws people. The question is—are we attracting them for all the right reasons? Are we leading others towards holiness? Or are we trapping them in a short-term, razzle-dazzle life, drained of meaningful substance?

Keep this in mind—we leave indelible impressions upon those who witness our dealings. In all our interactions, we are twice accountable. We are answerable to God and responsible for the people we sway. Whether we live to agitate or to inspire, we must take our accountability with serious, sober reflection. Let us leave an impact that's worthy of our Christian identity—for that is our calling!

The apostle Peter wrote in his epistle,

> But in your hearts revere Christ as Lord. Always
> be prepared to give an answer to everyone who
> asks you to give the reason for the hope that you
> have. But do this with gentleness and respect,
> keeping a clear conscience, so that those who speak
> maliciously against your good behavior in Christ
> may be ashamed of their slander. (1 Peter 3:15–16)

What do we learn from this verse?
Integrity!
By acting according to the dictates of a clean conscience, we silence our accusers. Integrity has a way of confounding people's frivolous judgments. It beats groundless presumptions to a pulp.

MENU 7: GODLY CHARACTER

Analyzing the Barbie story with logic and caution, I realized that Alvin had no choice but to look at the woman. She passed in front of him! Unless my husband intended to bump or trip all over her, how could he not look?

So what went wrong? My innuendos! I misread the situation and added malice where malice didn't thrive! My jealous eyes jumped at baseless conclusions, and these infected my heart with prejudice.

However, my husband's integrity—synchronized with his faith—stood in his defense. My blind judgment couldn't hold water against a man who honoured truth. God approved him as one who walked surefootedly and who diligently avoided wicked, corkscrew paths. Alvin had nothing to be ashamed of because he lived with authenticity. Through his uprightness, the tongue of the accuser was gagged to silence.

Integrity isn't a virtue you can enshroud in secrecy. A person whose foundation is built upon integrity will always broadcast his honesty and virtue by merely living.

You can't fake it.

You can't falsify it.

Even a person who follows duplicitous standards in his life—who masks his fraudulent intent with a cloak of sweetness—will sooner or later risk exposure.

This is because true integrity breeds consistency.

What lies inside your heart—your true nature—will find expression through your speech and behaviour.

What boils inside you will reveal itself as steam.

As it is written in Scripture,

> Whoever walks in integrity walks securely, but whoever takes crooked paths will be found out.
> (Proverbs 10:9)

I remember the day I learned what duplicity meant and what bitter aftertaste it left. A retail shop announced a 75 percent liquidation sale on all the merchandise they carried. The business went bankrupt and had to hollow its shelves within a month. I visited the store on the third day of the sale, knowing that these grab-and-go events depleted stocks pretty quickly.

I weaved through the crowd of shoppers and lugged my overflowing basket to the till. As the cashier rang up my bill, I realized that every item I bought was charged at full price. Thinking that it was a scanning error, I called the manager's attention.

"Aren't these on sale?" I asked politely.

"Oh no," the manager replied. "These are all regular price."

"I thought the ad said that everything's 75 percent off from now until the end of the month," I mildly protested without sounding pushy.

"Well, we just decided to do the sale in stages. You know ... uhm ... maybe 50 percent off towards the end of the month, then 75 percent when the stocks are almost gone."

What a double-dealing marketing ploy! My mouth flung open in unbelief. I forced a smile even though I felt a neurogenic shock coming.

To add to my emotional trauma, the manager reasoned, "We don't want the company to lose more money, right?"

"Then you should have advertised it as such!" The thought thundered in my head, but I was too diplomatic to retort.

What a disappointment!

Sadly, the world we live in often trades integrity for profit. People progressively exult Machiavellian ethics. Morality becomes irrelevant in the face of greedy, object-oriented gain.

Businesses maneuver policies to take the upper advantage. Men don't live up to what they say. Promises are worthless. Warranties on fine print are doubtful. Marriage vows are broken.

MENU 7: GODLY CHARACTER

Covenants are suspended on the basis of many caveats. Deception is a game ... and people find it exciting.

To sum it up—integrity has become a lost art!

But not for us Christians who are called to be different.

Friends, let us encourage one another to swim against the current even if it's an upstream struggle. Politically correct or not, the crowd is not always right. It is okay to be the nonconformist who upsets the standard and contradicts the flow. In fact, sometimes, this is the most righteous thing one can do.

God purposefully traced chalk marks around us to outline moral boundaries. Even if the world tries its hardest to erase them, these are lines we must not cross.

Soon, the day will be upon us. Soon, we'll stand before our Maker to take stock of how we lived. Get ready! He will test our hearts and weed out the iniquities.

We pray that, until then, we may remain incorruptible,
Unblemished,
Driven to a life of honour and purity,
Perfectly aligned with Christ,
Up to the very end.

> Finally, brothers and sisters,
> whatever is true,
> whatever is noble, whatever is right,
> whatever is pure, whatever is lovely,
> whatever is admirable —
> if anything is excellent or praiseworthy —
> think about such things.
> Philippians 4:8

Chapter 40

Just Pull the Plug

While working in the technical support department of an IT company, my husband received all types of inquiries from people of diverse backgrounds. In most occasions, he responded to legitimately complex procedural issues. Other times, the phone calls were plain silly.

During one of his shifts, Alvin received a call from a technologically challenged client. Quite advanced in age and apparently fiddling with a computer for the first time, the man didn't know how to shut down his system. The program malfunctioned, the screen froze, and he wanted to restart.

"Why don't you try pressing Control-Alt-Delete," Alvin suggested. This familiar solution launches a pop-up menu with a shut down option the man can easily click.

"What's that?" By the client's tone, it seemed as if Alvin addressed him in Aramaic language.

Alvin patiently walked him through the procedure. "First, press Control."

MENU 7: GODLY CHARACTER

After a brief moment of silence on the other end of the line, his client said, "I can't find it on the screen."

"Sir, it's not on the screen. It's on your keyboard, and it's spelled C-T-R-L."

"Okay, I found it. What's next?"

"Look for the Delete button. It's usually on the right side of the keyboard," Alvin instructed. The man took a couple of minutes before he stumbled on the right key.

Alvin continued, "Okay, sir? Now press Alt. That's A-L-T. Alpha. Lima. Delta."

"Okay," the man acknowledged.

"Now press them all together."

"At the same time?" The man sounded impervious to persuasion. He didn't trust his coach one bit.

"Yes, sir. Please press all the buttons at the same time."

Alvin heard faint scratchy noises on his headset. It sounded like the guy was wrestling with the keyboard. After a lengthy wait, the customer concluded, "It's not working!"

Puzzled, Alvin asked the caller to try the process again. The client, who was beginning to have a short fuse, replied, "It's really no use. It doesn't work."

As an afterthought, the elderly man said, "Wait a minute! I'll ask my wife to help me."

Before Alvin could say anything, the client hollered in the background, "Emma!"

After snuffing a few exasperated breaths, he went back to the phone and explained, "I need an extra hand to push down the keys."

By then, Alvin wondered what kind of bizarre computer his client fiddled with. "Sir," he said politely. "You only need to press down three buttons."

"Three? What do you mean three? I have to press five!"

"It's just Control, Alt, and Delete." Alvin wanted to make sure the guy picked up the right commands.

"Yes, I hear you," the septuagenarian was adamant. "Control, A, L, T, and Delete. Now count that. That's five!"

Alvin struggled to suppress his laughter. He didn't want to offend the awfully disoriented man. Adopting another approach, he put forward another two-cent proposition, "Okay, sir. Why don't we try something else. Can you access the restart button on your computer?"

The client must have only taken a perfunctory glance for he said, "I can't find it. I don't know where it is."

Alvin peeked at the clock and realized he already spent more than an hour with the same caller. The company's quality control and queue standards encouraged them to limit the service to thirteen minutes per client.

Thirteen minutes … max!

Unresolved cases beyond the target would reflect badly on the employee's performance evaluation. In spite of this fact, Alvin walked the caller through his problems—exhibiting patience and good nature along the way.

"Do you know where the on and off button is, sir? Can you press that instead?"

The man obeyed. Even so, whatever it is he pushed, he still came back with the same report, "That didn't work either."

Now what kind of computer wouldn't close after you force down the off button?

Pressed for time and finally running out of smart ideas, Alvin blurted out, "Just pull the plug, sir! Just pull the plug!"

I totally cracked up when my husband came home with this knee-slapping story. I'm a technically disadvantaged person as well. But I never thought there ever lived anyone slower in picking up directions than me. I marveled at how gracefully my husband

MENU 7: GODLY CHARACTER

handled the client who, by the way, was already snappish and prickly by the turn of the hour.

As I replayed the scene in my mind's eye, it dawned on me that just like the uncomprehending caller, we too are very slow on the uptake.

We are so slow in trusting God's provisions but too quick to bite our nails over the avalanche of bills.

We're slow on the apologies and the remorse, but we raise lame excuses for sinful behaviour in a flick.

We're slow in obeying God's will, but we're lightning fast in taking control of every ball game.

Like the elderly man, we are headstrong know-it-alls who insist on pressing five buttons even when God teaches us to press only three. We feel more comfortable getting an extra hand from other people although we're already directly hooked up in the prayer line, receiving heavenly wisdom that is as clear as daylight.

Nevertheless, despite our turtle-like strides and foolish determination, the Lord is ever so patient. He points us in the right direction. He picks us up from the muddy potholes in which we sloppily fall. He waits until we learn our lessons—even if we take longer than the "thirteen-minute rule".

God never runs out of ideas. Even when our brains are too dense to pick up, He'll still find ways for us to understand His drift. He'll speak in a language we can grasp. He'll never hide His wisdom from seekers of the truth.

Best of all, even when we drive him crazy, God will never pull the plug!

The Lord won't suggest an instant remedy just to keep our mouths shut in two shakes. He never dreams of getting rid of us though we call Him repeatedly. We have a God who already made up His mind to stay on the line with us for as long as it takes.

Do you know why God goes through all these troubles for the sake of slow-witted people like us?

Because He is a patient God, and He trains us by His example.

You see, none of us are born patient. None of us possess the innate ability to brush aside discomfort without the slightest whimper. None of us can calmly control our tempers, overlook inconveniences, and accept tragedies graciously.

Admittedly, we consider it an unnatural reaction when others shrug off delays without being upset. Who can stay cool when the wait is taking forever? What kind of oddball doesn't get agitated after he has tried a hundred times to explain the same thing to a person who still doesn't get it? Who remains sedate after a disappointment?

No one!

That said, patience is a quality that can only be mastered through Christ. If left to our own devices, we don't have what it takes to forebear without asserting our importance and rank. Without the grace of Christ, we do not have the backbone to endure opposition.

Humanly speaking, to pardon an offender seems ridiculous. Rather than reining in the urge to retaliate, we foolishly rattle our complaints. We feel vindicated after we give people a piece of our minds. In the face of irritations, we succumb to crankiness and all sorts of negativity because we are naturally impatient.

However, as children of God, we are called to grow in restraint. We, who bear the image of Christ, are called to develop calmness in spirit. The apostle Paul encourages,

> Therefore, as God's chosen people, holy and dearly loved, clothe yourselves with compassion, kindness, humility, gentleness and patience. (Colossians 3:12)

MENU 7: GODLY CHARACTER

It is our Christian duty to carry goodness as a baggage wherever we go. We embrace this call to holiness because an eternity with the Lord is exponentially better than winning points over petty arguments. We do not want to gamble our eternal salvation over a passing nuisance we refuse to bypass.

The next time you want to cave in to bouts of temper, think again. At what expense are you sweating the small stuff?

This might be a rude awakening for you, but let's deal with the truth. My friend, wrap your mind around this domino principle.

Every outburst of impatience dims your view of heaven. You take a step backwards—away from God's approval—when irritability defines your nature.

This is because impatience breeds anger.

Anger dematerializes love.

And a soul without love alienates himself from the Lord who is Love personified!

There's no way you can circumvent these cause-and-effect linkages.

So let me ask you again: At what expense are you sweating the small stuff? What do you stand to gain by unleashing your impatience over life's daily strains and pains, if you lose Christ along the way?

Is it worth the wager?

A person's wisdom yields patience;
it is to one's glory to overlook an offense.
Proverbs 19:11

From where the limitation of humanity begins, divinity takes off. Be Still! [THERE IS A] clearly-sketched plan behind the delay.

CHAPTER 41

On My Own Hiking Shoes

He says, "Be still, and know that I am God;
I will be exalted among the nations,
I will be exalted in the earth."
Psalm 46:10

During the fourteenth season of the reality TV show, *The Amazing Race*, participating teams flew into the hinterlands of Germany, in the picturesque state of Bavaria. Riding on enclosed gondolas, they reached the peak of a steep, rocky mountain where they faced their next challenge.

In the roadblock, aptly named "Fly Like An Eagle", team players had to run off the edge of a precipice and paraglide in tandem with an experienced guide from a scary 6,000-foot elevation, down into the green valley below. Meanwhile, the other partner would descend the mountain through a cable car and wait for his teammate near the landing spot. Those who wished to opt out of the spine-tingling parachute drop may take the 60-minute hiking trail down the slope.

MENU 7: GODLY CHARACTER

In this episode, most of the teams initially chose what seemed like the quickest and easiest route—the foot-launched, free-flying aircraft. However, turbulent winds made piloting the fabric canopy a high-risk sport. Understandably, paraglide instructors refused to fly until the atmospheric instability calmed down to a breeze.

Mel, an elderly player in this season's race, took the flight challenge for his son, Mike. Due to excessive wind speed that showed no signs of abating, he waited. So did the rest of the teams who wanted to paraglide. They all waited. Quickly, the clock ticked, but the gustiness lingered for what seemed like an eon.

Impatient to win the race, one by one, the players bailed out. They took the alternative course and journeyed on foot. Unable to keep still, their flurried minds decided to cede control of the situation to their own two hiking shoes.

When asked, "Why don't you stay?" Victoria, one of the racers, answered, "Because I have to move on."

Anxious to hold the reins and take charge of their game instead of risk the future to chance, almost everyone followed suit.

However, because of an injury from a previous challenge, poor Mel admitted, "It will cripple me to run down that hill."

As more of the latecomers caught up with the waiting father-and-son team, and as more of the younger players left the peak to beat the path, Mel's helplessness deflated his optimism. Repeatedly he whispered, "I made a bad decision. Oh no, I lost!"

Though worried about the possibility of elimination, Mel said to his son, "I can't pray for divine intervention. God has enough to do."

Admiring the Bavarian Alps with its autumn colors and the valley that swept away in every direction below, Mel said, "I can just thank you for this beautiful place. Thank you for having a son that is so great. I can't pray for God to intervene on my behalf with wind. But if it changes, I will be very grateful."

Though not intended as a prayer, God heard the plea. Immediately, the wind vane stopped stirring. The trees slowed their rustling. The uncalculated divine intervention peeked through the skies, and the miraculous intruded the hearts of two abandoned men.

Recovering his paraglide harness while delirious with joy, Mel soared like an eagle and outdistanced those who feverishly took the foot race.

Just like the *Amazing Race* competitors, many of us scoot through life like it is a marathon. We're constantly on pins and needles, impatient to see results. There are high-strung players among us who believe waiting is not in the program.

They think downtimes and roadblocks are an abomination.

Keeping pause is a waste of opportunity.

Fighting chances drop with every second of inactivity.

And gearing up on our own two hiking shoes is a sure formula for success.

However, there are interludes in our lives when taking upper command of the situation is not feasible. Turbulence hits, and we are helpless to subdue it. We are forced to stop.

Events do not follow our planned routes.

The narrative thread breaks with an unexpected scene-stealer.

And our money, talents, and business connections cannot bail us out.

Yet, like Mel, we think that disturbing God with our frivolous requests is an inexcusable intrusion. God is busy. He can't be bothered.

Psalm 46:10 says, "... Be still, and know that I am God ..."

Be still—two tiny words, almost negligible when standing apart. Yet, put together, they deliver an emphatic blow!

MENU 7: GODLY CHARACTER

Be still.

You can almost hear someone whisper ever so delicately, "Sssshhhhh... be quiet, child."

Be still.

It is a flaming scarlet flag waved at your face in warning—"Stop dead in your tracks right now! Calm down and don't even wiggle your ears."

Today's verse is an encouragement to sit on the mountain slope to enjoy the glorious alpine view. This post-it note has "pause" scribbled in glaring red ink.

God is not asking you to be idle and nap the whole day. "Be still" is not a whitewash to dress up one's laziness. Instead, it is an invitation to abandon your fears, to lean life's heaviness upon the broadness of God's shoulders. It is an appeal to steady the commotion in your mind, to declutter the heart, and to ease the tense muscles on your nape.

God has everything under control.

His marquee signboard reads, "Let go of the struggle. It is useless to panic."

Psalm 46:10 is a reminder that an all-knowing God takes you seriously when you whisper a wish—even when your prologue is incomplete and you can't phrase your prayers right.

Yes, know that God is God. You don't always have to be on top of your game. It is alright to fall apart, to be frenetic. Because from where the limitation of humanity begins, divinity takes off.

Be still. There is reason why the wind blows.

There is a clearly-sketched plan behind the delay.

And those who patiently wait witness the miracle.

Chapter 42

Earthen Wares

What prompts pastors, evangelists, and missionaries to say "yes" when God calls? Are they confident because they know they are smart and can jump over the barriers of public ministry without opposition?

I wonder.

Do they step up to the plate because they possess unique gifts that fit the job description? Perhaps the gift of gab and persuasion?

How does God choose harvesters for His vineyard? Does God read a hiring manual or consult self-help, how-to books? Does He follow a step-by-step selection process? Does He use a prequalification blueprint that sifts away the amateurs and recruits only the competent?

What kind of people does God tap to spread the Gospel? Is there a specific IQ or talent requirement? Perhaps a certain social stature? Or maybe a knockout, easy-on-the-eyes type of physicality to catch the crowd's attention?

MENU 7: GODLY CHARACTER

Today's society dictates stiff standards in practically everything. To gain entry into the employment sector, people parade training certificates, diplomas, awards, and trophies. School admissions and scholarships bank on test scores and academic transcripts. Doctors plaster a mosaic of degrees and fellowship credentials on their clinic walls.

In business, politics, or even churches, only the silver-tongued deliver speeches. Uneducated people rarely, if at all, make it to the corporate fast lane. The world demands excellence. And those who do not match up to the ideal are trimmed like deadwood. This is how the world's philosophy operates.

However, if we pit our paradigm against God's yardstick, we will be shamed by the divergence—for God doesn't pick servants from a motorcade of pop idols and superstars. He finds treasures in what the world considers a worthless heap.

Right in the middle of the dump, He spots a sparkling gem of opportunity. God singles out the best candidates for His mission from out of the commonplace—people with weak knees, trembling voices, fractured reputation, and blemished character.

God endorses the disqualified and entrusts to them the impossible. He even prefers the hesitant so that He can loosen their stiff necks and mold them to obedience.

God chooses the five o'clock workers, those doomed to failure, so that none may look down on the weak. Through them, He displays His glory, so none may claim credit for the victory.

If you want to understand what I mean, take a peek at God's dubious choices—

There was Moses, the murderer, whose momentary surge of pride and lapse of faith in the wilderness at Meribah, earned for him the cruel punishment of non-entry into the Promised Land (Numbers 20:7–13).

Aaron, his articulate orgy leader, who caved in to peer pressure and shaped the infamous Golden Calf (Exodus 32:1–6).

Jonah, the crabby and insubordinate prophet who had a personal encounter with a Moby Dick ancestor.

There was lustful King David, whose conquests included not just nations and Philistine armies, but a string of wives and concubines as well.

There was Solomon, who walked the same polygamist corridor as his father and who was eventually swayed to worship foreign gods (1 Kings 11:1–6 and Nehemiah 13:26).

Jacob, the crafty con-artist who deceived Isaac, his blind aged father, and who swindled his brother Esau out of his rightful blessing (Genesis 27).

The parade goes on with Ruth, the cursed Moabite. Tactless and impulsive Peter, the fisherman. Paul, the Christian persecutor. Matthew, the Roman government's extortionist and Jewish social outcast.

All were untrained nobody's.

Certified by God.

Endowed with grace.

And transformed through His influence.

Consider the prophets. Not all of them were gifted with oratorical mastery. Not all the disciples were scholars who were knowledgeable in the laws of Moses.

Saints were not born with pre-manufactured halos. These average humans had the same quirks and failures that beleaguer us today. They were haunted by the same worries and stresses. They were so ordinary; they could get lost in a carpet of people.

Isn't it comforting to know that God's heroes were human in every way? That His saints were deficient too? Since these people also struggled with guilt and sin, we can identify with their lives. This makes our personal call to discipleship less frightening.

MENU 7: GODLY CHARACTER

God is still in the business of hand-picking the unqualified from among scraps left by modern-day big shots. He is still rummaging through dumpsters for the most imperfect stones He can polish into exquisite diamonds. He is sifting through dirt in active search of the cheapest earthen pot. And within this damaged and modest vessel, God abides Himself as the very treasure we preach.

Men are God's clay pots, made worthless and unimpressive by a magnetic attraction to sin. But no matter how often we flub, God uses us for His service. Ultimately, He is the Gospel message we convey.

In God's perspective, our brokenness is of no consequence. Personality flaws and lopsided preaching techniques count for nothing.

At the end of the day, it is not us, but God who should be the core of attention.

No matter how fancy the vessel may be, we remain just that—a vessel.

We are not the banner to be waved, not the message to be preached.

We are just the messengers.

Just rugged treasure-bearers.

MODERN-DAY CLAY POTS

There are dozens of characters in the Bible who are fitting examples of how God chooses the nameless nobody's. There are thousands more who live in our day and age. Unknowingly, you may elbow them inside a packed bus, or sit beside them at a movie theatre. You can't easily tell because these people love to serve the Lord in obscurity.

Once, I had the chance to ask a missionary friend, "How do you know if the Lord is calling you to serve? How sure are you that you're not just getting the wrong impressions?"

I didn't receive clear-cut answers. For unlike in Old Testament times when God's messages tailgate celestial audio-visuals, God is relatively quiet in our generation. His voice no longer rebounds from a pillar of cloud or a burning bush as He did with Moses. He doesn't broadcast His breaking news with a thunderclap, an earthquake, or a vision of supernatural beings. If He did, I bet even the most calm among us will freak out!

If only the Lord has a more direct approach, there won't be any room for second-guessing. We can easily catch the drift.

Today, when God sees it fit to make a statement, He can either be plain-spoken or mysteriously vague.

The Lord does not follow a set pattern when He reveals His plans. There are no stereotypes or formulas. When He calls, He may either break convention, like He did with Saul who was blinded by heavenly light on the road to Damascus (Acts 9); or He can encroach through the ordinary, like He did with Andrew and Peter who were fishing along the shores of the Sea of Galilee (Matthew 4:18–20).

In my family's case, we were confounded when the rough sketch of our future was exposed through daily chores.

Our story began one dull day when I complained, "When can we hire a housekeeper?"

We used to live in a country where middle- and upper-class families typically indulged in the services of paid househelp. Such pampered lifestyle was culturally the norm.

[329]

MENU 7: GODLY CHARACTER

However, for two years, my husband and I single-handedly balanced the household chores—from cooking, cleaning, buying groceries, hand-washing dishes, laundry, and ironing, to the spine-breaking chores like uprooting knee-high weeds in the backyard, disposing maggot-infested garbage, and unclogging the flood-prone sewers. These, of course, were on top of my roles as tutor and chauffeur to my daughter. You name the job and my calloused, dry hand gave evidence to these stunts.

It wasn't by preference that we put up with the trouble. It was by force of circumstance. From the moment our three former housekeepers left the city, all attempts at finding replacements were fruitless. Often, we initiated arrangements with new applicants, but midway through, negotiations flipped cold. Either the fickle-minded maid was a no-show or complications in her personal life discouraged her from pursuing employment.

Never before had a suitable match been as difficult to obtain. Surely, if God allowed it, the search for competent housekeepers wouldn't be as tough as digging diamonds in depleted Botswana mines.

God didn't assure us that rest was forthcoming. Like a riddle, He simply hinted, "Let this be your training."

"Training for what?"

Instead of a straight answer, He said, "Have I not commanded you? Be strong and courageous. Do not be afraid; do not be discouraged, for the Lord your God will be with you wherever you go" (Joshua 1:9).

On hindsight, the Lord had brought up the subject of fear for four consecutive years that I already started wondering, "What exactly am I afraid of? I'm not scared. Why does God keep warning me against fear if this isn't really a baggage for me right now?"

> "See, I am sending an angel ahead of you to guard
> you along the way and to bring you to the place I
> have prepared." (Exodus 23:20)

As I was randomly flipping through my Bible, this passage struck a pleasant chord in my heart. However, I didn't necessarily claim it as mine. Sure, it was a sweet promise. But I considered it way out of my element to assume I was going anywhere.

In due course, the Lord proved me wrong. While in deep meditation, He opened my eyes to a soul-stirring disclosure.

> "Go from your country, your people and your
> father's household to the land I will show you."
> (Genesis 12:1)

> "Move out of your boundaries. I will give you the
> toughness and courage to start again. Do not cling
> to the events of the past. Look ahead for I will do
> something new. If you won't take risks for Me, you
> won't do great things for the Kingdom. Are you
> willing to accept the invitation and confront the
> challenge?"

God had not even finished His monologue yet when I broke into an avalanche of tears. Swiftly, doubts I never thought I had cascaded in rapid progression. I've never relocated to a foreign land, and I couldn't imagine life disengaged from my relatives and friends.

No wonder the Lord spoke of courage with such urgency and clockwork regularity. He knew that the second His roadmap is unfolded, I would bulldoze Him with questions.

Where will we go? Why do we have to leave? How can this be possible when funds are in short supply? When shall all of these plans happen? What are we to do? Where will we work? How

MENU 7: GODLY CHARACTER

can our daughter grow up in a culture so alien to us? Would our spiritual life be drastically affected by our separation from Church ministry?

That day passed. Not a single question was answered. I just sobbed, and the Lord just watched ... quietly.

AN UNFIT EARTHEN WARE

During one prayer assembly attended by hundreds of Christians, the worship leader addressed a prophetic message to unknown recipients sitting in the auditorium. He felt the powerful prompting of the Holy Spirit although he didn't know who exactly needed to hear the revelation.

My husband and I stood among the crowd. At that precise moment, the Lord impressed the preacher's message in my heart as clearly as if He Himself engaged me in verbal conversation.

> "You shall be my couple in mission. The harvest is abundant but there are a few people who are willing to take the risk to share, the risk to help, the risk to give," says the Lord.

> "Consider it a great privilege that you are at the threshold of a great spiritual time. I called you not to become settlers in the comforts of your home. I called you to work in My vineyard. Make yourselves ready this year and in the coming years. Open your hearts to Me, to what I will tell you to do, to where I will send you to go.

God Is In The Kitchen

"You are meant to go into the deep waters. Set your sights beyond your shores, beyond your little cities and cast the nets there for a great harvest. I will send you to places you have never imagined to be there. Allow Me to work with you and through you, in ways you have never known before. Today, I lay a burden that will be heavy in your hearts."

No doubt, God snatched my attention. So radically, in fact, that I momentarily forgot where I was standing. With no regard for the people around me, I wept openly until my eyes puffed out.

I couldn't believe it! God had so many surprises on reserve, and it was just too much to digest in one sitting. His challenge drew out my apprehensions afresh.

Why us? We were not specialists of any sort. By what credentials did the Lord count us worthy to carry such a noble task? We do not have licenses for public speaking, no spectacular gifts that can convince people to listen.

Why me? I was just an ordinary housewife. I had such a pathetic handle on Scripture that I didn't even know Jesus was David's descendant! That's how awfully ignorant I was.

What right did I have to preach when I had humongous sins of my own which I wrestled with daily? I badgered God to pick somebody else who wasn't a failure like me.

Instantly, previous encounters with missionaries filtered through my memory. I recall one worship rally where a couple who flew home from Pakistan spoke about their struggles in a non-Christian region. The lecture was meant to quicken people's hearts and stoke the desire for missions.

I remember how my friend and I sat at the extreme end of the gym, giggling and whispering foolish ideas to each other. A reluctant audience, we mischievously discussed how receiving

MENU 7: GODLY CHARACTER

countries would deport us even if we volunteered our services—all because our vanity wouldn't permit us to ditch the hair dryer and branded wardrobe.

In a separate incident, I recall the send-off party we had for a woman who sacrificed her status and wealth in order to establish roots on foreign soil. She gambled her future without clues on the aftermath. With the weight of God's promise, she moved forward as a missionary for the Lord, with only heroism and stoutheartedness as her ammunition.

After her farewell speech, I congratulated this woman for her conviction and resilience. I even insisted, "I can never do what you're doing." For who would have the rashness to compromise their stability and purposely go out on a limb like that?

Against these backdrops, the question floated, "Why me, God? Aren't you making a colossal mistake here?"

Our family's future hung by a thread, and I felt a tightening in my stomach. I was shaken up ... and awkwardly out of joint.

Even so, while in prayer, the Lord continued to inject His message,

> "I have been using ordinary people for thousands of years. Why would I stop now? If you look through history, My work was not accomplished by great tribes but by humble and weak servants who were committed to Me. Look at Moses. He was hesitant and inarticulate but I used him to lead Israel to freedom. Look at the disciples I handpicked. They were not kings, rabbis, or officials of high political or social esteem. I called fishermen, farmers, and men of herds and flock to evangelize multitudes and to record My words. I call you because it is

My desire to choose 'the foolish things of the world to shame the wise' and the 'weak things of the world to shame the strong' (1 Corinthians 1:27). 'Although you were once small in your own eyes', I have anointed you and I will send you out with orders (1 Samuel 15:17)."

These words tipped the balance against me. I felt like a recent addendum to God's long list of treasure-laden misfits. I became one big-time garbage bin dweller—an awfully cracked earthen ware.

An imperfect choice for a perfect mission.

I was no different from Ruth who was compelled to leave her homeland. No different from Caleb, the spy who conquered a mountain. His was a fortified land in Judah, mine was fear. My tarnished nature was no different from Matthew's notorious history.

But my response was so diametrically opposed to their open acceptance. I wanted to switch my gear to reverse, do a Jonah, and run where I was not told to go.

IN GOD'S GARDEN

The time came when my family decided to have the backyard landscaped. After four years of patiently pulling stubborn weeds and seeing these mushroom again after a light rainfall, we finally gathered funds to have a professional clear our insect- and toad-infested "wasteland". We thought the timing was perfect because the gardener, who for the most part of the year was occupied, had his calendar freed up for the month.

MENU 7: GODLY CHARACTER

Thus, the work progressed and the wilds that once were, became transformed into an eye-soothing carpet of fresh Bermuda, punctuated by a palm tree and a hedge of flower-bearing tropical greens. My skilled gardener transplanted most of the shrubs from our previously landscaped front and side yards. The finished output was so pleasing that my daughter romped around in the garden for the first time since the house was built.

We knew March was a summer month, but we never expected the temperatures to rise steeply beyond historical peaks. The weather bureau predicted it to be a La Niña year in which torrential rains would be the norm. And so we were dismayed when the 34° to 35° Celsius heat wrinkled the leaves and sapped the life out of my lawn.

Morning and night, my husband and I painstakingly soaked the garden with as much water as the grounds could absorb. Not for a single day did we suspend this laborious regimen, for we knew that our hard-earned savings could be trashed if the greens became permanent browns.

One late evening, while my husband was engaging in this taxing routine, the Lord drew him into a reflective pose.

"Look at your garden," God spoke in Alvin's heart. "What profit would there be in having the side and front yard teeming with fresh blooms and healthy shoots when the larger part of the backyard is crawling with unsightly weeds and annoying pests. Wouldn't it be better if you uproot the thriving shrubs and plant them on the other side, so the whole garden will show beauty and life?"

"The world is My garden," the Lord continued. "But not all parts are full of life. What splendor can I witness if only one speck of My creation believes and follows Me while the rest of the world is still glued to vice and indiscretion? It is My desire to uproot My faithful servants from homes that breed complacency. I wish to replant them in places where they can overcome weeds and make bountiful harvests for the Kingdom."

"But look," Alvin argued, pointing at the partly dried up grass and hedges. "Look at how my plants are struggling to live. They're dying! Will you transplant your servants only to see them die in a foreign land?"

"In as much as you provide water and extra care to this dying garden to assure its survival," the Lord said, "I shall give you a double outpour of compassion and favor to keep you alive. Do not worry. Your needs shall never exhaust My supply."

God spoke His marching orders.

And attached to the package was the hope of provisions.

Clearly, He already made up His mind. He didn't want to pick any other intellectual guru, money-spinning businessman, or religious scholar.

He opted for a simple, quiet man and his scripturally non-conversant housewife! Name dropping the likes of Moses and Peter didn't make the assignment easier, but it did broaden my perspective of the master plan.

SERVANT I WILL BE

Even before God chose us to be His treasure-bearer, He knew we still needed hefty patch-up work. To prepare us for the journey, He had to refine my prickly behaviour, and He did so through the ordinary.

The month my mom first toured Canada fell at the same time four of my best buddies also flew out of the country, either for a two-month holiday or for permanent migration. During their

MENU 7: GODLY CHARACTER

absence, I experienced separation pangs which progressed into depression.

When I wanted to uncloak my heartaches, it was my habit to run to friends and burn phone lines with chatter until the blues disappeared. However, since all my tried-and-true confidants lived continents away, sadness stuck on me like a disease. I craved for their presence. This seemed like a superficial issue, but God used it as springboard for deeper pruning—"Let it be your training."

Not again! The remark began to rub me the wrong way.

"Training for what?"

The Lord's message breached barriers and rested peacefully in my spirit.

"Notice how you react to trial," He said. "Instead of drawing near Me, you seek consolation in strange places. The time is coming when these temporary crutches on which you lean shall drop out of sight. None will remain to take the sting off your scrapes. Keep in mind this feeling of alienation, for this shall intrude your life on northern ground. Be detached from human sources of short-term relief so that you can cleave to Me. I alone can bail you out of hot water. I am your sole source of comfort now, and I shall remain your stability in the future."

Detachment.

That is the key.

God taught me the painful lesson of detachment from people or possessions that offered a quick fix. But that's not all!

I thought preparation for relocation entailed mere physical arrangements. By no stretch of the imagination did I think His preparation also implied the unveiling of other gaps in my character—including my foul temper.

At any rate, I figured that if God wanted to shape a genuine missionary out of me, He also needed to deflate the bloated opinion

I had of myself. What a tough task to make a meek servant out of a real bigheaded lady!

A meek servant.

Sounds funny!

I am light-years away from being a meek servant, and God had to glaringly point out this truth.

As the ruggedness of daily chores sapped my energy, I gradually lost graciousness of speech and became an impatient, complaining brat. I flew towards every occasion to compare my plight with others. I snapped at my family for messing up the house and grunted fiery breaths at my husband whenever he couldn't lend me a hand with the dishes or the garbage. This went on and on as the odds of getting a housekeeper narrowed to a bleak possibility. I wasn't even aware that I was fast becoming a nervous wreck until God bore it out.

During my time of meditation, the Lord reproved me with a stern, fatherly tone. Yes, I was the grouchy clunkhead that needed some discipline. And He didn't spare the spiritual rod as He spoke—

> "How can you be a true disciple, carrying authentic witness to strangers, when you can't even serve your own family without clamoring for appreciation for every favor done? Must you grumble, when you have only completed the duties of your vocation, as My anointing requires of you? Make each day sacred through meekness. Consecrate your life in My honour and do as I bid, even as I send you to labor unrewarded, to serve unpaid, unloved, uncelebrated, under the eclipse of the unknown. Be My nameless saint, working behind the scenes, happy without the notice, provoked not by credits but by heavenly joy! I commission you to toil for Me

MENU 7: GODLY CHARACTER

without lust for rewards. Rejoice in your obscurity. Embrace humility.

"When the trifles of daily life drag you down, see the dry, unpoetic routine as My work. Let the kitchen be your vineyard, the odd jobs your gateway to virtue. Then alone can you be a true servant yourself. Only then can you be best qualified to convey the gospel message to others.

"How is the pitch of your voice?" the Lord continued. "Learn to bridle your tongue. There is no need to flare up or snatch people's attention by your commotion.

"Instead of invoking peace when you speak, why do you demand urgency by a tyrannical voice? Many are the sins that drip from your mouth. Put your words under the Holy Spirit's control, that you may not cause further division and pain. Do you realize that each hurtful word is like a whip that lashes My skin and opens up My wounds afresh? You crucify Me again and again by your untamed speech. Learn the virtue of silence. Surrender to gentleness. A person set on God is not argumentative. Unleash your irritations and seal them in a tight vacuum. I tend to the political malaise of nations and the conflicts of every living soul. I manage the rising and setting of the sun. Do you hear me yammering to get the job done?

"I am the Prince of Peace. My ways are tranquil and true. I do not bark at you to push you into My service. I allow flexibility for human error. There exists no dog-eared book where I keep tabs on your mistakes. Therefore, let go of the obsession to prove yourself right. Such effort only feeds your ego; you already have enough pride that will take years to tame.

"Give love in copious rhythms—in packed barrelfuls weighing tons. When you drive others to do things as you want, you claim headship in a power structure. No force is necessary if I am in charge. So release the pressure and let the Creator handle the created."

Such were God's piercing words.
Deep, painful lessons.
Yet, fundamental for transformation.

God has a heart for people like you and me. Individuals who are broken. Defective. And raw.
You wonder why?
Because we are perfect for the pottery wheel.
We fit snuggly on the Shaper's hand. We are clumps of clay suited for the kneading. We are most in need of refining through the heat of the kiln. The more blemished our nature, the more fit we are for use as God's earthen vessels.
We are clay pots at work in the Potter's kick wheel. The process of twisting, turning, squeezing, and moulding continues until we learn our lessons.
And God alone knows when the work is complete.
He knows when we are polished enough to carry Him as a treasure, the sole message we preach.
Therefore, my friend, do not vote yourself out of God's roster. If He recruits you for a job that leaves you twitching with

MENU 7: Godly Character

worry, enlist in His service with faith. Keep at it like there's no tomorrow.

Shed the anxiety, and believe you are qualified—because God is the one who builds your credentials.

In 2001, after six years of discernment and groundwork, we finally migrated to Canada, the land God promised. But unlike David, Ruth, Matthew, and all the rest whose histories are complete, the architecture of our lives is still taking definition at the Potter's mould.

It is a story outline still unwritten.

> So I went down to the potter's house,
> and I saw him working at the wheel.
> But the pot he was shaping from the clay
> was marred in his hands;
> so the potter formed it into another pot,
> shaping it as seemed best to him.
> Then the word of the Lord came to me. He said,
> "Can I not do with you, Israel,
> as this potter does?" declares the Lord.
> "Like clay in the hand of the potter,
> so are you in my hand..."
> Jeremiah 18:3-6

Chapter 43

Judging by the Looks ... and the Tooth

I had the perfect outfit. A peach Gap cashmere sweater with matching black slacks. A knee-length wool coat with a slender cut at the waist. The wardrobe hid all my twenty-pound, post-partum flab and made me look less like a potbellied pig.

I wore my brand spanking new leather high heels to give me a ramp model's height. I even took pains in adding volume to my grotesquely limp hair. To top off the haute couture, I wrapped a knitted scarf around my neck and donned dangling earrings made of semi-precious gems. I knew I was drop-dead gorgeous that day, if I do say so myself.

I thought, "It's Christmas! Might as well shed off the housewife look, at least for a day."

Off we went to the town center to shop for gifts. As we walked around, I received a few inspired stares. A young lady even approached me and said, "I love the outfit."

Menu 7: Godly Character

Even as I thanked her for the generous compliment, inside my head, silly thoughts ran—good thing you can't see me on normal days. I start and end the day with bad breath, tangled hair that hasn't known the feel of conditioner for weeks, and pajamas that look the worse for wear!

For our family, a day in the mall was never complete without Purdy's ice cream. The sweet cravings were too intense to ignore, so we stopped by the shop and bought our favourite maple walnut flavor.

With a purse on my shoulder and a sugar cone on one hand, I pushed the stroller where two-week-old Chiara napped. I kept an eye on Pajo who tottered in his steps. Suddenly, the most awkward thing happened.

Pajo threw a caterwauling fit that drew unwelcome stares from shoppers who walked past. He wanted a lick of the ice cream to which I said "no". The last time I gave him a treat, he had diarrhea on his diapers which I regretted immensely.

But Pajo never reacted well to a "no". With all the petulance a little tyke could manage, he flung himself on the floor, kicked, and cried, as if headlining his sob story would reverse my decision.

I never realized an eighteen-month-old toddler could be so strong. One tug and I was down on the floor with him—outfit, poise, and all. It was such a rude way for me to realize that I was only as agile as an eighty-year-old grandma on a skateboard.

I tried to salvage my lost dignity. With the ice cream cone still on one hand, I smoothed down my sweater, pulled up my chin, and with the gentlest voice, coaxed Pajo to calm down. I guess all the ladies who passed were mothers too. Because none of them laughed at the embarrassing scene we made. They just gave me one sympathetic gaze that said it all—"Don't worry. We've been there, done that."

Now, forget the prom queen flamboyance. This mom needed to tie up her hair in a neat bun to keep tiny fingers from pulling them from the scalp. Ever been strangled by a scarf before? I just did.

And high heels! Who needs them unless you want to fall flat on your face with maple walnut ice cream on your nose (which, by the way, I also did).

Wool coats. Nah! My babies' mouths were like Yellowstone geysers that squirted all sorts of gooey disgorged matter left and right. Vinyl tablecloths were created for such a time as this. It would have been wise to wrap myself in one.

Suffice it to say, I embraced motherhood with all its scents and beauty—or lack of it. I tried to convince myself that God dug under my harried, battlefield look and spit-up milk scent to behold my true, inner person. I wanted to believe that mothers like me were not judged according to the barf stains on our clothes, the peanut butter on our hair, or the six-pack, postnatal fat on our bellies.

Eventually, I learned that my optimism wasn't totally misplaced. The Lord does pierce through the surface and examines the inner workings of the heart. In fact, there's a page in the Bible where this is printed in clear ink!

> But the Lord said to Samuel, "Do not consider his appearance or his height, for I have rejected him. The Lord does not look at the things people look at. People look at the outward appearance, but the Lord looks at the heart." (1 Samuel 16:7)

The Lord does not look at the things people look at. Don't you find these words comforting?

We are not sized up according to human standards of superiority. We are so much more than the clothes we wear, the

MENU 7: GODLY CHARACTER

liquid assets we hoard, the mansions and cars we brag about, or the professions we keep.

Swell-headed men and women, trumpeters of their credentials, may catch the spectators' applause—but not God's. Because life is not about the moolahs and blings that people seize with tight fists. Deep pockets, business empires, and high-stakes portfolios can't buy a seat in heaven. What's meritorious by God's yardstick has nothing to do with cosmetic touch-ups and airbrushed faces.

If I can venture a guess, I'll say that there's only one thing God is crazy about, hidden from plain sight. It is seated right there, tucked at the very bosom, where the authentic "you" resides.

God covets one thing alone—your heart!

> A person may think their own ways are right, but
> the Lord weighs the heart. (Proverbs 21:2)

God judges the ways of the human heart, with all its righteousness or disgrace. He grades each heart on scales of holiness to appraise where it is lacking.

He sifts through its motives and gathers evidence to invalidate its guilt. He does all these with the heart because God created us good. He believes the human heart, pumped by divine grace, has the potential to preserve this uprightness till our journey's end.

Knowing that the Lord judges us by the condition of our hearts, not by our multi-layered disguises, we too should learn to withhold judgment of our neighbour.

There's no point in wagging our tongues when we don't see the entire picture. We can't read the stream of consciousness that influences one's decision. Life is more complicated than just adding two and two together. Therefore, never second-guess another when the truth is masked, mysterious, and Greek to you.

Unverified speculation that descends from the mind to the mouth is simply gossip.

Once, I witnessed firsthand how easy it was for people to jump to conclusions. My kids were at the age when baby teeth fell off quicker than the Tooth Fairy could earn money. Understandably, the kiddos were anxious over the bloody uprooting. However, the butterflies gradually calmed down after Tooth Fairy honoured their bravery with little gifts.

By morning, the kids held their breaths in anticipation as they reached under their pillows for surprise treats. There, they found Tooth Fairy's squiggly handwritten messages, a few coins, and pocket-sized toys. While waving their goodies in the air, huge grins exposing toothless gaps, I took a mental snapshot of the scene and clung to the childhood memory with all its sweetness.

The routine went on, tooth after tooth, year after year. Soon, Pajo and Chiara grew more inquisitive, deeply insightful, and gazillions too analytical for their age.

Like a forensics detective on the trail of hot clues, the siblings connived to trap the Tooth Fairy in a bottle or in the flesh, whichever came first. They did some exhaustive handwriting analysis. By witty inferencing, they concluded that Tooth Fairy's and Santa's letters were scrawled by the same left hand! Although they had no empirical evidence—only half-formed opinions—my kids weren't too far from hitting the mark.

As all tales normally unfold, the protagonist cracks the code after a whale of effort. One afternoon, my little heroes almost cried in unison, "Mama, we know who the Tooth Fairy is?"

Acting above suspicion, I asked, "Who?"

MENU 7: GODLY CHARACTER

"You!" Pajo said triumphantly.

"Who told you that?" You bet, I could win the Oscars for pulling this one off with the most guiltless facial expression.

"Our friends," Chiara chimed in.

"Which friends?"

"Trish asked her dad directly if he is the Tooth Fairy. He said 'yes'. And as you know, Uncle Thomas is a Christian so he doesn't lie!" Pajo watched my reaction with a playfully mischievous smile.

Not wanting to let the cat out of the bag, Alvin jumped into the conversation like greased lightning. "Aha!" he exclaimed. "Now we know!"

I looked at my husband and wondered what he was up to.

"The Tooth Fairy is NOT Mama ... it's Uncle Thomas!"

"Papa!" Chiara and Pajo spoke in chorus, half-amused, half-bewildered. Their faces said it all, "I can't believe you still don't get it!"

"Think about it," Alvin presented his case. "Uncle Thomas works the night shift. What's up with that? Because he has to deliver everything while kids are sleeping."

"Oh!" Less skeptical Chiara was won over. "Now I remember! When we saw Uncle Thomas at church, he said 'Chiara, you're so pretty-ful'. I corrected his grammar but he still kept calling me 'pretty-ful'."

Turning to Pajo, Chiara continued, "Do you remember in one of the letters, Tooth Fairy also wrote 'pretty-ful'? Papa's right! Uncle Thomas IS the Tooth Fairy!"

With new avenues of thought open for scrutiny, my children gathered more evidence to pin upon Uncle Thomas the fairy identity.

The perfect opportunity arrived shortly. Uncle Thomas volunteered to serve as usher in our church. One of his responsibilities was to take up the collection from pew to pew.

And so it was that midway through the liturgical prayers, the ushers stood to facilitate the task. Row by row they walked. It happened that Uncle Thomas was designated to pass the hat along our aisle. Being new to the service, this was the first time my kids saw him with the wicker basket full of money.

My kids' brain waves seemed so synchronized that evening. Without any verbal exchange, and with just one glance at our usher, they both shaped the same opinion. The little detectives immediately glued mismatched puzzle pieces together to draw up a picture based on coincidental evidence.

"Look, Chiara," Pajo pointed. "Uncle Thomas is carrying the basket."

Eyes round with wonder, Chiara had a eureka moment. "That just makes a lot of sense!"

"What do you mean?"

"Where else will Tooth Fairy get the money?" Chiara said.

"From the basket! Of course! Why didn't we think of that before?"

Pajo's and Chiara's hearts pulsated with so much glee, you'd think they hooked a big fish. They were so thrilled with their meteoric success. Finally, they solved the riddle after three years of groundwork and silly scheming!

If only we weren't in the thick of solemn adoration, I would have scolded the two for turning good ol' Tooth Fairy into a collection-basket embezzler!

I do give them props, though. Their character profiling was creatively out of this world! Who else would have dreamed that a night-shift worker plus poor grammar plus hieroglyphic handwriting plus a tray of church tithes equals Tooth Fairy? You should give my kids' copious imagination some credit for assembling something so epic.

MENU 7: GODLY CHARACTER

The whole teething business kindled for me this pulse of thought—we twist reality when we draw conclusions from skin-deep appearances.

The Lord tells us never to pass judgment. It is not our place to form false opinions, to criticize, and to needlessly meddle into others' affairs.

We are all guilty of doing this. Ours may not be as funny as the little darlings' Tooth Fairy fiasco. I dare say, at least once in our lives, we've falsely accused through back-fence talks, hearsay, or poisonous thinking.

Perhaps we've painted malice upon a married man's relationship with a female office colleague without giving them the benefit of the doubt. Have you looked down on an associate whose career stagnated for years only to discover that he waived promotions in favor of critical family issues?

Friend, the Lord wants you to be intentional in taming your assumptions. Tattling isn't a leisure sport. And you don't need to be a link in the grapevine.

With or without reasonable grounds, snuff out the appetite for presumption. Woman, you are not the critic of the human race, so suppress those urges—they're as dangerous as acid that warps the soul.

Instead, be selective and refined in speech, positive in perspective. Don't rely on your gut instincts to evaluate others for you don't really know what lies under their skin. You can't always get to the crux of their motives because people are not onions with layers you can peel.

Bless others even in your thoughts. If you must form an opinion, judge in favor of your neighbour, regardless of outward appearances.

Remember, we are a myopic race.

No one but God, the ultimate Judge, knows our neighbour's true heart.

> For in the same way you judge others,
> you will be judged,
> and with the measure you use,
> it will be measured to you.
> Matthew 7:2

Chapter 44

Dunk

My son wasn't two years old yet when I guessed he would have a future career in professional basketball. With remarkable speed and precision, he could throw a three-point shot from his corner high chair into the center of the dining table. He flung anything his hands touched—his Playskool car, toddler spoon, Sesame Street board book, or milk bottle.

There was one major problem, though.

There were no baskets to shoot. Instead, he aimed at his three-month-old sister who slept quietly on her carrier!

Knowing Pajo's knack for launching objects into space, we always tucked Chiara away in a safe distance. But my little Harlem Globetrotter still managed to toss the bottle on to her forehead or cheeks, eliciting a shrill cry from my otherwise sweet-tempered daughter.

Being a one-sided referee, I favored the losing team. In this case, I played Chiara's defense and blocked all of Pajo's slam-dunks.

MENU 7: GODLY CHARACTER

My son finally got tired of my tight guarding, so he decided to switch baskets. Next, he angled for the toilet bowl! It gave him greater thrill to see water slosh at his every dunk shot. And he scored better too!

I didn't know how much longer I could take the disruption. Hoisting sunken fridge magnets, slippers, hair accessories, and pencils from the bottom of the john wasn't exactly my cup of tea. I never signed up for the job of dredging lavatory water. What an unholy mess!

But again and again, with Pajo's improved dodging skills, he somehow managed to lift the toilet cover and stir his brew with a wooden spoon. If I wasn't lucky enough to hijack the spoon before he whipped his combo, he'd still run into the bathroom and swirl the mixture with his bare hands!

It was never a waltz for me to look after a hyperactive boy. Sometimes, I desired a change of scenery to bail out of my obligations. Of course, that was impossible. I'm a mother and would always bear the stretch marks of a mother. I wished, intead, to be as cool as the first breath of spring and respond to these antics with the patience of Job.

But I was hardly a patient person. In fact, I believed that impatience came with the territory of an overworked mom. I hoped that under the circumstances, my family would understand if I came unglued more often than expected. I easily blamed the rush of hormones for my lack of emotional control.

However, estrogens had nothing to do with my rudeness. My irritability and outbursts were clear symptoms of a temper needing repair.

God has made it plain to me that my lack of character tests His patience too. Pajo's fascination with the toilet is no different from my attachment to sin.

His repeated dunk shots are no different from my repeated mistakes. But instead of shouting at me for my stubborn misconduct, God forbears and waits until the day I learn my lesson.

God teaches His children by example. He remains for us a model of even-tempered behaviour. Though we are repeat offenders, God demonstrates patience towards us. He does so in order that we too will learn to extend the same grace and composure towards others.

God never hammers our guilt in our hearts when we fail to be as patient as we ought. He doesn't drill a finger at our foreheads to remind us of our delinquency.

Instead, God understands our daily struggles with moderation and tolerance. He accepts the frame we're built in. He honours our individuality but adds His own flavor into our character. He loves us—complexion, thumbprints, and all. But He works on us until our habits reflect His integrity, until His nature is stamped in our conscience and becomes our nature too.

God works on us until we learn to be as mild-tempered towards others as He is with us.

Therefore, brothers and sisters, may we appoint in our own lives the same message the apostle Paul preached to the Colossians. Let us "…live a life worthy of the Lord and please him in every way: bearing fruit in every good work …" (Colossians 1:10).

Please the Lord in every way.

This one's a meaty statement, isn't it?

It covers many bases including our need to cultivate patience. We please the Lord even as we keep our cool when days turn sour and plans go awry. We please the Lord when we zip our mouth a second before it poisons someone with the venom of our sarcasm.

We, the Created, become worthy of the Creator, and give Him pleasure when we personify His kindness in the daily runs of life.

MENU 7: Godly Character

Friend, if patience is an area of combat for you, pray that you may slowly grow in it. But be ready. The more you ask for good temper, the more God will bombard your week with troubles in which patience will be the choice weapon to overcome.

The more you seek gentleness, the more irritants you'll encounter.

The more you ask for forebearance, the longer you sit in the sand traps and water hazards of your life's course.

Have you noticed?

Moments after you pray for patience, traffic hounds your lane while everyone else moves just fine. A child suddenly wants to go to the bathroom just as you're loading in the car for a time-sensitive appoinment. A waitress in a restaurant mixes up orders and serves new customers first while your table is twice bypassed.

The receptionist informs that the doctor will see you in thirty minutes, but you end up wasting three hours in the lounge. You stop at an intersection, shift gears in less than five seconds after the light turns green, and receive disharmonic honks from short-fused drivers behind you.

I tell you! Ask for patience and you're asking for trouble.

The nuisance and delays will not cease until you embrace them without screaming your annoyance. Even so, these are inconveniences worth taking. These are abrasions that will smoothen your rough edges to a glittering shine.

Remember, God will continue to agitate,

Until your patience activates,

To the point where your character captivates.

Chapter 45

Of Pixels, Quilts, & Homecoming Misconceptions

I have a confession to make.

I dread reunions.

At the mere thought of a homecoming, my heart pulsates so fast you'll think that the hooves of a thousand race horses are rampaging in my chest. It is not that I don't long to reconnect with old friends and swap memoirs, children's misadventures, aging symptoms, wrinkle control secrets, and what-nots. Neither do I mind the pageantry of reengineered noses, dyed hair, tucked tummies, and cream-pampered skins against my non-athletic, sagging features. I have long accepted my unwanted extra poundage and have tricked myself into believing that I'm not old—I'm just a recycled teen-ager.

If this isn't it, then why do I get the willies?

MENU 7: Godly Character

It's really simple.

For me, a reunion is a time of reckoning. It is a painful moment when I need to confront my pride and assess my true worth.

I always thought people carry their resumes and brag sheets to reunions. It is an occasion to underscore the string of letters attached to their names—M.D., PhD., Atty., D.M.D., or whatever. It is also an opportune moment to set under klieg lights the successful businesses people incorporated, the charitable organizations they founded, their network of clients that pushed sales figures upwards, the saga of their world travels, or even the Rockefeller-league spouses that made the women's married names sound more impactful.

Don't get me wrong.

I'm not saying that there's anything lame or crummy about these. Accomplishments earned under the sweat of one's brow also need a periodic shower of applause.

My problem? I have none of these things.

My profile sheets are too undecorated and empty; they're non-marketable. My career path had more stops and gaps than starts. I was academically outstanding, but I have nothing to show for it. I have no wealth stashed in foreign bank vaults or blue Hope diamonds in tightly-guarded museums.

Yes, I was able to infiltrate the military ranks as a General—that is, "General Housekeeper" in my own home. I don't have a shelf of certificates and trophies except the ones my daughter won in her bowling tournaments.

I do not have anything to gloat about in a reunion because I am an unsophisticated person with very rudimentary needs. Migrating into North America, I launched myself into oblivion and had to prove my worth once again to a bunch of people who knew nothing about my value in the human race.

Dropping to the bottom of the pecking order, I lived happily in my puniness and didn't want it disturbed by resume-swapping showdowns.

This was the source of my anxiety.

Homecomings force me to question the judgments and compromises I made. They force me to journey back to my past and probe my steps.

Did I discern the right choices?

Am I anywhere closer to God's purpose for me?

Am I a one-dimensional character, defined only by credentials and helter-skelter plans? Or did I invest my life on non-random things which carry eternal weight and glory?

It then hit me.

All of us are strategic parts of one body. In the general scheme of things, we are all important—lawyers and clerks, doctors and hospital janitors, front stage actors and backstage operators, restaurant proprietors and dish stackers, board directors and receptionists. We are all spokes of a fully-functioning wheel.

Each one is a stitch in an embroidery or a fabric on a complex quilt. Each one is a small pixel in a digital photograph. The picture just wouldn't be complete without the presence of one tiny pixel.

This paradigm shift brought a whole new meaning to the homecoming. The reunion is no longer an opinion poll on who succeeded and who failed. It is not an occasion to see who tipped the weighing scales closest to the yuck-I'm-too-fat mark, or who can best disguise the receding hairlines.

It is a moment to rekindle old memories—a time to thank the Lord who turned our life's toneless monochromes into charming rainbows.

MENU 7: GODLY CHARACTER

More than any earthly reunion, there is one Grand Homecoming we should all anticipate with feverish excitement. It is a time when all of us pilgrims enter into our true heritage.

In Paul's letter to the church in Philippi, he says,

> But our citizenship is in heaven. And we eagerly await a Savior from there, the Lord Jesus Christ.
> (Philippians 3:20)

Like a beachside sandcastle that is gradually whipped and flattened by rolling waves, our earthly home has no permanence. Everything we hold dear will soon crumble into nothingness.

Death is proof that all things are temporary. Christ's resurrection is proof that we are destined for a higher purpose.

Therefore, we should not be too invested in a world that has no capacity to endure. Let us wrap our minds, instead, on our future homecoming. We, who were created for Heaven, must hold on to our blessed hope that Christ will grant an eternal inheritance to those who persevere in the faith.

On the day of your final homecoming, you too will carry your brag sheets. But you will no longer be marked against the yardstick of shifting desires in a drifting world.

The Lord will lead you to a thorough examination of conscience, and you'll be weighed according to the purity of your soul. On this grand reunion, your true credentials shall be exposed to throngs of witnesses. Whether it is righteousness or heinous misdeeds, nothing will be hidden from sight.

Even now, prepare for the return to your roots. Examine what's written on your brag sheets.

How much of the world did you give up in order to gain Christ?

Which words from your lips stoked a brush fire of gossip? Which words dried tears of desperation and uplifted a browbeaten brother?

Jesus approached you as a homeless, disheveled man. He knocked on your car window, begging for mercy. Did you offer a ray of comfort and leave him a hopeful man? Or did you drive without a single care, annoyed at the grimy fingerprints that soiled your polished car?

Were you so dazed by the flash mob of fame and fortune that you compromised truth to swim with the crowd? Or did you frown on swellheadedness and greed in order to live humbly, detached from the pursuit of vain glories?

Were you choked by unquenchable ambition? Or was social status in this perishable world a burden—and your identity in Christ, true freedom?

Can you honestly echo Paul's words, and make it the central psalm that your life sings?

> But whatever were gains to me I now consider loss for the sake of Christ. What is more, I consider everything a loss because of the surpassing worth of knowing Christ Jesus my Lord, for whose sake I have lost all things. I consider them garbage, that I may gain Christ. (Philippians 3:7–8)

You and I ... we're going back to heaven.

Back to our roots.

Therefore, do not sit on the bleachers nor wait in the sidelines, observing from a distance how Christians behave. Get your feet wet; embrace righteousness with scrupulousness and rigidity.

Menu 7: Godly Character

Experience the joy of discovery and learn the fruitfulness of loving Christ ... right now!

Don't wait for a morning that may never dawn. Your breath can be snuffed out in a nanosecond, and tomorrow may only be a wispy dream.

Thus, let your hearts beat for the Lord and your life be Kingdom-bound ... right this minute.

Put this in mind—the easy freeways of the world lead to doom. Dusty gravel roads of the suffering Messiah lead to rewards that never decay. Which homecoming do you choose?

We are all homeward bound.

But which home?

You decide.

```
For here we do not have an enduring city,
but we are looking for the city that is to come.
                Hebrews 13:14
```

About the Author

Ginger Umali is an artist, math tutor, and homeschooling mother of three. As down-to-earth as her writing, she is a bucketful of quirks who cries at the sight of rainbows, creates eye-catching paintings when troubled, considers math textbooks perfect coffee-table reading, and talks to plants in her Surrey residence. She writes from a heart that suffered a twenty-year odyssey through the wilderness where pain was soul-racking and God seemed more than an arm's length away.

Ginger is an active member of Vancouver-based Families for Christ Community, a lay Christian organization that is part of The Sword of the Spirit, an international network of more than seventy-five ecumenical communities. There she serves the Lord through music.

Printed in the United States
By Bookmasters